I0559890

A TREK
WITHIN

Embracing Unexpected Truths

BY ROB RYAN SULLIVAN

A TREK WITHIN: Embracing Unexpected Truths

Copyright © 2023 By Rob RYAN Sullivan

Cover and Interior Design by Josseline Ross

Megan Close Zavala and Josseline Ross, editors

All rights reserved. No part of this publication may be reproduced, distributed, or transmitted in any form or by any means, including photocopying, recording, or other electronic or mechanical methods, without the prior written permission of the authors, except in brief quotations embodied in critical reviews and certain other non-commercial uses permitted by copyright law.

Printed in the United States of America.

This book is dedicated to the countless angels in my life.

Whenever I take time to reflect on the vast number of people who have knowingly or unknowingly changed the trajectory of my life, I am inevitably awestruck. On the one hand, I am humbled by the nameless angels who show up and provide seemingly endless opportunities to practice patience and compassion. Given my penchant for screwing up the lessons, it comes as no surprise that these angels are more likely to have horns than halos. They are angels nevertheless.

I am equally grateful to the angels who give me so many reasons to smile. In addition to my amazing parents, who have always been my most loyal cheerleaders, I am grateful to those who have had the biggest impact professionally and who I am blessed to consider friends: Ted Simon, Judi Carpenter, Tom Cutler, Kari Lehman, Jennifer Schlott-Rouzan, Ross Parr, John Drake, Norm Goldring, Aspasia Apostolakis Miller, and Asa Baber.

Among the angels who have helped me grow as a person, I am most grateful to Jackie Hart, Amber Gentile, Harry Wilson, Richard and Megan Brasser, Sue Davis, Chris Hennes, Nadia Ochoa, Kevin, Tommy, Annabel, Azrael, my siblings – ML, Clare, Bill, John, and Matt – and so many others.

I love and thank you all.

ACKNOWLEDGMENTS

My sincere thanks to the many people who generously shared their stories and talents in the creation of this book. May the experiences you shared inspire others to watch for the signposts and follow their inner compass.

I also extend my sincere thanks to Megan Close Zavala and Josseline Ross who each contributed profoundly to the shaping of the manuscript. Many thanks as well to Kate Morrissey and Pat Lee whose early editorial contributions were also quite helpful. This book would not be what it is without the insight and expertise of these wonderful people.

Table Of Contents

PART ONE:

Opening Your Mind – Finding Your Roadmap

Part TWO

Applying What You Have Learned: Embarking On Your Journey

NOTE TO READERS

They said:
I should learn to speak a little bit of English
Don't be scared of the suit and tie
Learn to walk in the dreams of the foreigner
I am a third world child
*-- from the song **"Third World Child"***
Written by Johnny Clegg
® 1986. Scatterlings Pty Ltd.

Johnny Clegg, the late songwriter/musician/anthropologist from South Africa once said, *"If you truly want to understand someone, you need to start by learning that person's language."*

This is important because, as a reader of this book, you will benefit from the perspectives of people around the world who shared their very personal stories and experiences. In many cases, English is not their native language. To preserve the integrity of what they have written, I intentionally left alternative spellings (sceptic/skeptic) and unique phrasings intact rather than "Americanize" the book.

As much as I like consistency, I feel more strongly about accepting and embracing our cultural and linguistic differences.

Rob

FOREWORD

I am – by definition – a sceptic. At least a great part of me is. This is likely due to my upbringing and less a product of my conscious decision-making and thought process. I would love to consider myself a very open-minded, curious, and spontaneous, always-willing-to-try-out-new-things person. Still, many books I have read so far, which claim to be able to help you, improve your skills, broaden your mind and soul, break with your undesired habits, overcome your fears, achieve nothing less than optimizing yourself as a human being, bring this suspicious and cynical sentiment forward. I am aware that this is a very generalizing statement. There are (for sure) books that do a divine job in helping people who feel trapped in their daily routine, who are seeking for motivation, answers, an alternative path to the one they are on. However, there are many that claim to have THE solution. THE answer to most if not all of your problems and questions. Very often, they claim, the key to success is simply believing in yourself. Believing in the equation of luck and happiness, the author provides you with. A simple list of bullet points, which, if you rigorously tick them off every day, you will be a happy, peaceful, successful, and wealthy person. I don't know... is it because I am a sceptic, or do you also get this scrunching thought that if life would really be that simple, we would – as a society – not be where we are right now?

When Rob asked me to read his book and give him feedback, I was indeed a bit nervous. Not at all due to the number of pages in front of me. I always love reading and listening to Rob's stories. There are only a handful of people who can tell their stories in such a vivid, engaging, and funny way as Rob does. But rather because I had a vague idea what it was about, since Rob continued to share his thoughts and we had several conversations on many different chapters of this book. Knowing Rob for almost a decade, I knew many of his experiences in life and all the challenges he had to tackle on his way. I knew he is not only a warm, extremely empathetic, strong, open-minded, and adventurous man. He is also someone who will never give up on others or on himself. Therefore, it wasn't a surprise to me, when he – after being diagnosed with cancer – didn't stop looking for alternative and additional healing methods. But even before that, he always seemed to be able to surprise me with a new experience he had, a new healing method, a new discovery on how human connection works, what we can learn from our dreams, and how synchronicity can be explained. I don't know why I ever doubted that this book would be any different to himself and his way of telling me about his experiences in person. Why was I afraid that he might also claim to have the answer, the solution? Truthfully, I am ashamed that this thought even crossed my mind.

This book does not claim anything. It holds no promise to change your life or to make things easier. It does not pledge to improve your daily routines, your way of thinking or performance.

And yet, it changed me.

And quite frankly, it did improve my way of thinking, facilitate my daily routines, gave answers to many (un)conscious questions I had been carrying around with me for some time. All of this without forcing you to believe in anything to make it happen.

There is no shortcut to happiness or self-fulfilment. And yet, this book helped me to at least circumvent some mistakes. To skip some diversions. To feel understood, connect to several stories, be moved and cry but also laugh throughout so many chapters in this book. By reading these pages, I may not have found all answers to my questions, but I started thinking about several new questions that might be even more important to solve – to look at new or alternative ways to solve my problems or behave in different situations.

By having the courage to share his stories, to open up about his struggles in life, I was able to learn from many of his mistakes without having to tap into them myself. Of course, I did already have an idea of what was important for myself, what I wanted (and didn't want) in life. In Rob's words, I had an inner compass that I was following already. However, reading this book, I simply discovered new paths, a new grid that helped me make decisions or at least be aware of different ways to approach my challenges. Moreover, I felt less alone. As if the navigation of my inner compass received an extra validation. And that is worth more than I could ever explain in words.

— Josseline Ross

INTRODUCTION

This is not the book I expected to write — it's better. Let me explain. What started out as a driving desire to share the experiences that changed the way I view energy, spirituality, and our relationship to ourselves and each other, felt strangely unfinished after four years writing, editing, and restructuring. That changed on February 18, 2015, my 48th birthday, with the most unusual, and most soul-expandingly powerful gift I have ever received — malignant tumors in my chest and neck.

But I'm getting a little ahead of myself.

The seeds of this book first began to sprout on January 7, 2009, when Mike Falcone, a friend from college, and I had an email exchange on Facebook about our mutual interest in acupuncture. We met working at WCHC-FM, the alternative radio station at the College of the Holy Cross in Worcester, MA, where Mike, who went by "Francis" at the time, and I spent several years as Music Director and Assistant Station Manager, respectively. Had you asked at the time what role I thought needles might play in Mike's future career, I would have chosen tattoo artist long before acupuncturist. Nevertheless, there we were, 20 years later, exchanging emails about alternative medicine and his decision to pursue a career as an acupuncturist.

I remember the night vividly. When Mike asked what sparked my interest in acupuncture, I started to type a reply when I suddenly remembered a lengthy article I had written seven years prior describing my experiences working with various alternative healers including acupuncturists, Chinese herbalists, Reiki Masters, medical intuitives, and hands-on healers. I had originally written the article as a submission for the inaugural issue of magazine focused on alternative medicine.

I'm honestly not sure what happened after I submitted the article. Either the magazine never got off the ground or the editors decided they had a better chance of success without my input. What I do recall is saving the article and consciously moving the file with each new computer knowing I'd someday find a use for it.

On that cold January evening in 2009, rather than rewriting the story I'd written so long ago, I searched through my files, found the article, and posted it as my first-ever Facebook note. At the time, I had about 300 Facebook friends and the newsfeed wasn't the tractor-beam-like feature it is now with the heaviest users checking status updates multiple times per day. Within a day, 16 people posted comments and many more contacted me privately. Almost immediately, I began receiving friend requests from friends of friends who heard about my story and wanted to read it. The response surprised me because nothing I had written professionally touched people the way my experience with alternative medicine did. Having written a job search book a few years before, I knew that my professional missteps and other business experiences helped people, but I never expected my personal experiences would someday have an even greater emotional impact.

The comment I remember most came from my friend, Carolyn, who said, "Just a heartfelt WOW! I am one of those skeptics and hearing a story like this from someone I actually know makes me think."

Carolyn's comment got me thinking as well and inspired me to share more of the experiences that have changed the way I view the world. Shortly after that first Facebook note, I started collecting ideas and other stories in an app on my phone I'd someday use to create other chapters. Like most of the writing I've done, it took some time for the information to process internally before I was ready to sit down and write. I'm also a practiced and proficient procrastinator. So, between the processing and procrastination, it took another two years before I did any substantive writing.

Even after much of the book was written, I developed a sense that it wasn't finished because I hadn't yet lived some of the experiences that were supposed to be included. What I struggled with most was my strong feeling that this book, while autobiographical in nature, was never meant to be an autobiography. The experiences happened to me, but it isn't about me. That's why we later decided to incorporate similar stories from other people so it is clear none of this was a fluke.

Around the time I was experiencing that unfinished feeling, it occurred to me that there might be a life experience I hadn't yet had that might tie all of the stories in the book together. Of course, my hopeful side had visions of something aspirational and life-changing like meeting the perfect woman or a huge, unexpected inheritance. So naturally I found myself feeling impatient. Had I known the gift I awaited was lymphoma rather than love I might not have been in such a hurry.

At this point, you might be thinking, "So, what on earth is the book about and how could lymphoma possibly have been helpful in the process?"

Only when I made it far enough along the path was I able to turn around, appreciate, and fully understand the experiences along the way. It was as if every experience, every lesson, every teacher, and every moment had somehow conspired to give me access to the perspective and positivity that enabled me to get through 30 days of inpatient chemotherapy over a four-month period with relative ease and without the need for a blood transfusion. While I am proud of the strength I was able to demonstrate physically in handling and recovering from over 545 hours of chemotherapy treatment, I was genuinely surprised at the exponential spiritual growth triggered by the tumors. I would never have expected such a serious diagnosis to result in such profound, authentic feelings of happiness and connectedness.

It's been even more gratifying to see the impact this journey has had on others. It would take an entire chapter or three to share the heartfelt comments, private messages, and stories people have shared in a staggering display of love and support. When I first opened up about the tumors, it felt incredibly weak and vulnerable to admit that I needed treatment and was facing something I couldn't deal with on my own. Nothing about the situation felt strong or masculine.

Nevertheless, I knew I had to be open because I didn't want people to think I was dying. Moreover, reaching out to people made me feel alive and connected to the world outside of the hospital. It was a two-way road, a mutual path of appreciating what we have right now.

I never expected so many people to use words like strong, graceful, insightful, and inspirational to describe my approach to the diagnosis and treatment. From the beginning, people encouraged me to continue sharing. More people than I can count, including a few professional writers, urged me to turn my lengthy Facebook notes into a book. That didn't take too much convincing because I realized almost immediately that this journey was the missing chapter that tied everything together. This was reinforced by the many beautiful comments I received like this one from my college classmate, Elizabeth Greabe Antony:

"After my own journey back to health, I really thought I'd learned every lesson about life, love, appreciation of friendship/God/family. I really thought that my faith in people had been strengthened to a point it couldn't grow any more. Ha! What do I know?! Thank you for sharing here. My guess is that I'm not the only one who has grown from reading your posts and contemplating your shared perspectives. You sharing your journey has reinforced my own healing. Reinforced good things in my life. Thank you."

One of my other favorite comments came from Annette, one of the nurses at the hospital. She posted a picture on Facebook with the teams from the two units who took care of me and a note that read:

"Rob has gotten through chemo with the most positive attitude anyone has witnessed...Because of him, good vibes and good music brightened up our units."

Shortly after my last treatment, my dear friend, Amy Harris, saw me at the gym, smiled, and said: "No one does cancer like you do."

I love that.

But it wasn't the treatment experience or the tumors that made this part of my journey the missing chapter. After all, millions of people have experienced tumors and treatments. What made this experience a unifying thread is the way it incorporated Western and Eastern medicine, prayer, meditation, visualization, and spirituality, as well as the contributions and insights of intuitives. For the first time, it finally made sense how my previous experiences and shifts in perspective had prepared me to handle adversity in a way that surprised everyone, myself included.

In my case, the tumors were a gift that came with multiple lessons. In reading the following pages, my hope is that you find opportunities in your own life to learn and grow from adversity and emerge a more positive and powerful version of yourself. I am also clear, however, that my experience is my experience. We are all on our own journeys with different lessons to learn based on our unique experiences and histories. It isn't always easy, or even possible, to see the gift in certain types of adversity. I get that. For this reason, my goal isn't to convince you of anything or to change your beliefs. Instead, my goal is to encourage you to see if any of the insights that brought me health, happiness, and sense of love and connection beyond anything I have ever experienced might have value for you. If, like the many people who have already heard some of these stories, you gain insight and perspective that helps you in your own life, that would be fantastic, and this book will have been well worth the effort — for both of us.

PART I

OPENING YOUR MIND – FINDING

YOUR ROADMAP

CHAPTER 1:

Some of the First Signposts

So many miles I have travelled
So many a dim lit bar
Because when things start to unravel
You're gonna find out who you are
*-- from the song **"I Know a Place"** by Michael McDermott*
Reprinted with permission: Michael McDermott/Pauper Sky Songs (ASCAP)

The second oldest of six, I remember my childhood as a happy one. I was born on Kincheloe Air Force Base in Sault Ste. Marie, Michigan but have no recollection of the military because my parents moved back to Chicago with my older sister, Mary Lisa (ML), and me when I was a baby. Five years later, my younger sister, Mary Clare (Clare) was born followed by Bill, John, and Matt four, six, and nine years after Clare, respectively.

My perception at the time was that I had two of the strictest parents among my peers. That may have been true, but they also did an amazing job fostering independence and initiative. For example, my request to have the training wheels taken off my little red bike at the age of four would have been completely unremarkable were it not for the walking casts I had on both legs from a series of operations to repair severe club feet. Even though my parents knew operating the foot brakes would be borderline impossible, they didn't say no. Nor did they say no when I discovered the only way to stop was to dive off onto our lawn. Most importantly, it meant keeping what was probably a collective gasp to themselves when diving off the bike onto nearby lawns at progressively faster speeds became the whole point of getting on my bike in the first place.

From second or third grade through my freshman year in high school we lived on the 20th floor of 1000 N. Lake Shore Drive, an apartment building just north of Michigan Avenue. I didn't realize at the time just how special that was because I didn't have much to compare it to. Although relatively few children grew up in the heart of downtown Chicago during that period, I was fortunate to have a few close friends within a block or two. Everyone else was a short bike ride away.

The only people who ever questioned my parents' hands-off approach when it came to bike riding were the two police officers who visited our house after I had my five-speed bike stolen on the east side of Oz Park after Little League practice. Over the past 20 years, the area has improved immensely. But Oz Park, which is now surrounded by expensive houses and townhomes, was once a favorite area for gangs. Some of those gang members, including the two six-foot gentlemen I encountered, apparently decided stealing locked bikes was too much of an effort. So, they started stealing unlocked bikes. The only problem is that most unlocked bikes in Chicago have riders on them. My little 5-speed was no exception. Apparently, my menacing four-foot, six-inch, 75-pound frame was something short of a deterrent.

As the officers took my report and squashed any hopes I had of seeing my bike again, they didn't miss the opportunity to encourage my parents to rethink their decision to let me ride into the Lincoln Park/Oz Park neighborhoods.

When I wasn't riding my bike along the lake or playing baseball, I filled my time with Hardy Boys' books, football, floor hockey, trombone, piano, video games, and dropping water balloons and paper airplanes complete with side-mounted fireworks from my friend Richard's apartment on the 45th floor of the building next door.

In seventh grade, I joined the Boy Scouts but only as a way to get out of the house on Tuesday nights. The idea of camping on weekends and playing tag on Tuesdays was fun, but I never considered getting a uniform. Strangely, I don't even recall being asked about it during my two years with the organization. Only years later did I discover the significance of my aversion to uniforms. We'll talk more about that later.

If you consider wearing jeans, high tops, and a white t-shirt to our meetings slightly rebellious, cheating to get my one and only merit badge would probably rank as my most memorable achievement — and I use the word achievement lightly.

I'm not even sure what possessed me to do it because I didn't care much for most scouting-related activities. It's even more bizarre in my mind because it wasn't as if I was gunning for a merit badge in camping, climbing, or canoeing; I cheated to get one in dentistry.

The night of my un-scout-like offense was a typical Tuesday except that instead of learning about knots or wilderness survival, the Scout Master brought in two young dental students to inspire our interest in all things oral. After sitting through a riveting presentation about tooth anatomy and oral hygiene, we were given a quiz. After passing a less-than-rigorous test, which was probably around the same degree of difficulty as the one professional football players are required to pass before joining the National Football League, I was surprised to learn the only other requirement was to build or carve a model tooth. I vaguely remembered having heard about the assignment the week before, but since I only joined to play dodgeball on school nights, the required carving and creativity wasn't something I made any effort to do.

Carving a tooth seemed like such a pointless requirement I was surprised so many of my friends made the effort. One by one, my fellow scouts walked into a small room adjacent to the larger room where we played games and presented their carvings. My friend Steve, who already had a uniform full of merit badges, was the second-to-last to go. Knowing how much Steve liked whittling and carving, I wasn't surprised to see him walk out a few minutes later with a new merit badge in his left hand. In his right hand, though, he still held the large molar he carved out of a bar of Dial Soap. I fully expected the dental students, like the Tooth Fairy, would consider the tooth a trade for the badge. But they didn't. In the moment, I had a flashback to the night a few years before when I swindled the Tooth Fairy by slicing the edge off a bar of Ivory Soap and putting it under the pillow so I could keep my tooth (for what I have no earthly idea). Armed with the confidence only a history of tooth-related larceny could inspire, and completely unconcerned with the lack of integrity and honor, I convinced Steve to let me use the bright orange tooth he carved for the occasion.

With seconds to spare, I secured the last place in line before the dental students packed up for the night. I honestly don't know why I thought they wouldn't recognize a bright orange molar they examined three minutes before, but I presented the tooth with all the earnestness I could muster. Perhaps they were too stunned to say anything. After all, they probably never expected to come face-to-face with the anti-Scout in the basement of Fourth Presbyterian Church that night. But there I was. It was such a brazen act, I can only imagine they let me get away with it because they correctly sensed I wasn't destined for scouting greatness.

The First Verse - Poignant Memories and the Power of Music

My father, in large part, was responsible for my passion for music. Whenever he heard Arlo Guthrie sing Steve Goodman's "City of New Orleans", he talked about how accurately the song describes the journey he made so many times between Chicago and New Orleans with his own father. Whether it's a beautiful melody, a deep and brooding minor key, or an intense bass line or drum beat, music is a powerful force in my life because it gives me access to what I experience as pure emotion. Judging by the tempo alone, music probably has a similar impact on the composers themselves. No matter how fast or slow the song, the vast majority fall in what would be considered the normal range of the human heart rate. Considering the way our heart rate changes with different emotional states, it makes sense that there would be a strong relationship between music, heart rate, and our emotional response — and that doesn't even factor in the impact of the melody and lyrics.

On some level, I had always seen the link between music and my moods, but it took a long time to fully grasp its importance on an emotional level. When I was in kindergarten and grade school, music was something that brought me joy. At recess, my friends and I would often stand on the playground and sing Beach Boys songs like, "Fun, Fun, Fun" and "Surfin' U.S.A." and pretend we were harmonizing. In high school and college, when typical teenage angst set in, my tastes evolved to the harsher sounds of The Ramones, The Sex Pistols, and The Clash.

In the midst of dealing with some long-forgotten issue, I created the *I'm Pissed Off Mix* that started out with "Bonzo Goes To Bitburg" by The Ramones, a song with the instantly recognizable chorus, "My brain is hanging upside down". For more than an hour the tape wound through a collection of fast and loud songs by The Clash, The Psychedelic Furs, Shriekback, and Ministry. About halfway through the mix, I began to recognize the power of the music to help me move beyond resistance to a place in which I was ready to release my anger and frustration. In less than one hour, music could take me from anger to a state of relative peace and contentment.

Over the next few years, whenever I found myself feeling upset, I put on my headphones or turned up the stereo and worked my way through the feelings by listening to music. In a way, the approach makes sense because feelings are, by definition, not something that can be dealt with rationally. Without music, my logical mind, like a hamster on a wheel, would have continually replayed whatever scenario I found upsetting. Music, on the other hand, gives my thinking mind a break and allows me to feel my way through the experience.

It often happens that people associate songs with a particular period or moment in their life because the song was an important part of the experience. For example, a remake of Chuck Berry's song "Rock 'N Roll Music" was on the first album I ever purchased, The Beach Boys 15 Big Ones. Whenever I hear songs from that album, I am immediately transported back to the time I was 9 or 10 years old. "Yellow Submarine" and "Octopus's Garden" by The Beatles have a similar effect as do countless other songs I have fallen in love with over the years.

When we have a chance to look back on this life from a higher perspective, I'm sure we'll understand the reason for some of these situations. But for now, certain songs like "Good Things" by The BoDeans remind me of the time I wasted in my twenties spinning my wheels without a mentor. The melody stirs up a powerful sense of loss and missed opportunity. At the same time, my inner optimist would like to reframe my thinking about this lost decade and instead focus on the many wonderful people I met and experiences I had. When I do, I am immediately reminded of Fr. Michael Ford, a priest I met as a student at Holy Cross. Fr. Ford, more than anyone else, gave me perspective on those aspects of our past with which we struggle.

"God draws straight with crooked lines," he said.

I've thought about that line a lot over the years because it captures so well the idea that sometimes the wrong path is precisely the one that leads us to the right path. I love that concept, not because it provides an excuse for bad behavior, but because it acknowledges the importance of experiencing what we don't want in order to focus on and appreciate what matters most. Jerry, a character in Edward Albee's play *Zoo Story*, described the same phenomenon in a completely different way: "Sometimes you have to go a long distance out of your way to come back a short distance correctly." (Many thanks to David Murphy, my gifted improv instructor, for pointing out this great quote.)

Early Faith

I remember praying a lot as a child, but mostly out of fear that people I loved wouldn't make it to heaven. You could say I had a strong relationship with God, but when it came to Sunday school, I had an equally strong relationship with McDonald's.

Sunday school was a little confusing, for starters, because it took place on Wednesday afternoon. The first few years, I took it at least somewhat seriously and looked forward to making my First Communion. At that point, we were living at 215 E. Chicago Avenue, one block east of Michigan Avenue, in a space now occupied by Lurie Children's Hospital. At the time, the Veteran's Administration Hospital was two blocks south and slightly east of our building so my parents let me walk by myself to the chapel on the fourth floor of the hospital where I attended mass every day after school. I don't remember much about my motivation for attending mass daily, but I cut back to weekend mass almost as quickly as I started.

The sudden spike and subsequent drop in mass attendance was reminiscent of my decision to quit kindergarten a few years before. I had asked to go to the public school with friends in the afternoon after spending the mornings at Montessori but found the concept better than the execution. I remember almost nothing except one girl who threw up every day and the fact that I didn't like racing home to find I had missed the beginning of Felix The Cat or Speed Racer.

The last few years of grade school, I distinctly remember walking from Ogden School at the corner of State and Walton south on State Street to Chicago Avenue to Holy Name Cathedral for church school or CCD (Confraternity of Christian Doctrine) as it was known. Other than the four or five block walks, the only thing I remember was sneaking into the McDonald's on the corner of Chicago Avenue and State Street, a place we weren't supposed to stop, to buy french fries.

Anyone who has ever walked within a block of someone holding a McDonald's bag can appreciate the utter impossibility of smuggling McDonald's food unnoticed into any enclosed space — including a cathedral. Nevertheless, it became part of my weekly routine to walk in late, sit in the back of class, and do my best to eat french fries or the occasional Quarter Pounder unnoticed.

The only somewhat religious lesson I recall was not directly from the nuns or lay teachers, but from my sister, ML, who laughed when she told me she was reprimanded for saying, *"Gesundheit!"* when one of her classmates sneezed. The indignant nun retorted, "'God Bless You' would have been more appropriate."

Early Health

I vaguely remember complaining about spending virtually every Wednesday from 1st grade through 8th grade at CCD. What I'm quite sure I didn't complain about was the number of operations I had during that same period to correct my severe case of club feet.

I actually looked forward to each surgery because every admission to Weiss Hospital in Chicago meant a new large manila envelope filled with cards from my classmates. It also didn't hurt that Weiss had roast duck on the menu — a dish my dad and I both loved. Only years later did I realize that most people don't necessarily look forward to being in the hospital.

The summer after I turned 15, our family moved from downtown Chicago to Winnetka, a suburb 20 miles north of the city. Not long after we moved, I noticed a large file cabinet in the basement and was curious to see what was inside. To my surprise, there were files for my five siblings and me, each containing everything from Social Security Cards and birth certificates to reports cards and pictures. In addition, my file also contained a few pictures taken the day after I was born.

Until that moment, the only baby pictures I had seen of myself were black and white photos taken when I was a few months old by a photographer at a Sears studio. Even though I had casts on both legs, they were completely hidden by my one-piece pajamas. I looked so happy in the pictures I was surprised when my parents pointed out the casts. However, the pictures I found in the basement file were not of my smiling, happy face, but of my feet. Until that moment, I had no idea how disfigured and bizarre my feet looked when I was born.

Shortly after I was born, Dr. Levon Topouzian, the orthopedic surgeon, remarked that I had the worst case of club feet he had ever seen. My feet literally looked like golf clubs. I had all the required bones but they weren't properly aligned and my Achilles tendons, which connect to the heels and play a pivotal role in movement and balance, were half as long as they should have been.

I knew all of this consciously because Dr. Topouzian and my parents had shared all of the details of the operations. Nevertheless, since I lacked a frame of reference, I didn't fully comprehend the extent of the issue.

The photographs seared unforgettable images in my mind. At the same time, my heart ached for what my parents must have experienced seeing me for the first time.

Discovering these pictures set off a wave of thoughts and emotions I didn't expect but, strangely, didn't feel unprepared for either. It almost felt like one of those scenes in a movie that flashes back and ties everything together once story-changing information has been revealed. I had been through the operations and had a basic understanding of what had happened, but nothing makes the case like photographic evidence. After experiencing a small sense of what my parents must have felt, my focus shifted to a deeper appreciation of my own resilience and upbeat nature.

This picture of my feet was taken the day after I was born.

I immediately remembered a story my parents had told me about an operation Dr. Topouzian performed on both feet around my first birthday. After a lengthy procedure in which he realigned the bones and inserted temporary pins to keep them in place during the healing process, Dr. Topouzian and his team came out to debrief my parents and prepare them for how much pain I'd likely be experiencing. When the nurses wheeled my crib in from the recovery room, I opened my eyes, smiled at everyone, and immediately pulled myself up to a standing position.

Horrified, Dr. Topouzian said, "Strap that kid down. He's going to ruin everything we just did."

Dr. Topouzian thought my feet would hurt so much I would never consider standing. Until recently, I always thought of that story as an example of my mostly upbeat personality that has been apparent from my earliest days. In many respects, that is still true. It's also a strong bit of evidence supporting what was, even at that point, a well-developed ability to repress unpleasant feelings. More about that later.

I don't remember sharing my discovery with anyone but kept the pictures and the shaky sense of helplessness I felt to myself. I didn't tell anybody because I was somewhat self-conscious to begin with and had no intention of doing anything to scare off my new friends. After transferring from St. Ignatius College Prep in the city, I was so grateful to start sophomore year with a clean slate. There were 4,400 students at New Trier High School — and all but five had no idea we shared the same planet. They didn't know about the lisp I had until I got my braces off the year before and they didn't know about my abnormally skinny calves. I had a chance to start over and I was intent on not blowing it.

Walking with Lymphoma and Dancing with the Obstacles

In hindsight, my journey into the realm of alternative medicine was even more important than I previously thought because it introduced me to people and practices that turned an even bigger challenge – the discovery of malignant tumors in my chest and neck on my 48th birthday – into the most unusual, and most soul-expandingly powerful gift I could ever have imagined.

I mark February 3rd as the start of this part of the journey even though it seemed a non-event at the time. On that night and the one that followed, I had difficulty sleeping because my chest hurt. I convinced myself that I had pulled a muscle in my chest while working out at the gym. Two nights later, when the discomfort had all but disappeared, I assumed my assessment was accurate. The next week, however, I awoke feeling as if someone had karate-chopped me in the throat, just below my Adam's apple. Still, I didn't give it too much attention.

The following night, the pressure in my throat returned, and I discovered an egg yolk-sized swelling immediately above my right collar bone. It was a lot lower than any other swollen gland I had ever had and a trainer at the gym advised me to get it checked out.

I stopped by my dad's office and had him take a look. He thought it might be a goiter or a thyroid cyst, but also wanted me to get an ultrasound to be sure; the ultrasound techs, in turn, recommended a CT scan. Before I knew it, I was meeting with Dr. Stephen Becker, an ear, nose, and throat surgeon. After a chest x-ray, Dr. Becker, not liking what he saw, decided to do a needle biopsy on the spot. Then, on my birthday, I got a CT scan and heard words I never thought I would hear: "You have an eight centimeter by five-centimeter by seven-centimeter tumor in your chest just below your sternum and above your heart. We don't know exactly what it is, but it's most likely either a lymphoma or a germ cell tumor."

Dr. Becker went on to say that the odds were overwhelming the tumor would be curable with chemo and radiation. To get a more definitive diagnosis, Dr. Becker scheduled a surgical biopsy of the lymph node in my neck, and a few days later, he called with the preliminary diagnosis: Large B-Cell Lymphoma. Later, the oncologist, Leo Gordon, added a bit more specificity: Aggressive Primary Mediastinal Non-Hodgkin's High Grade Large B-Cell Lymphoma – Stage 2.

Soon afterward, I began a five-day inpatient chemo treatment that repeated every 21 days through the end of June. As I began to share the news with family and friends, I remained optimistic. A few people, including my dad, said, "If you have to have a tumor, lymphoma is the one you want."

As you might imagine, I did a lot of thinking over the first few weeks and months. After my previous eye-opening medical experiences, I was open to any methods to cope with and recover from this diagnosis. Almost immediately, the situation changed my thinking about the language around this diagnosis.

From the start, I never identified with having cancer. This was not denial as much as it was the simple recognition that the words cancer and chemo are far too broad. Instead, I began to think about health and disease as a range from zero to 100, with zero being perfect health and 100 being close to death. With that in mind, a common cold would be a one. A small cut requiring stitches might be a two. Broken bones, depending on the severity, might start around three or four. Cancer, the way we currently define it, could legitimately take up 85 or more positions on the continuum ranging from the low teens or so up to 100. Such a broad range is a bit confusing, especially when you consider the associations many of us have with words like cancer and chemo.

Overcoming, beating, or kicking cancer's ass, were also concepts I never related to. At all. Phrases like these conjured up images of battle and swimming upstream. I did not see it that way.

When I first heard about the tumors, I was not seeing the experience as a gift. The first twelve days between the discovery and the diagnosis were the most difficult emotionally. To be fair though, it did not take too long before I slid into a place of relative peace, acceptance, and openness. Somehow, I knew at a soul level that the tumors brought lessons for me. My goal was to accept the situation, walk with it, learn from it, and resolve it. I had no intention of fighting because I knew in my heart that resistance would only tempt nature to fight back harder. I may be strong, but I would not give myself particularly good odds in a battle against life and nature.

I was also careful about the way I referred to the tumors. Shen Robinson, a gifted medical intuitive I will say more about later, pointed out the importance of separating myself from the tumors both verbally and energetically. For this reason, I worked hard to avoid using personal pronouns like "my" and "mine" with respect to the tumors. They were something I was experiencing. Most importantly, they were not permanent.

The days before the treatment began were filled with a wide range of procedures including a PET scan, a test designed to determine how advanced the lymphoma was. After the test, I pulled out of the hospital parking garage and turned on my car radio. To my horror, I heard the song "Don't Fear the Reaper" by the Blue Oyster Cult. I love the song, but that wasn't exactly the sign I was looking for as I wondered about my prognosis. Fortunately, my friend Robbie Schaefer from the band Eddie from Ohio called about one minute before the song ended.

I just love Robbie. Besides being an incredible human being with a huge heart, he also has a peaceful energy and the ability to put everything in perspective. When I told him about the song and thanked him for his perfect timing, Robbie laughed and said "Never doubt that the Universe has a sense of humor." In that moment, he instantly changed my perception. Thinking of the moment as a cosmic joke rather than a sign made a huge difference in my outlook. One might legitimately wonder how you tell the difference between a sign and a joke. The honest answer is that I don't know. But when the recipient is too dense or wrapped up in earthly issues to sense the humor — as was the case with me — at least some of the time the Universe will send an angel like Robbie to make the point. Sensing that, it makes me laugh to think how often my guardian angels must shake their heads in utter disbelief.

Throughout the treatment, my more spiritual friends helped in many ways – offering the use of a crystal healing bed; taking my concerns to John of God, a famous Brazilian healer; and putting me in touch with, Dave Choi, a chef who prepares special meals for people going through chemo.

What I did not realize at the time, but see clearly now, is that dealing with uncertainty was a huge part of the lesson. Once the diagnosis and prognosis had been determined, uncertainty showed up in other forms. How would my body handle the chemo treatments? What side effects would I experience? What would be the impact of increasing the dose for the first four treatments? How would I handle six five-day inpatient treatments as I watched the weather get progressively warmer? Would I be so sick that I would need someone to stay with me?

The strangest effect from the first treatment was gaining 13 pounds of water weight in a 36-hour period. Fortunately, that situation was remedied with an infusion of Lasix, a diuretic that worked almost instantly. By the time I returned home, the extra weight was gone. The first chemo treatment reduced the pressure in my neck and chest so much that I only noticed slight discomfort once or twice between treatments. The only other side effects were fatigue and a strange stomach cramp. The fatigue was manageable in the sense that I learned to work around those days when I found myself needing a nap. The stomach cramp was different. The cramp lasted three days, stayed in exactly the same spot, and intensified when I ate.

The second treatment was an almost exact repeat of the first, despite the dose being 20% higher. It was also more fun than the first time around since I had now come to be familiar with the many friendly faces of the people at the hospital. Everyone was incredibly nice and upbeat, a feat I found amazing considering the number of serious-looking leukemia and cancer cases on the unit.

Considering that three of the six chemotherapy drugs they gave me had hair loss as a side effect, I knew there would be no escaping baldness. I also knew I did not want to watch the hair on my head thin and fall out. I am strong; but I am not that strong.

The best part about losing my hair had nothing to do with function and everything to do with appearance. It was great having women at the gym tell me I looked younger and hotter, but the funniest memory was the night I had four female couchsurfers from France and Slovakia over for dinner. They got into an animated discussion about the actors I resemble with and without hair. I must admit, I liked the comparisons to Bruce Willis and Matthew McConaughey, but they lost me with Lord Voldemort. When I finally had to admit that they had a point, I updated my Facebook profile with a split picture with Lord Voldemort on one side and me on the other. Half my friends thought it was hilarious. The other half found it horrifying.

Despite the ongoing uncertainty, I quickly found myself in a place where, except for the strange and unexpected side effects, I felt happier and more connected than I had ever felt in my life. As the journey progressed, I made it past milestone after milestone. The more milestones I passed, the more certain I felt that the lessons were over.

After the final treatment, I had to wait five weeks to repeat the PET and CT scans to confirm what I already knew in my heart: that the tumors were gone. Although there was one small area in my chest at the site of the largest tumor that showed some activity on the PET scan, it was not unusual and happens in about half the cases with only a 5% chance of being abnormal. To eliminate the uncertainty, Dr. Gordon sent me to a thoracic surgeon for the robotic removal of the suspicious area under the sternum.

What fascinated me most, besides the state-of-the-art surgical procedure, was the fact that the three-week wait for the procedure meant that the uncertainty at the end of the treatment was almost twice as long as the uncertainty of waiting for a diagnosis. Another opportunity to learn the lesson.

Putting It into Practice

This is a good time to stop and reflect on your own journey. First, what are the moments, issues, or challenges that stand out as particularly memorable or important — even if you weren't sure why at the time. Add to that list experiences or feelings you had along the way that didn't necessarily fit with your beliefs or what you had been taught. Trust your intuition. If an experience seems worth recording, write it down. It may make sense later. It may make sense years from now. It may never make sense. For now, trust the process.

CHAPTER 2:

Identifying the Roadblocks

"

When patterns are broken, new worlds emerge.
– Tuli Kupferberg

When I work with people one-on-one as a career coach, my approach is to learn as much as I can about their experiences, accomplishments, challenges, interests, and goals, as well as the decisions they have made along the way. Once I have enough of the pieces, a clearer picture emerges that accurately reflects who they are, what they have done, and why a particular path may or may not make sense as the next logical step in their personal and professional development. At first, I thought of the process as a putting together a puzzle, but it eventually occurred to me that a better way to describe the process is that of creating a mosaic.

Viewing the individual experiences as a collective is a classic case of the whole being greater than the sum of its parts. Better still, it is more accurate because a puzzle implies there is only one correct picture, when that is not the case at all. Our experiences can be combined in myriad ways to create different images of ourselves as they relate to what we want to do and who we want to be.

Like many people I have met over the years, my life has been a series of sharp twists and turns on a path that, for the most part, felt less like a smoothly paved road and more like an untraveled trail through a heavily wooded forest on my way to some unknowable destination. It reminds me of the scene in the movie *Romancing the Stone* in which Kathleen Turner follows Michael Douglas through the rainforest as he uses a machete to slice away at the underbrush. When she asks, "Where are we going?" he replies, "I don't know. I think it's a path." In my own journey, only as I reach what feels like a halfway point and look back does any of the scenery along the way make sense.

Adopting a New Mindset

The expansion of my beliefs from a traditional Catholic upbringing has been an evolution. I have friends who experienced a crisis of faith that caused them to question and ultimately reject the Church, but it did not happen that way for me. During the same journey in which I hit various milestones within the Catholic Church – First Communion, Confession, Confirmation – I made a series of discoveries outside the Church that unexpectedly shaped my experience and belief system.

More than any other, the concept of past lives made me question what I had been taught. I first heard about past lives in the George Harrison song "Give Me Love (Give Me Peace on Earth)":

> *Give me love*
>
> *Give me love*
>
> *Give me peace on earth*

Give me light

Give me life

Keep me free from birth.

This song was released the year I turned six, and I remember asking someone what Harrison meant by "keep me free from birth." This was when I learned that in the Hindu religion, people believe in reincarnation for souls that didn't get it right and have more work to do in order to reach moksha or liberation. In the Hindu tradition, Moksha is one the four goals of human life, collectively referred to as Puruṣārtha. Moksha represents a release from the cycle of life, death, and rebirth. The other three goals are dharma, a virtuous and moral life, artha, prosperity and financial security, and kama, pleasure and emotional fulfillment.

At first, I didn't like the idea of reincarnation at all because I thought the goal was to get to, and stay, in heaven. But, over time, that began to change. One of the people most influential in the evolution of my thinking was psychiatrist and author, Dr. Brian Weiss.

Through hypnotic regression therapy, Weiss helped patients uncover and understand their soul journey across multiple lifetimes. The more my mind opened to the possibility, the more evidence seemed to appear.

According to many historians, reincarnation was an accepted part of the early Church belief system until 545 A.D., when Emperor Justinian forced the ruling cardinals to draft a papal decree forbidding the belief in reincarnation. It might seem odd that a Roman Emperor would take the time to refute the possibility of reincarnation, but in a twisted way, the logic makes sense: if people thought they had more than one lifetime to get it right, they would be more difficult for the Romans and Church leaders to control.

Despite efforts to remove passages from the Bible that mention reincarnation, there are a number of references that remain. For example, in John 1:21-27, John the Baptist denies being Elijah when asked; the fact that they were asking the questions at all strongly suggests reincarnation was an accepted possibility:

They asked him, "Then who are you? Are you Elijah?" He said, "I am not." "Are you the Prophet?" He answered, "No." Finally, they said, "Who are you? Give us an answer to take back to those who sent us. What do you say about yourself?" John replied in the words of Isaiah the prophet, "I am the voice of one calling in the desert, 'Make straight the way for the Lord.'" Now some Pharisees who had been sent questioned him, "Why then do you baptize if you are not the Christ, nor Elijah, nor the Prophet?" "I baptize with water," John replied, "but among you stands one you do not know. He is the one who comes after me, the thongs of whose sandals I am not worthy to untie."

The historical context is fascinating, but whether my beliefs align with what the Church once taught or currently accepts is not particularly important to me. Nor am I on a mission to get other people to change their beliefs. Instead, I have come to view reincarnation not as a punishment that keeps you from reuniting with loved ones in heaven, but as an opportunity for souls to re-experience what it means to be human and, in many cases, to help others on their journey.

The best examples I have seen come from the patients at Lurie Children's Hospital, formerly Children's Memorial, where I volunteered for 34 years starting when I was a junior in high school. Seeing children who lived a few hours, days, weeks, or years not as victims, but as souls who came to help and teach others important lessons about love and loss – or even to further medical knowledge – is so much more hopeful and inspiring. It does not make sense to me that if God (Creator, Source, the Universe, or whatever you like to call it) is truly loving, there would be souls who only get one short chance to experience the miracle of life.

Reincarnation is not the only point on which I have a different view than the Catholic Church, but it isn't necessary to get into a long discussion about it. I carry with me the life-affirming lessons I learned about loving one another, make my own decisions on other issues, and focus on a more spiritual approach.

I had long since left the house when I made the decision to stop attending weekly Mass, so there have not been any issues with my family as it relates to what I believe. It is not a topic we have spent much time discussing, though I do know that my dad was definitely open to the possibility of reincarnation. After three of my siblings studied in Rome, we decided to take a family trip to experience Christmas Eve Mass at the Vatican. My dad frequently spoke with amazement about how he would walk down the streets of Rome and know what was around the next corner, even though he had never been there before. He was convinced he had a lifetime in ancient Rome. Given his passion for Latin and Ancient Greek, the fact that he even majored in those languages in college, and his insistence that my siblings and I study Latin, I am not at all surprised.

Identifying an Emotional Block

We can learn a lot from young children and infants who are able to shift from agitation to amusement in a moment simply by having their needs met. Once crying newborns get fed, held, or changed, they don't brood for another hour about how mad they are that it took so long for their caregivers to respond; they shift instantly. Unfortunately, we lose this ability and develop instead a habit of thinking and rationalizing our way through problems. That doesn't always work, however, as I discovered through my session with Therese Rowley, Ph.D., a gifted, Chicago-based intuitive.

I met Therese through my good friend Jackie Hart. Jackie had a strong sense that Therese and I needed to meet so she arranged a lunch. Several years later, I found myself reaching out to Therese again and scheduling a private session with her.

To my delight, the time with Therese proved even more enlightening than I hoped. My goal was to explore the inescapable feeling that, despite modest success for my first book, *Getting Your Foot in the Door When You Don't Have a Leg to Stand On* (McGraw-Hill), and the speaking and coaching career it inspired, I felt like my progress had come to a grinding halt. After years of applying the principles of the Law of Attraction and doing my best to remain focused and positive, the financial rewards remained elusive.

Since Therese had seen me speak a few years before, she was aware of my writing and speaking. Nevertheless, she would have had no way of knowing how stuck and frustrated I felt, nor did I want to give her any clues. After a brief prayer, Therese shut her eyes and began to tune in to what she was seeing. Throughout the following 90 minutes, Therese rarely asked any questions, and instead focused on what she was seeing energetically. Whenever she came across a block in my energy, she would describe what she was seeing and do her best to interpret each image before snapping her fingers in rapid succession, waving her hands, and blowing forcefully to clear out whatever might be holding me back. She did not know it at the time, but the first image received of me toiling away at an unnecessarily complex project accurately depicted the tedious, frustrating years leading up to our session.

Twenty-five minutes into the session, after describing several past life or archetypal scenarios that correctly represented aspects of my relationships with a few immediate family members, Therese went on to describe what she saw as the beautiful, elaborate method I had devised to "stuff my feelings." As she admired the beauty of it, she was quick to point out that what may have once served a purpose was no longer working for me. After asking for permission to look further, Therese had me to say my full name aloud three times. After I replied, "Robert Ryan Sullivan" for the third time, Therese paused, sighed deeply, and proceeded to snap her fingers 15 times before speaking again.

After a long three minutes of Therese's energetic digging and a growing look of surprise on her face, my curiosity was high as it had ever been and I was on the verge of flying out of my seat screaming, "What? What is it? TELL ME!"

Therese went on to describe seeing a life as a soldier in which I performed my duties so well I received multiple promotions and, in the process, became more accountable for my behavior and the impact it had on others. Upon further exploration, Therese uncovered a pattern of punishing myself for not having had the courage to speak up and suffer the consequences. These observations proved insightful in a few unexpected ways. My extreme dislike for uniforms, as it turns out, started much further back than my boy scout days. So many memories that previously seemed disconnected and insignificant suddenly made sense. What also made sense was my fear around the time I was 17 about being drafted and whether I could use my feet as an excuse for not serving. My strong aversion to military service was particularly interesting given how much my dad loved being in the U.S. Air Force.

Apparently, I was so hard on myself after the lifetime as a soldier that I decided to use subsequent lifetimes to serve humanity without reward. As Therese talked about this decision, I remember thinking, "Well, that would certainly account for the lack of financial traction in my current life."

Therese then wondered aloud if my commitment to serve humanity, at a soul level, was an agreement or a vow. Sensing I was not clear on the difference or the implications of each, Therese explained that a vow was more challenging in the sense that it would represent a more formal commitment I made to myself on a soul-level. A less formal agreement would have been more akin to a decision I could easily reverse, in much the same way a donut can derail well-intentioned decisions about dieting.

Had it been an agreement I was ready to consciously release, Therese could have cleared the energy in alignment with my willingness to do so. As it was a vow, she explained, I would have to recognize the seriousness with which I created the vow, and be the one to clear it. In that same session, Therese guided me through a brief exercise in which I envisioned the commitment memorialized on parchment. To eliminate the vow, Therese then guided me through a visualization in which I acknowledged no longer needing the vow and proceeded to visualize myself burning the parchment thereby releasing myself from its power. Unlike the charlatans of the psychic world who might have used the opportunity to extort money and additional sessions, Therese recognized and addressed the issue in the same session without requiring additional payment. I mention this because I have met with psychics who do not share Therese's sense of integrity; instead, they try to sell everything from candles and prayers to additional sessions.

Letting go of the vow proved to be a sudden shift, not one that required focused attention, but one that occurred on a soul level. A week later, I experienced a powerful dream in which a being claiming to be "That part of you responsible for stuffing your feelings" begged me to not let him go. When he realized I had already made up my mind, he left. Almost immediately following the dream, I began to gain significant traction in my business.

I am well aware many people will question this. That does not bother me because I know what happened. And I know what is true. Believe me, it would be easier – and more believable – to find a way to take credit by pointing to a particular action I took to get my financial life back on track. But that is not what happened.

In my case, expanding my beliefs was more about remaining open to new ideas and entertaining the possibility that not all church teachings are helpful, empowering, or even particularly Christian. For others, the questioning of faith marks a much more powerful moment with life-long implications. For Lora, the moment proved to be a turning point that led her from an evangelical Christian upbringing to a more open mindset toward spirituality:

> *I remember the moment quite clearly, though nothing about it would have been memorable to anyone watching me. I was driving down a road in the northwest suburbs of Chicago at night, on my way home from a 12-step meeting for an eating disorder. At 23 years old, the road I was more focused on was an internal one, and I saw a fork in it: if I kept my current religion – I was an evangelical Christian and had been for 10 years, a devoted, Bible-packing, street-evangelism, door-to-door, prayerful, Bible-studying, church-attending-three-times-a-week, remain-a-virgin-until-marriage Christian – I was going to die.*
>
> *I'd entered 12-step groups four years prior because of a budding eating disorder, and by the time I took that car ride, I was intermittently suicidal and fighting to find my way out*

of the darkness of bulimia. My evangelical faith could not lift the darkness, and the harder I tried, the more I felt like a failure, an imposter. I wanted to follow Jesus, but there seemed to be only one right way to love and serve God, and I did not fit that mold. I made a decision that night: I would drop the evangelicalism of my last decade. I did not know what lay down the other road. I feared it might be eternal damnation. It seemed a real risk at that time. But I knew I could no longer be a part of that religion, and so I decided in that moment that what I could hold on to was the initial, mystical connection I felt with something, something I thought was God, and let go of the evangelical interpretation and prescription for what that experience was and how it should be lived out. Twenty-six years later, I'm grateful for the courage I had to take that unknown fork and for the life it made possible.

Now Lora's spiritual practices include mindfulness, meditation, connection with nature, and working with art. Most importantly, she spends her time connecting with others in deeply authentic ways — teaching meditation and yoga and facilitating a safe transformative and healing place for others. Though she does attend a Unitarian church, her path of inquiry is about what is meaningful in life and how we can best love another. As the Dalai Lama says, "My religion is kindness."

Beth also found her ideal connection away from the organized religion her family continues to practice. Here is how she describes it:

I grew up Orthodox Jewish and attended an Orthodox Jewish day school so I was very, very sheltered. My parents, particularly my father, are quite religious. My mother, who grew up conservative, decided to become Orthodox as a teenager and my father attends synagogue twice a day. Judaism is the main, identifying force in his life, bar none.

I, on the other hand, have always been a strong-willed and assertive woman. Naturally, I started to question certain things at age 12 or 13. More specifically, I had trouble accepting the fact that women don't have a visible part in the Orthodox Jewish community at all. Worse, they were relegated to subservient status. I also began to wonder why I had to observe the laws of keeping kosher and the Sabbath — practices that didn't seem to have a common-sense basis or that resonated and made sense as to why I should follow them. But I did.

After high school, everything changed. I attended a seminary in Jerusalem, but felt so far removed from what they were teaching that I left halfway through the program. At that point, one of the rabbis told me I was "a waste of a Jew." The intention behind the statement made it particularly horrifying – it's one of the most disgusting things anyone could say to someone else. Up until that point, I had been questioning my connection to Orthodox Judaism, but that really solidified it. That's when I started to pull away.

What made my decision particularly difficult is the fact that I never wanted to disrespect my parents because religion is so important to them. I kept up appearances out of a sense of guilt until my mid-30s, when I finally told them I was no longer religious and no longer observant. Seeing their reaction and knowing they felt they had failed as parents made it especially difficult, [but] at the same time, I was tired of pretending. I feel strongly that religion is so personal and so private that one person can't dictate what another person's relationship to a higher power ought to look like.

A lot of my peers got married in their 20s, but my life has taken a very different turn from what was expected of me in the Orthodox Jewish community. I don't go to services at all for high holidays because I don't want to be resentful in a house that is dedicated to the observance of God. I do believe in God or a Higher Power, but I don't believe anyone should tell me what that looks like. Also, I never wanted to feel shameful or guilty for the choices I made that diverged from everyone else's.

At this point, I'm somewhat of an outsider looking in on my family of origin. From this unique perspective, I see one brother who is an atheist and attends a synagogue with his family primarily because he wants to pass the traditions down to his children. Then I see my other brother who buys into the religion and the traditions but doesn't live a life that adheres to all of the requirements and commandments. I feel like I am the only person in my family being honest with it.

When it comes to my spiritual life, I don't want to have to follow rules. I don't like anyone telling me what to do — particularly if I don't have an understanding as to why I need to do it. I've always felt very much like a second-class citizen being an Orthodox Jewish woman watching men get certain privileges afforded to them simply because they are male. The fact that I am intelligent and successful was never going to matter as much as whether I got married and had children. I'm comfortable with the fact that I am, and always have been, a very spiritual person and more of a free spirit. There's too much connection and too many serendipitous things happening for it to be a coincidence. There's something bigger than all of us.

My current spiritual practice involves yoga and meditation. In the summer, I sit by the lake or in the middle of the park and meditate. I reflect on things more. The older I get, the more grateful I am for certain things I have. Yoga is the thing I do the most. I practice four days a week. When I look at the wonders of the world and the beauty and how nature changes, that gives me more perspective on the bigger picture and that there is something bigger that oversees everything and it is not just science in a box. There's something else. I feel most grounded being out in nature; sitting on the ground amidst the trees is particularly cleansing to me.

Despite my decision to pursue my own path, the religious traditions continue to hinder a big chunk of my life. For example, I've never seen myself wanting to marry anyone I've dated and I've never seriously dated anyone who is Jewish. One reason I've dated people who don't have real long-term potential is that my parents would never come to my wedding if I married someone who wasn't Jewish. That would be a colossal, devastating blow to them. It would also be a huge embarrassment to them in their community. For a long time, the impact on my dating life was subconscious. Now it is something I am more cognizant of. Nevertheless, it is sad to realize I've chosen partners with no long-term potential because my parents would never come to my wedding and I'd never ask anyone to convert, given that the request would be solely for the sake of my parents. My parents are super proud of me now and they are happy that I'm successful professionally, but I don't know that they will ever fully come to terms with the decisions I've made.

Unlike Lora and Beth who were exposed to organized religion from an early age, Veronica grew up with a different understanding of the divine that nevertheless evolved:

Throughout my life I have always felt a strong connection to the Divine, even though I did not have a name for it, or a way to put it into words. I was raised by two hippie parents who taught me "God lives in you, as you." Even still the word "God" always triggered me. I imagined it referenced some man sitting on a cloud agreeing to answer some prayers and ignoring others. I found the concept of God to be conditional and limited. I was a self-proclaimed agnostic.

Through many dreams that have come true, personal spiritual growth work, the connection with my guides, and the help of a broken ankle, I have grown more and more into a relationship with this energy presence that exists in everything (call it Source, Life Force, Creator, or God) – I have come to experience it more tangibly in my life. There is a clear sense of knowing that is present. We all have access to it, however many of us choose not to listen.

For a long time, I felt like religion was a limitation – belief systems that had been created to control people and keep them in line. However, I now see within each religion are elements of greater Spiritual Truths – some of which have been distorted over time. And rather than give us access to the big space of God and all Life Force - religion has led us to believe we are separate from it. However, we are not, and cannot be separate from that big space. It is in us; it is the essence of who we are.

Spiritual teachings that lead us back into connection with our own true essence – that point the direction towards the ever-expanding God space – are the ones I have come to respect. I believe all of the ascended masters and saints have come forth to remind us of these Spiritual Truths. However, their messages and teachings have been altered over time and through translation. Anything and anyone who leads us back towards our own personal connection and highest knowing is on the right track.

The more I expand in my relationship with this God presence, or God energy, the more I perceive it as pure peace, a vast, ever-loving presence which holds no judgment or anger. It is completely without condition or expectation, and has created this huge playground for us to remember who we really are. And even that remembrance – is a choice! What will you choose?

[Note: Veronica sends out spiritual and thought-provoking emails every night she refers to as "Today's Practice".]

The passage below is a Today's Practice I wrote a few years back. I was just guided to reread it and send it to you.

The idea of God is a confusing one. Many of us have fear of God or mistrust in God. We have a sense of unworthiness, lack, reaction or distortion about what God means – what God is. Many of us were raised to believe God didn't love us unless we were good. Or that we should fear the wrath of God. We have been told stories of a vengeful God – or of no God at all. Perhaps we have had moments where we felt so victimized that it would seem impossible for there to be a God! How then can we trust people who speak of a loving God that they know - and if this exists then why does it only show up for those people?!

These are all thoughts I have had.

Growing up my parents would tell me "God lives in you, as you." And while I liked this version a whole lot more than the religious version I heard others speak of - I still did not know God.

The deeper my spiritual practice became, the more I meditated, the more I learned how to speak with my guides and listen, the more I trusted that the Universe had a place for me, the more I began to wonder and question what God really means, what God really is. It certainly didn't seem to me it was some man who looked like Charlton Heston sitting on a cloud who decided some people were good and should have their prayers answered and others were bad. But this is the God we are fed through religion, media, society and pop culture. If that's not God, then what is? The logical answer - God must not exist. But if God doesn't exist than how is it that my heart beats every day? How is it that trees exhale exactly what I need to inhale? How is it that the presence in the eyes of a child can be so healing?

If God lives in me, as me, if I am God then isn't God living in everything? If I am God, then my brother is God, isn't my dog God as well? What then of the terrorist who chooses to blow himself up for his beliefs, is he God too? What of an emotionally abusive ex, or the jerk who cut me off on the highway?!

These are all legitimate thoughts and questions - and so who better to ask them of than God Itself. And so I did.

One day a few years ago while deep in meditation in Brazil I asked Creator, (Creator was a name for this indescribable presence that I felt safe with). I asked Creator, "If you live in all things, if everything is You, how then can there be toxic waste? How can there be wars and crime? If you are everything, what are You?"

The answer was so simple - as God usually is:

"There are different types of food. Yes?"

"Yes." I replied.

"There are twinkies and there are fresh organic apples. One can choose to eat whatever they like. Because each person, each being, has freewill. You could eat Cheetos®, or a salad. Both these items are food, you may think one is 'better' for you than the other, but they are both food. There can be 'good' food, and 'bad' food, but it's all food. What you choose to eat is your choice. Just like me - I am everything, I am in everyone - how you choose to act is your choice. How you choose to perceive me is up to you."

What I have come to learn is that there are levels of God, just as there are different types of food. Which version we choose to align with is up to us, just as we can choose what to eat. McDonald's or home cooking?

The God I know is all loving, all forgiving, non-judgmental, open, kind and very neutral. It does not look like a man or a woman, it does not have a form. It is an energy, a presence, a cloud, a fire, an ocean. We are a candle of light in the fire. We are a drop of water in the ocean. The more I align into this knowing, the more I feel held, safe, connected and supported in each and every moment.

God's arms are always open to us, often we are the ones who made the choice to turn left when deep down we knew to turn right. Then after things have gone south, we blame God for it, "How could YOU let this happen to me?" When it was us who veered off course. We blame God and state God must not exist.

In Aramaic, the word for sin actually means missing the mark. Meaning we have an intention about why we came in - we had some level or version of God we were connected to and then somewhere along the way we veered off. Somewhere along the way we made a choice that led us off course. God doesn't judge us for this, because God does not judge Itself. It is up to us to forgive (ourselves and anyone else involved) and course correct (each and every time we veer off course, which can happen daily!). As I said, God's arms are always open. We make the choice to go back into it - back into the ocean of light, of love, of presence. This is the Source of life, the Creator of all, the God that has been so misconstrued and used against us.

If the word God does not work for you, replace it with Creator, or Source. This is what I used to do. Until one day I felt that hiding from the word God was holding me back from really stepping into that ocean, from really living it and being it in my day-to-day life (outside my meditation in my bedroom). The God I know is not a religious God, it is a non-denominational presence of ever-expanding love. It is inside and I cannot be separated from it, nor can you. It is the essence of who you are, who we are. It is what makes your heart beat every day. It breaks down the food you eat and turns it into energy.

I will leave you with this message I received a few months ago from this presence of God, "When you look at your hands, know those are not your hands, they are My hands. When you look in your eyes, know those are not your eyes, they are My eyes. When you look in the mirror, you are looking into My eyes..."

Whether or not our beliefs evolve, change, or shift radically, what matters is that we remain open to new ideas and experiences. For some people like Lora who moved away from her evangelical upbringing, it becomes a matter of health and survival. In my case, it happened as a way to better understand and come to terms with life as I have experienced it. I also view my beliefs and spirituality as an evolution. No one can claim to have it all figured out. Reaching that point would be a warning sign that we are no longer open to new experiences. I prefer to think of it as a buffet of sorts: if a belief or experience helps me understand myself and others better, makes me more loving, and helps me develop the patience and compassion I know I need to work on, then it is worth exploring.

Putting It into Practice

A few questions to consider as you reflect on your own journey:

- What beliefs were you taught as a child?

- Which beliefs resonated strongly with you?

- Which beliefs did you find challenging or difficult to accept?

- To what degree have you shared your thoughts with others — family, friends, priests, rabbis, etc.?

- How have your beliefs evolved?

CHAPTER 3:

Improving Communication
Through Awareness

Nothing goes really to waste if you're determined to learn.
-- Isaac Asimov

Considering the importance of communication in our lives, it is not surprising that so many of life's lessons are often related to that. However, there is a prerequisite for effective communication: we have to have a message or point to communicate. Dreams, which we will cover later, encouraged me to dive into my emotions and helped me understand what I was thinking and feeling at a deeper level. Likewise, a lesson I learned from my accountants gave me something — namely boundaries — to communicate in situations where my previous approach would have been avoidance. Once I became aware of the necessity of being an effective communicator, I was determined to become one.

To do so, I first had to develop the ability to recognize, feel, and communicate the range of emotions that came into play in relationships as well as everyday interactions. Not feeling particularly in touch with my own emotions, whenever I experienced a subtle shift in the way I felt, I began to ask, "What am I feeling right now?"

By repeatedly asking that question in the moment, I challenged myself to pick up on subtle differences. Looking below the surface, I eventually realized the powerful underlying emotions are often masked by anger. For example, when the root cause of anger is embarrassment, I have found it much more helpful to focus my attention and energy on forgiving myself. When fear is the underlying emotion, simply allowing myself to feel vulnerable, or powerless, or whatever the situation calls for helps the wave of emotion pass without me making it worse through words and actions.

Until the last few years, not being in touch with my emotions at a deeper level was one of the biggest obstacles standing between me and a meaningful, long-term relationship. Dr. Michael Tansey, the psychologist I saw during my senior year of high school, described the phenomenon in visual terms. First, he stretched his hands far apart to represent the distance between two people who are at the beginning phases of a relationship and do not know each other particularly well. Then, as he brought his hands to within four or five inches of each other, he described my ability to quickly connect and feel comfortable with someone in the context of a relationship. Unfortunately, in Dr. Tansey's example, it was the last few inches that represented true intimacy in an emotional sense: the willingness to trust myself and another person enough to let go and be completely vulnerable and open.

Much like directions that do not seem to get complicated until the last mile or so, the gap between immediate rapport and true intimacy has been a reference point that simultaneously haunts me for my past failings and inspires me to become the partner some loving woman deserves.

When I look back to past relationships, it makes me cringe to realize what a horrible communicator I really was. What seemed like a small four-inch distance in Dr. Tansey's relationship continuum proved to be a chasm it would take most of my adult life to understand, address, and navigate. The worst part of the process has been the awareness of the pain I unintentionally caused along the way.

The harsh truth is that quite a few of my relationships looked like a game of chicken. We would race at each other at top speed and swerve at the last minute to avoid genuine connectedness. In most cases, I was the one doing the swerving. Having grown and evolved, I am determined to be the person in relationships I would want as a partner. The best part is that it feels so much better to communicate honestly and openly. That is an incredible relief compared to how soul-wrenchingly difficult and uncomfortable it can be to hide one's feelings. No matter how hard the conversation is, if it needs to happen, my commitment is to have the courage and courtesy to be present in the moment and communicate openly.

Without question, the relationship that suffered most from my communication challenges was with Amy. The heartbreak I experienced from losing her proved to be a catalyst for personal growth on multiple levels. For this reason, it is not especially surprising that she is one of only a handful of people who has ever made frequent, repeat appearances in my dreams. What I find genuinely confusing though, is why she continued to appear in my dreams more than 15 years after our last contact.

In the book *Conversations with God*, Neale Donald Walsch writes about the important role each person we encounter plays in our lives. In the book, God challenges Walsch by saying that every person we meet, even the ones who hurt us, are angels who are in our lives for a reason. Our challenge is to see and accept the gifts that each one of these people provides. In my life, Amy is one of those angels, not because she hurt me – although the break up was painful – but because she was the first woman I ever dated with whom I recall having deeper spiritual conversations.

In addition to her work as an occupational therapist, Amy is also a Reiki Master. Along the way, she introduced me to a number of intuitives and healers including Shen Robinson, a woman who played an important part in my own healing journey.

Not long before Amy and I began dating, I had moved back to my parents' house to work on my first book. Since I was not making any money, it was wonderful to have that kind of support from my parents. However, money became a big issue in my relationship with Amy because I found not having a steady income incredibly frustrating. At that stage of my life, financial well-being was the way I erroneously measured success and happiness.

For most of our relationship, my struggle with limiting beliefs and my scarcity mentality about money kept me from seeing how much fun Amy and I had without spending much money. We often went bike riding, made dinner at her house, or simply enjoyed each other's company. We were especially compatible when it came to music as we enjoyed many of the same bands. Better still, almost everyone in her family seemed musically inclined. That led to occasional jam sessions with her dad and brothers. To my delight, Amy also played banjo. I didn't expect to fall in love with her family as well, but that's exactly what happened.

One of the highlights of our relationship was the summer trip we took to Jackson Hole, Wyoming to stay at the home of one of Amy's good friends. We jogged through the cool mountain air, hiked challenging trails, drove to Yellowstone, visited a beautiful chapel with a bay window overlooking the Grand Tetons, swam in Jenny Lake, and relaxed in the backyard hot tub at sunset. It was a spectacular couple of days.

Toward the end of our relationship, money was less of an issue because I had begun working as an executive recruiter and was making more money than I had ever made up to that point. What continued to be an issue, however, was communication: more specifically, my lack of it. I clearly remember one day when Amy surprised me by saying, "Let's move in together." Stunned, I replied, "I'm not ready for that," and immediately dropped the subject. When I think back to that moment, I cringe. There was no discussion. No exploration of her thoughts or feelings. Nothing. Just me stopping the conversation.

The truth is I was scared. I felt closer to Amy than anyone I had ever dated and knew she would make a phenomenal partner. At the same time, I was paralyzed by a fear of commitment I interpreted as a desire to date other people. The breakup itself, because I was not ready to let go, was not an event, but rather an extended period of hopeless gestures. In a way, it reminds me of one of my favorite quotes from my brother, Bill. When asked if he was interested in watching the July 4 fireworks a few years back he replied, "If I want to watch things explode colorfully, all I have to do is reflect on my past relationships."

During the extended breakup, Amy and I saw each other less and less over the first few weeks. A month or so later, we bumped into each other jogging down Central Street in Evanston. We stopped and held both hands as we faced each other. Amy had tears in her eyes but lamely blamed it on being "that time of the month." I thought to myself, "Yeah, right. You never once used that as an excuse in the 18 months we dated." I didn't say that though. Instead, I offered to go to couples counselling — a suggestion she flatly rejected. Even though it seemed she had some residual feelings for me, I was eventually forced to accept that she had moved on both physically and emotionally.

In hindsight, I cringe at some of the needy, desperate things I said to try and get her back. Not once did it occur to me that I was only killing whatever attraction there may have been. Knowing what I know now, I respect Amy for breaking off the relationship the way she did. I'm also sorry I made it unnecessarily difficult for both of us.

After a few months without any contact, Amy called and asked me to dinner. Looking across the table, I was struck by how stressed Amy looked, but she insisted she was happy. Then she told me she was moving to Salt Lake City, Utah. My parents and siblings loved Amy so they were sad to see the relationship come to an end. Seeing how devastated and depressed I was, my dad encouraged me to make a trip to Salt Lake to propose. He wasn't quite ready to give up either. Knowing I didn't have the funds for an engagement ring, he generously fronted the money. Armed with little more than a ring, a cell-phone number, and an address from a résumé I helped her write shortly after she moved, I landed in Salt Lake. Oddly, I was also somewhat at peace in the sense that I wasn't attached to the outcome. My primary goal was to be able to look myself in the mirror knowing I had made every effort.

Upon arriving at the small apartment building, I quickly discovered that Amy had moved without leaving a forwarding address. My first calls to her cell phone went straight to voicemail because her phone was turned off. Knowing those calls wouldn't show up as missed calls, I didn't leave a message at first because I kept hoping she'd turn the phone back on and answer. When that didn't happen, I left as nonchalant a message as I could about being in Salt Lake and how I'd love to see her. With nothing to do and no one to see, I set out in search of a hotel. After dropping my luggage off, I wandered back to town in search of live music. To my delight, I found a band called Velour playing their own version of surf rock in a downstairs bar. Losing myself in the music, I almost forgot why I was there in the first place. Almost. After the show, I was shocked to hear that the band had never played publicly before. As a result, they also didn't have any CDs for sale.

My original plan was to stay a few days — or as long as it took to find Amy. However, I awoke the following morning feeling both strangely content and absolutely certain I wouldn't hear from Amy. Needing a friend, I called Shannon Nelson, a friend from high school who invited me to visit her in Denver on my way back to Chicago. Under the circumstances, that seemed like the perfect plan so I changed my flight and gathered my belongings. Since I already had the number for a taxi in my phone, I hit redial and waited. The moment I heard the phone ring, I was overcome with a strange and overwhelming nervous sensation in the pit of my stomach. I didn't understand the feeling until I looked at the phone and realized the phone dialed Amy's number instead of the cab company — only this time it was ringing with my number flashing on the Caller ID.

With each reach ring I could feel Amy's overwhelming shock and uncertainty as if she were looking at the phone unsure of what to do. There was an almost indescribable angst that seemed to say, "If I answer, this is going to complicate things, and I'm not ready for that. I don't want to question myself anymore." The feeling hit me so hard I was literally shaking with nervousness. I can't account for why or how I happened to sense what Amy may have been feeling, but it all made sense later when I heard that she married the person she was almost certainly dating at the time of my arrival in Salt Lake.

It didn't occur to me until I sat down to write this part of the story but sensing Amy's feelings at that moment was actually a gift of healing because it made me realize with absolute certainty that she had begun another stage of life that didn't include me. The experience also made me far more understanding. Under the circumstances, it would have been easy to leave Salt Lake upset that she never returned my call. But after experiencing what she may have been going through, I found myself filled with so much compassion there was no room left for bitterness. That was truly a gift from the Universe. The experience also reinforced my belief that loving someone means wanting what is best for that person. What makes this belief challenging in reality is the graceful acceptance required when what is best for the person doesn't happen to be you.

Help Along the Way: Learning from others

The most important lessons we learn in life do not come from books. Instead, they are lessons we learn from interacting with each other and experiencing what it means to be human. If you accept the premise put forth in books like *The Little Soul and the Sun* by Neale Donald Walsch and *Radical Forgiveness* by Colin Tipping, it is clear that some lessons are so important that we have agreements, on a soul level, with others who will help us learn the lesson.

We learn and grow through our interactions with others because, if we are even somewhat aware, thoughtful, and empathetic, we see how our behavior impacts others and how we must adapt to get along in society. Even in face-to-face conversation, much of the feedback we get comes not from the spoken word, but from our interpretation and understanding of the non-verbal cues like tone and body language that account for so much of the total communication.

When I interviewed candidates as a volunteer recruiter at Leo Burnett, one of my goals was to find out what people were most committed to improving. Even though we are all human and all have opportunities to improve, many candidates are not forthcoming because they are too worried about saying the wrong thing and damning themselves to a life of unemployment. To complicate matters, ineffective interviewers ask stupid questions like "What are your weaknesses?" that everyone who has ever interviewed knows to expect. Rather than provide an honest, insightful response, the vast majority of candidates offer meaningless, irrelevant answers like "chocolate" or "I'm a perfectionist." The "perfectionist" answer, which is the most common, is also the most unbelievable. Judging from the current state of our world, it is clear there are not nearly as many perfectionists as people who claim to be.

To avoid this dilemma, I used a technique Tom Cutler, one of my supervisors at Burnett, shared. Rather than ask about weaknesses, I would wait until about halfway through the interview and say, "Someone who doesn't know you well doesn't like you. What are five adjectives that person would use to describe you?"

It is a great question because you cannot fake your way through it. There will always be people who do not like us at first for a variety of reasons; that is life. The issue is not whether it happens, but whether we are aware enough to know how we are sometimes perceived. This may sound straightforward, but you would be amazed how many otherwise intelligent people lack the insight and self-awareness to know how others perceive them. Awareness, however, is only the first step. Using your insight to address what may be a legitimate weakness is what really counts. Perhaps the best way to illustrate this point is to share how I became aware of a few of the adjectives people who do not know me and do not like me use to describe me: I attended an intense personal development workshop.

The most powerful experience of the whole session occurred on the first day when the woman leading the workshop told us to turn around and face someone we didn't know. She proceeded to say, "For the next three minutes, just 'be' with that person. Don't talk or introduce yourself. Don't touch them or shake their hands. Just be with them." The next thing I knew, the woman said, "Go!" and there I was, standing two feet in front of a man I had never seen in my life and silently looking into his eyes. Before I had a chance to think about what was going on, the last line of the song "Sometimes" by the British rock band James started playing in my head: "Sometimes when I look deep in your eyes, I swear I can see your soul."

My initial impression was, "Hey, that's pretty cool." Then I recoiled and thought, "Yuck! I don't even know who this guy is; I don't want to see his soul."

For the next three minutes, our encounter deteriorated into what felt more like a staring contest than a genuine human interaction. After three excruciatingly painful minutes, the instructor finally said, "Stop!" and asked people to share their impressions. Not surprisingly, quite a few people laughed nervously and talked about how uncomfortable it was. Once a few people had spoken, the instructor surprised everyone by saying, "Now, turn to a different partner and do it again. Go."

The second time played out in a completely different way. Once again, I was face-to-face and two feet away from a man I did not know, but for whatever reason, it felt different. To my relief, I did not feel threatened or uncomfortable, but instead experienced what I can only describe as a wave of empathy and compassion. That is when my conscious mind took over and I thought, "I don't know this person's name or anything about his life, but I do know that he cares enough about himself to sign up for this workshop." That was when it finally occurred to me to smile. This might sound deceptively simple, but as someone who grew up in downtown Chicago, smiling at complete strangers is not something I do naturally.

The effects of this exercise lasted well over a week. Without any conscious effort, I became aware of a human connection with everyone around me.

Over the next several weeks, as the friendships blossomed, a number of my new friends were so struck by the difference between their first impressions and what I was really like that they felt compelled to say, "When I first saw you, I thought you were..." Then, they would share a few adjectives that typically included words like arrogant, aloof, cocky, and condescending. While it was great to hear people say, "But you're so nice and you're really not like that at all," it was humbling and disconcerting to know how I had been coming across before.

From that moment, I became committed to working on that aspect of myself. In my role as a speaker and coach, it is a serious weakness if people do not see me as kind and approachable. Unfortunately, it is not always easy to change. To this day, it disturbs me that I still come across as angry and intense, even when I am not feeling that way at all. At the same time, it does not feel natural to smile all the time either.

Communication issues, like the ones described above, are not limited to personal relationships. In my work as an executive coach, I see similar issues in the work place all the time. One case I found particularly intriguing involved Linda, a C-level executive who was referred to me for presentation skills training. Knowing how pervasive the fear of public speaking is, and how critical communication is at the executive level, I fully expected to find the usual challenges. Not wanting to prescribe a solution before fully diagnosing the problem, we spent the first coaching session looking at the symptoms. When Linda opened up about personality conflicts she had with people at work, a different picture emerged. My gut level impression was later confirmed when I watched one of her presentations.

Linda's issues had nothing to do with her public speaking skills. Instead, her biggest issue was the complete absence of acknowledgments in her conversation style. Acknowledgments are powerful statements we use to let people know we are listening and paying attention to what they are saying. Without them, a conversation can come across as confrontational.

To appreciate the importance of acknowledgments, picture an overly-eager salesperson who is genuinely interested in what a client is saying, but only asks questions. It doesn't take long for a meeting like that to deteriorate into an interrogation. Acknowledging what the client has said before asking a follow-up question prevents this from happening. For example, if the client says "Our goal is to grow topline revenue by

34% this year," an effective acknowledgment would be, "Wow, that's an aggressive goal." The salesperson could then follow that acknowledgment with, "How do you plan to do that?" Without the acknowledgment, the follow-up question, while legitimate, could easily and unintentionally come across as confrontational.

In Linda's case, the absence of acknowledgment came across as a lack of empathy. For instance, at the end of a very complex presentation Linda gave, a participant raised his hand and said, "I'm confused." From there, he went on to question an apparent contradiction between one of her last charts and a comment she made earlier. Had Linda prefaced her answer with an acknowledgment along the lines of, "This can definitely be a complicated, confusing topic," the participant would have felt understood to some degree. From there, she could have diplomatically explained the flaw in his thinking. Instead, Linda, who no doubt felt misunderstood herself in that moment, quickly explained why he was wrong with no acknowledgment whatsoever. From an empathy standpoint, that was not an ideal response—especially considering the person's willingness to be vulnerable by saying he was confused.

Over the next few sessions, Linda and I focused on ways she could incorporate acknowledgment into all aspects of her daily communication. It was challenging at first because Linda incorrectly equated acknowledgment with agreement.

What makes acknowledgments so powerful is their versatility; we can easily let people know we heard them without agreeing or saying, "I understand" or "I hear you." To continue the sales example, let's imagine you have a client who says, "Your prices are too high." Launching right into a question would sound defensive for the reasons highlighted before. Agreement, which might sound like, "We hear that from everybody" also is not a great option because it basically says, "You are right to be concerned." A more neutral acknowledgment such as "Price is an important consideration" is a better choice because it neither agrees nor disagrees with the person's statement. Nevertheless, it still lets people know they have been heard.

Recognizing the value in this approach, Linda committed to practicing neutral acknowledgments in a range of situations. Enthusiastic about the impact this behavior change would have, I predicted that people would quickly begin responding differently to her without knowing exactly why. Less than two weeks later, Linda sent an email describing a chance elevator encounter she had with the company's chairman in which he said, "I can't quite put my finger on what is different, but whatever you are doing, keep it up. I like it."

I am fascinated by the way common words and phrases have an unintended, negative impact on our communication, and as an executive coach, I pay particular attention to the words we use. For example, as part of an executive coaching assignment, I once watched an entire team at a commercial bank engage in a finals presentation to a prospect via telephone.

By the time a team gets to a finals presentation with a commercial banking prospect, months of work by analysts, underwriters, treasury people, relationship managers, and others have gone into the proposal because the deals typically range between $50 million and $200 million. Sometimes they are closer to $1 billion. As the meeting began, the relationship manager who led the team said, "I think we've put together a recommendation you are really going to like. I think we will be able to help you hit your goals for next year." Even though he seemed to have the right energy, over the course of the next five minutes, he used the phrase "I think" eight times. Unfortunately, "I think" introduces doubt. It is the equivalent of having a person look at you and say, "Well, it's your money, let's give it a shot."

What is fascinating about the situation above is that the prospect clearly did not know why he was feeling the way he did. Nevertheless, his response was predictable. At the end of the presentation, he said, "I can't quite put my finger on it, but I'm not feeling confident moving forward." No wonder he didn't feel confident; the salesperson wasn't confident. It would take a miracle for a prospect to buy from a salesperson who isn't confident.

When it comes to communication, salespeople are a fascinating bunch to watch because most are under the misguided impression they are being paid to speak. If they truly believed they were being paid to listen, they would all make more money.

I once did a ride-along with Bryan, a classic example of an old-school rep who thought he could win potential customers over with cute stories rather than substance. It was painful to watch because this mindset created a situation in which he constantly interrupted everyone. The body language of the prospects made it obvious that no one felt listened to or acknowledged by Bryan either. When we debriefed after the call, I said, "Bryan, the best coaching I can give you is a suggestion I am confident will have a positive impact on your personal relationships as well as your professional ones. The good news is that you only have to remember five words: 'Allow yourself to be interrupted.'"

Bryan was receptive to the coaching because, like so many of us, he had blind spots with respect to how people perceived him. He and I did not see each other after that because he accepted a position at a different company. Nevertheless, if he kept his commitment, I am confident his family and customers would have perceived a significant, positive change in his behavior. Small changes can make a big difference.

What gets in the way of our communication is not always what we say but often what we don't say. I once did a mock interview with a woman named Debbie who often made it to the final round of interviews, but was not getting offers. After about 20 minutes, I sensed intuitively what her issue was. She wasn't evasive in answering my questions, but it was clear there was something she didn't want to talk about. I knew if it was coming across to me in her practice interview, the hiring managers were almost definitely getting the same vibe.

When I shared my perception, Debbie had a very surprised look on her face. After a few moments of silence, Debbie looked up and said, "You're right." She proceeded to tell me that she had checked herself into treatment for an eating disorder the year before and was deathly afraid people would not hire her because they would notice the gap on her résumé and view her as a risk. Her story caught me by surprise, not because of the eating disorder, but because of her fear about how the experience might be perceived. On the surface, the fear makes sense, but it ignores a few critical facts.

First, when Debbie checked herself into treatment she did so after approaching her boss and saying, "I can't do the job you are paying me to do. I've tried to deal with this on my own, but I can't. I need help." The integrity Debbie demonstrated is all the evidence a potential employer might need that she is one less person the company will have to worry about. Even if she were to have a relapse, there is every reason to believe Debbie would take action before her sliding performance becomes a liability to the company. Once Debbie had a strategy to share her story if needed, I could literally see the weight of fear and doubt lift. She looked like a different person. Better still, she got a job offer two weeks later.

Another aspect of what is unsaid, but loudly heard, in conversation is our intention. A number of years ago, I watched a woman who ran a New York talent agency lead a workshop for people who wanted to get into acting and modeling. What fascinated me about her approach is that she delivered candid and, at times, harsh-sounding feedback, yet everyone in the room – without exception – literally begged for more. If you read a transcript of her feedback, you would wonder how she made it out of the room alive. Her style worked, though, because it wasn't about the words, it was about her intention. What people heard, although she never once said this, was "I get that your dream is to be an actor or model and to get cast on commercials, TV shows, and in movies. I also know that you are willing to do whatever it takes. You are willing to change anything about your appearance or personal presentation that is standing in the way of your dreams. I am the person who will tell you the truth no one else has the courage to say because I know it will make a difference for you."

I was so struck by her gift for delivering honest, direct feedback that I sent her an email acknowledging an ability I hadn't seen before or since. To my surprise, she called me the following day to thank me and said, "I have always wanted to be the person you described in the email. Until I received your note, I didn't realize I had actually achieved it. Thank you. No one has ever told me that before." She laughed when I replied, "That's because people are afraid of you."

I'll never forget the experience because it was a powerful example of the fact that many people crave honest, direct communication as long as the intention of the person speaking is pure. When we take the time to understand another person's perspective and we speak with that in mind, it's amazing how much more smoothly conversations go. I've even found it helpful to preface some conversations with the phrase, "I've been thinking about this from your point-of-view." If you have succeeded in seeing a situation from a different viewpoint, it can help the outcome of the conversation. At the same time, it tends to increase the level of listening of the other person because he or she will be curious to see if you truly did see and understand their viewpoint.

Clarifying the Vagueness

When you look deeply at the way we communicate, it is almost shocking how vague we are at times. It's a wonder we don't miscommunicate even more than we do. One of the words that is the biggest source of misinterpretation is the word "fine". Fine once meant exquisite, as in "fine" dining. Now, the more common meaning is "OK" or "acceptable". One Chicago restauranteur who appreciates this distinction has forbidden his staff from asking customers any question that could be answered with the word "fine". Similarly, salespeople encounter this with prospects when they ask ineffective checking questions like "How does that sound?" that practically beg for a one-word answer, rather than a thoughtful discussion of pros and cons. Likewise, when someone says, "It's fine", if there is a tone of frustration, it really means, "This is not fine and you're going to pay for this later."

Even though I cover this specific issue in workshops, I still laugh when I remember that I'm not immune to its impact. When I was going through chemo, I went to the oncologist's office for blood tests once or twice a week to check my blood counts. Within a half-hour or so, Betsy, the nurse practitioner, would always call and say, "Your bloodwork looks good. Everything is fine."

Despite this, with each passing treatment, my endurance at the gym plummeted. I still made it to the gym almost every day, but I didn't have the energy to do my usual workout. In particular, the 10-minutes I previously spent doing intervals on Jacobs Ladder™ were down to three minutes with big breaks in between. Wondering if I was hopelessly out of shape after just two months of treatment, I expressed my concern to Betsy who said, "Rob, that's because your hemoglobin is so low." Confused, I replied, "I thought you said my blood counts were fine." Somewhat shocked, Betsy exclaimed, "It's fine for being on intensive chemo. It means you don't need a blood transfusion. It's not fine for being healthy." I had to laugh because I seriously thought fine meant normal.

Communication lessons

In no way do I claim to suddenly have figured out the secrets of effective communication, if for no other reason than that effective communication doesn't lend itself well to secrets. Nor do I think everything is black and white when it comes to sharing what is important. Life isn't that simple. Nevertheless, there are two guidelines I have found helpful. I purposely avoided the word "rules" because there are very few absolute truths in the world.

The first guideline, which I've mentioned before, is really more of an internal alarm that warns me when to keep my mouth shut. The basic idea has its roots in a Buddhist principle that encourages you to ask yourself: "Is what I am about to say an improvement over maintaining silence?"

If the question even pops into my head during a conversation, I treat it as a warning to be careful about what I say. This might seem to contradict my earlier statement about the importance of open and honest communication, but that isn't necessarily true. First, we have all, at times, probably made hurtful comments that may have been true, but were destructive rather than constructive. In other cases, we may want to speak the truth, but, for reasons beyond our control, the person isn't ready to hear it.

I faced this exact scenario a few years back when I dated a woman we'll call Sophia whose erratic behavior turned out to be the result of a serious drug and alcohol problem she wasn't interested in addressing. Though I did my best to encourage her to get help, she wasn't ready or willing to take that step. Unfortunately, cowardice, rather than the principle of maintaining silence, is often what motivates people to avoid unpleasant conversations. The person in the best position to judge your motivation in this regard is you.

Sadly, this cowardice shows up as often in business communication as it does in personal communication. For example, a common complaint among job hunters is getting rejected via email. While it would be wonderful if job hunters received some indication that their résumés had been received and didn't drop into an abyss, it isn't practical for companies to formally acknowledge every applicant. Actually, a huge percentage of applicants, thanks to the Internet, probably don't even remember applying. This also means, unfortunately, that qualified applicants frequently get lost in the sea of unqualified applicants who are under the misguided impression that job hunting is a numbers game.

The real problem, though, happens after the interviewing process. A disturbing number of companies think it is appropriate to email a rejection to people who have invested time and energy going through formal, face-to-face interviews. Ideally, this news should be communicated by phone and, I shouldn't have to say this, by an actual, living, breathing human. At the very least, the company should send a formal letter on company letterhead. But an email? Come on. That is the ultimate in lazy, cowardly, and inconsiderate behavior. Have we become so gutless as a society that we can't even deliver bad news by phone anymore? These wimps make all human resource professionals and hiring managers look bad.

Any company that sends rejections via email needs to rethink this policy because it leaves a seriously negative and unprofessional impression. Is that really the way these companies want the world to view them?

Sadly, horrendous business manners are not limited to interactions between companies and potential employees. Every day I see and hear examples of people who text when they should be engaged in meetings or allow themselves to be interrupted continuously – no matter what they're doing. When someone answers a call in the middle of a face-to-face meeting – without first managing expectations about the possibility of having to deal with whatever emergency might be occurring – that person is conveying a strong message. In effect, the person is saying that whomever happens to be calling is more important than the person with whom they are meeting with at the time. This is rude and disrespectful. And it happens millions of times every day.

Unfortunately, conflict avoidance and other disrespectful behavior via email and text are even more prevalent in our personal communication. Not long ago, I had a disturbing conversation with a woman who decided to stop dating a guy she had been seeing for several months. As she talked it over with her female friends, she was shocked by how many of them encouraged her to break up via email.

She was so disappointed in her friends it actually made her wonder if she had as much in common with them as she had thought. In any case, it clearly illustrates how quickly rude behavior has become the norm. This conversation made me wonder if any of these women had ever had a guy break up with them via email or text. My female friends who have had that experience didn't like it at all. I know I didn't appreciate it when it happened to me. Unfortunately, too many people are so self-absorbed that they don't think about the long-term damage they are doing to their reputations when they take the easy way out.

If you have ever called it quits in a relationship via text, email – even voice mail – you owe the person a serious apology. This is a disturbing trend I see as our society becomes more technology-focused. Any communication that could potentially hurt, upset, or disappoint someone should never be delivered via text or email. It's insensitive, rude, gutless, cowardly, thoughtless, and classless. I like what my friend, Sherry, had to say about this disturbing practice: "It's a pansy-ass move and the wimpiest thing ever."

Talk face to face. If you can't do that, pick up the phone. But don't send a text or email and pretend you are being honest. By the way, not returning phone calls as a way to avoid a difficult conversation is just as lame. These principles apply to men and women equally.

Putting It into Practice

Communication is such a broad and important topic I have literally made a living teaching the many aspects of it. The examples in this chapter highlight a few of the common challenges I have seen either in my own experience or in coaching people to be more effective communicators. It isn't intended an as exhaustive list of issues, but simply a thought-starter for people committed to improving in this important area.

If your personal and professional relationships aren't what you would like them to be, first, observe yourself to see if you are acknowledging people when you speak. Many people don't acknowledge at all. As a result, their comments come across as cold and their questions sound more like an interrogation.

Next, check your intention. How candid are you with people? Do you feel the need to hide your thoughts because you worry about how people will react? You don't have any control over the reactions of others. You can only control your side of the conversation. Before you speak though, ask yourself three questions:

- Does this need to be said?
- Does this need to be said now?
- Does this need to be said by me?

This is another variation of the Buddhist principle: "Is what I am about to say an improvement over maintaining silence?"

If any of the questions above even cross my mind, I treat it as a warning sign to keep my mouth shut. Sadly, I don't always listen.

CHAPTER 4:

Overcoming a Scarcity Mentality

If you think happiness is a rare bird, you won't see much of it.
-- Marty Rubin

erhaps because he never went to college, my maternal grandfather, Grandpa Ryan, was a big believer in education and left enough money for all eleven of his grandchildren to earn a degree. After he died, my mother learned about a variety of generous donations he had made — often anonymously — including putting a friend's child through college. His quiet generosity, which has always been an inspiration, is one of the many ways I aspire to be like him.

I also appreciate Grandpa Ryan's sense of humor and the fact that he didn't appear to be sad or disappointed about not having the opportunity to go to college. Whenever someone asked where he went to school, he'd say, "I spent most of my time between Harvard and Yale." After a short pause he'd explain with a playful grin that Harvard and Yale were two streets on the south side of Chicago between which was a pool hall.

Early Working Years

My first full-time job was in advertising account management at Leo Burnett, where I worked after grad school. From a financial perspective, that was a great period because the steady income enabled me to do more trading and investing, keep my bills paid, and take a few scuba trips every year.

I was having so much fun trading and following the markets that I decided to leave Burnett to join Cooper Neff, a proprietary options trading firm. My financial goal, at the time, was to make a few million dollars, retire when I turned 30, and spend the rest of my life volunteering. But the Universe had other plans.

Cooper Neff offered me a salary for the first year in the firm's training program that was slightly less than half of what I was making at Burnett. By curtailing my music addiction and being more careful about my spending, I was able to adapt and keep my bills paid. Unfortunately, I loved and hated the job from the moment I arrived. The male-dominated trading floor was like a locker room in the worst sense. Even though I truly appreciated the company's willingness to train me, I began to realize that trading full-time was not fulfilling.

Around this same time, I was diagnosed with narcolepsy. Against the advice of everyone I knew, I quit my job without a backup plan. Unemployed at the age of 27, I decided to have fun for a few weeks and accepted a seasonal job at Tower Records in Chicago. After paying a few bills, I used what little I had left to take full advantage of the employee discount and add to my growing music collection. What I didn't anticipate were the sideways glances of my former Burnett colleagues who said, "Oh, so you're working here now."

Had I had the benefit of a crystal ball or other glimpse into the future and seen the 15-year financial roller coaster ride that would follow, I might have accepted the open invitation to return to Burnett rather than carve my own path. I have no regrets about my decision to start the entrepreneurial journey, but I do regret my decision to do so without creating a safety net or back-up plan. I also regret the ignorance that allowed me to proceed without a business mentor.

Around the time I went on my own, Mike, a colleague I did not meet until much later, made a similar decision. Knowing that it would take time to get his headhunting business off the ground, Mike worked all day on his business and worked nights as a bartender. In this way, Mike created the financial freedom to let the business grow at its own rate without any unnecessary financial pressure. As a result, Mike now has a successful business with no debt. For several years, he continued to bartend simply because he enjoyed it and used the money to pay for his vacations.

Unfortunately, I did not have Mike's wisdom or foresight. Instead, I operated under the misguided impression that I had to appear successful from the beginning. For some stupid reason, I thought a side job would undermine my credibility. In truth, the only thing I undermined was my own financial peace of mind.

Around the same time, people who wanted to get into advertising started coming to me for help with the job search. One afternoon, after coaching my neighbor for a few hours, I stood in my parents' kitchen and commented offhandedly about how surprising it was to see so many smart people struggle. My mother, ever the intuitive one, said, "Why don't you write a book?"

And so it began.

In that moment, I decided to write the guidebook I wished I could have read before I ever interviewed with Leo Burnett. Writing the book took two years. Realizing what a mistake it was to initially self-publish took a lot less. But by that point, I had already invested over $50,000 into the process.

The first glimpse of success came within a year of the book's release when Judi Carpenter, owner of a successful headhunting firm, read the book and wanted to meet me. A few months later, she recruited me to interview and place candidates. Financially speaking, the two years I spent at Carpenter Associates were quite good. I was making money and investing again. Better still, I made enough on one investment to pay cash for my car. But from a personal standpoint, I was not happy. Sitting in front of a computer and talking on the phone all day made me feel like a caged animal. This was the first real desk job I had ever had and I disliked the office aspect intensely. At Burnett, I spent my days running between studios, meetings, printers, and production houses. My friend BJ Trausch used to joke, "I don't know why you even have a desk. You're never there." Trading was not a desk job either. But headhunting was. A few months after I left Carpenter Associates, the rights to my book sold. With visions of an impending financial windfall, I once again drained my investment account. But I did not stop there: I made one of the biggest mistakes of my life and used those evil blank checks credit card companies send to create debts I still owed more than 10 years later.

I did not feel financially irresponsible at the time because I was making sacrifices, never had any money, and stopped taking vacations. Every nickel was spent on business expenses and basic necessities like food. I made some money from coaching and book sales, but lacked the steady income my friend Mike was busy making as a bartender. Recognizing I had an issue with money did not take long; coming up with a plan did. I read and reread classic books like *The Dynamic Laws of Prosperity* by Catherine Ponder and *The Richest Man in Babylon* by George Samuel Clason, but knowing and applying the principles within proved a different challenge entirely.

I first read *The Dynamic Laws of Prosperity* when I was dating Amy, the former girlfriend I mentioned earlier. Shortly after we started dating, Amy invited me to spend a week with her in Jackson Hole, Wyoming. She was excited because a close family friend offered to let us stay in their million-dollar ranch at no charge. Our only expenses would be the $400 airfare and food. It sounded like a fantastic opportunity, but $400 was exactly $800 more than I had in the bank at that moment.

In *The Dynamic Laws of Prosperity*, Ponder writes at length about the importance of trusting the Universe to provide whatever money you need. I loved reading stories about unexpected inheritances but remember thinking, "Yeah, like that will ever happen to me." Deciding to have faith in the process, I bought the airline tickets, trusting that the money would somehow appear. I was not disappointed. Two or three days later, Grandma Sullivan called to tell me that my great uncle, Jim Dever, who had died six months before, left what little he had to all of his grand nieces and nephews. After the money was divided, each of us would receive exactly $400. My check would arrive the following week. I was stunned.

Despite such compelling evidence of the power of our thoughts and attitudes, my financial situation deteriorated over the next few years. One worry and one bill at a time, my thoughts shifted from a belief in abundance to a scarcity mentality. The Law of Attraction states that whatever you give attention, energy, and focus to, you will get. Unfortunately, I used my attention and energy to focus on the awareness that I did not have enough money. As a result, the Universe delivered exactly what I was focusing on: the condition of not having enough. The most disturbing part of this process is the fact that I did not even know it was happening.

Anyone who knows me well has probably heard me say at some point, "The Universe has a way of throwing the same lesson at you until you get it." Many of the lessons we learn and re-learn through life are presented in an obvious, straightforward way. I distinctly remember a few nights after I moved back to my parents' house when my dad expressed concern about the lack of progress in my career. The more he talked about what he perceived as "spinning my wheels," the more defensive I became. Unfortunately, I did not approach the conversation openly. If I had, we might have come up with a creative solution like getting a side job while I worked on the business. Instead,

I interpreted my parents' concern as a lack of support and a desire for me to go back to the corporate world.

It was not until I finally grew exhausted from swimming upstream that I understood my parents' concern and learned the lesson they were so anxious to teach me. It has been said that when the student is ready, the teacher will appear. It is equally true, in some cases, that when the resistant student is drained and disheartened, the lesson will finally make sense and take hold. Fortunately, another teacher appeared as well, in the unexpected form of Amber, a woman I dated after Amy.

Amber the Angel

Amber and I met playing beach volleyball on North Avenue Beach in Chicago. Early in our relationship, Amber's excitement about my openness to spirituality in general, and psychics in particular, prompted her to schedule back-to-back meetings for us with a psychic she knew. During the session, Grandpa Ryan, my maternal grandfather who had been dead for almost 18 years, was apparently concerned enough about my financial situation to come through and tell me I needed a "swift kick in the assets." This candid observation was absolutely consistent with what I remembered about his no-nonsense personality and sense of humor. Even though the message was delivered in a loving, concerned, and slightly humorous way, it hurt to hear because I knew he was right.

At the time, I was still in the early stages of building my speaking and coaching business, so my income was erratic at best. Speaking gigs paid well, but they were not nearly as predictable as my rent and utility bills.

As a result, I was more than a little dependent on overdraft protection, a habit made worse by my resistance to balancing my checkbook. Before long, my unwillingness to deal effectively with the issue began to impact people close to me.

A few months after a teary breakup initiated by Amber, she called one afternoon and said, "I have something I really want to tell you that I think will help you in future relationships." Her words came as a shock. My first reaction, I am embarrassed to admit, was to be defensive. She then said, "But I don't have time to talk now. Will you be around later?"

Three of the next four hours were spent doing the equivalent of winning imaginary arguments in the shower and defending myself against an impending attack. When it finally occurred to me that Amber was giving me a great gift, I immediately shifted my mindset from defensiveness to gratitude. After all, there was absolutely nothing in it for Amber to share whatever candid observation she might make. She was doing it with the belief and hope it would help me. With that in mind, I was able to listen with an open mind and heart.

When Amber and I spoke later that day, she started by recalling a conversation in which I had told her about Grandpa Ryan's generosity to complete strangers and how I hoped to do the same someday. Then, like a great coach, she went on to give specific examples in which I was anything but generous.

One painful example Amber shared was the night we went to Schuba's Tavern to see the band Eddie From Ohio perform. Before the show, we joined the band and a few friends for dinner. When the check came, and everyone chipped in, I turned and asked Amber for $20. I don't remember doing it, and it is embarrassing to admit, but I was completely disconnected from reality, chivalry, and the feelings of others. It makes me wonder if having an extreme scarcity mentality and being so focused on the lack of money impacts judgment and decision-making in the same way severe alcoholism does. Based on my experience, I consider it a disease in the same sense.

Seeing how open and receptive I was to her feedback, Amber closed by telling me the real reason we broke up was her observation that I was being cheap and her belief that the behavior would never change. Until that point, I was under the impression our relationship had simply run its course.

To be clear, it is not that I saw myself as generous. But I definitely did not see myself as cheap. I bet if you asked me at the time, I would have mistakenly imagined a strong correlation between generosity and income. But that clearly isn't accurate. Some of the most generous people on earth are also the poorest. Just ask anyone who has backpacked in a third world country. I have heard story after story about travellers who have been given food and shelter by families who barely had more than a hut in which to live. That is why I look back and see my own profound disconnection from reality as the disease that it was.

When I say my behavior changed in an instant, I mean it. At a foundational level, I reacquainted myself with Catherine Ponder's book, *The Dynamic Laws of Prosperity*, balanced my checkbook, and avoided overdrafts. On a spiritual level, I focused on my gratitude for whatever money I had as well as the new clients who would be coming into my life. On a social level, I apologized to friends who had experienced my lack of class and actively looked for and embraced opportunities to be generous and chivalrous. The embarrassment of my previous behavior was motivation enough to remain aware and never be driven by scarcity again.

Not surprisingly, my financial situation improved. When I gave attention, energy, and focus to my beliefs about the scarcity of money, scarcity manifested in my life. When I shifted my focus to gratitude and appreciation, abundance appeared.

Lessons from a Homeless Man

When I am the most open, opportunities to be grateful come from unexpected moments and seemingly random encounters that transport me to another place and perspective.

I had one of those a few years back on a business trip.

I awoke that morning with TMJ (jaw pain) and a very unsettled feeling about life in general. Unfortunately, traveling from Chicago to Albany to Baltimore starting the day before in the afternoon didn't exactly give me a chance to rest and recover. Despite my efforts to start the day with a healthy breakfast of fruit and oatmeal, all I managed to find was a diner that made the uninspiring continental breakfast buffet at the hotel look like gourmet fare. Lacking proper nourishment, the hunger headache and short-tempered feelings that quickly followed came as no surprise.

After a few early logistical frustrations I won't recount here, I gave that day's workshop a strong effort and even managed to keep the group laughing throughout the session. By the time I got to the airport though, I was feeling even worse than before. To complicate matters, I had no fewer than three consecutive reminders of unresolved issues that had been constant, unwelcome companions.

At 7:30pm, I landed in Baltimore. Desperate for a healthy meal, I asked the concierge at the hotel for directions to the nearest Whole Foods. Fifteen minutes and one cab ride later, I had a shopping basket filled with Perfect Bars, great local kombucha, pomegranate seeds, kiwi, mango, and protein shakes. I could feel my smile return as the fog in my head slowly dissipated.

After finishing one of the protein shakes, sampling the kombucha, and eating one of the large containers of pomegranate seeds, the mile and a half walk back to the hotel seemed like the perfect plan — especially after spending 8 ½ hours in a windowless training facility.

Four blocks from the store, I crossed the river on Pratt Street and looked left to behold the largest Coast Guard vessel I've ever seen. It looked more like a Navy ship. At that moment I heard a voice say, "Hey man, do you have a cigarette I can buy?"

Turning to my right, I saw an older homeless guy with long, grayish white hair and a matching full beard. He stood only about 5' 5" and would have been taller had he not been slouched over. Picture a 52-year-old Willie Nelson with the posture and borderline frenetic energy of Dobby from Harry Potter and you'll have the right idea. When I said,

"Sure don't," most homeless people would have continued on their way. Not Jay. He slowed down, looked at me, flexed his arms like an ape and said, "Hey, anyone ever tell you that you look like Arnold?"

"Schwarzenegger?," I asked in disbelief.

"Yeah," he replied.

Occasionally people will tell me I look like someone famous, but Arnold? This was a first.

As I looked Jay in the eyes, I was surprised to see deep red scabs running down both of his temples. In addition, the white part of his right eye was almost completely blood red. He had either fallen down or been in an altercation of some sort. But what struck me most weren't the obvious signs of trauma. Instead, it was the kindness and light in Jay's faded, but vivid blue eyes. Even in the dark, Jay's eyes had an almost supernatural glow. For the next hour as Jay and I walked, he shared his story. I didn't hear the beginning until later because Jay started in the middle with the 23 years he spent in prison. He talked openly about his experience with the lawlessness of a notorious motorcycle gang, drug addiction, and severe alcoholism. At one point, Jay managed to survive hospitalization with a blood-alcohol content so high it earned him a featured spot in a medical journal — much to the embarrassment of his now ex-wife, the Director of Nursing at a prominent local hospital.

Throughout Jay's story, I found myself admiring the utter absence of bitterness, regret, or self-pity. He even spoke lovingly of both his ex-wife and her new husband, a military man he clearly admired and respected.

I also noticed that Jay didn't talk about his struggle in the past tense. Instead, he spoke honestly and compassionately about his ongoing challenges. Just minutes before he saw me on Pratt Street, Jay walked out of an AA meeting in which he shocked everyone by receiving what he called his "Day 1 badge." After seven years of sobriety, he slipped recently and had less than a shot glass full of alcohol. Miraculously, it didn't lead to a binge. Pointing to the sky, Jay said, "Until tonight, He and I were the only ones who knew about it." Nevertheless, he made no attempt to hide what he had done or excuse himself. He simply said, "Today I started the count over at Day 1."

Only after we had been talking for 45-minutes did I come to appreciate how far Jay had fallen. He was raised in a 17,000-square foot mansion complete with a 625,000-gallon pool, a gas pump, 31-foot ceilings in the entryway, crystal chandeliers, helicopters, and house guests that included well-known bands at the peak of their popularity. But Jay didn't tell me that to brag. Or so I'd feel sorry for him. It was simply part of the mosaic of his life.

Through it all Jay has found peace while he continues to struggle with his addiction issues. He also finds both strength and compassion for himself in the insight of his ex-wife's new husband who once told him: "Jay, you are in a battle far more challenging than what the military faces in Afghanistan because the enemy is you — and you know every move you're about to make." Reflecting on the lessons of the evening proved to be a wonderful and timely reminder of an affirmation my friend Herschel Lazaroff created for me not long ago:

"I love who I really am, not who I thought I would be."

My challenge is to fully accept and appreciate the truth in this statement. Jay, on the other hand, seems to be already there. Or extremely close. Jay and I parted ways expressing the deepest gratitude for what we learned from each other, what we have learned from the many people and teachers in our lives, and for the many opportunities we have every day to create a new story of possibility for ourselves. For this reason, I am grateful, amazed, and energized.

When I awoke that morning, I never could have predicted a stranger on the streets of Baltimore would alter my perspective so powerfully. As I put my head on the pillow that night, I was in awe of the gift I had just received. But I'd be lying if I didn't say how humbled and happy I am to know that Jay, this angel of wisdom and compassion, made sure I knew that I had enriched his life as well. That may have been the best and most unexpected gift of all.

Scarcity at the Corporate and Societal Levels

What makes the scarcity mentality so interesting is that it is not limited to an individual issue. It is one we deal with at the corporate and societal levels as well. Consider the fact that there are ancient Roman roads still in existence and modern roads that need to be repaved every few years due to potholes and deterioration.

I have heard stories about companies that purchased inventions for everything from long-lasting products and razors that do not dull to cures for cancer, but one of the most compelling is a light bulb designed by the Shelby Electric Company and installed in a firehouse in Livermore, California. The bulb has been burning continuously since 1901 and has logged more than 1.1 million hours of use. This has been documented by the *Guinness Book of World Records* and verified by Snopes.com, a website that investigates the veracity of various stories.

We have the technology to design and build better and longer-lasting products, but a scarcity mentality on the part of corporations prevents this from happening. In other words, companies believe that their future income and ability to thrive will suffer unless they design products that need to be replaced at frequent intervals. This belief reflects a well-entrenched scarcity mentality. It also stems from the inability of these companies to position value.

So, what would it look like without a scarcity mentality? First, quantify what we will save in time, money, and materials not having to replace light bulbs and streets as often as we do and you can justify a much higher price. With the exception of Black Friday, consumers and the free market behave somewhat rationally. Show me the value and I'll gladly pay a higher price.

Second, companies should invest the higher profits from higher priced, higher value products into research and development. That way, the companies would be able to deliver even more advanced products and technologies rather that repaving the same roads over and over or filling our landfills with replaceable products.

Putting It into Practice

The first step to resolving scarcity issues is recognizing when and how they impact our lives. Begin to notice when you catch yourself thinking you do not have enough love, time, money, or any other resource. What are you telling yourself in that moment? How do you feel about the situation? Hint: if you are feeling sadness, disappointment, frustration, or any other negative emotion, you are not helping your situation. Instead, you are reinforcing the absence of whatever it is you desire.

A better choice is to be grateful, in advance, for the appearance of whatever you want to manifest in your life. For example, I recently had a situation in which I did not have speaking gigs booked in January or February, historically two of the slowest months of the year. As a backup plan, I put together a budget to make sure I would at least have enough to pay my bills through the end of January. Rather than worry about the situation and project negative emotion into my current and future state, I chose to be grateful in advance for the financial abundance coming my way. I also resisted the temptation to do the "responsible" thing and cancel my end of the year scuba trip.

A week or so later, one of my clients called to ask how much business I had done with his department in the previous year. When I gave him the number, he exclaimed, "Wow! That was a great investment. I consider you my best sales guy. We'll use you even more next year." Another client followed suit a few days later. Within three short weeks, I booked more business in those first two months than I have done in other years combined.

The Gratitude Journal

My favorite method for practicing gratitude is to keep a gratitude journal. Before I go to bed or when I wake up, I write down five things for which I am grateful. Some days, the list includes health, family, life, and other aspects of existence that are difficult to quantify.

There is no right or wrong way to do this. Whatever thoughts get you smiling and feeling happy are perfect. My only caution would be to avoid using the word "want" as is, "I want this income" or "I want that relationship." The distinction is subtle but important – the word "want" has "lack" as one of its definitions. When you use the word "want," you are expressing to the Universe that you are lacking. As a result, you risk bringing more lack into your experience. Instead, be positive in the way you speak and write. Rather than say, "I want more business from new clients" say, "I am grateful, in advance, for the clients who come to me knowing the value they receive far outweighs their investment."

When my brother, Bill, and I got into a conversation about gratitude journals, he said, "I used to keep a gratitude journal, but stopped doing it because the lists can get a little rote at times. I think there is some value in being more intentional and thoughtful about it." In that moment, Bill helped me realize something that hadn't occurred to me. Keeping a gratitude journal can seem repetitive at times. The secret to making it work — and to avoiding this pitfall — is to make sure you are FEELING whatever you are writing. If you are truly grateful for the abundance of health or love present in your life, allow yourself to feel the joy that naturally accompanies deep gratitude. If you only write the words, you'll miss the point.

CHAPTER 5:

Identifying Your Patterns

If you've been dealing with it for a long time,
you have to ask yourself what you are getting from it.
You won't be able to let go of it until you can see it as a blessing.
-- Shen Robinson, Shaman and medical intuitive

Have you ever noticed how the same scenarios and struggles seem to play themselves out repeatedly? Not long after one difficult situation ends, an almost identical one begins with different people playing essentially the same roles. What has impressed and frustrated me most is the way the Universe finds so many creative ways to help us grasp the lessons we most need to learn. With each successive scenario, the stakes get higher until we can no longer ignore the underlying issue.

In some cases, the clues are fairly obvious and the lessons, although painful, can be faced with focused effort and attention. Other lessons are more cleverly disguised and require introspection, insight, and, at times, a dose of divine guidance.

Establishing Effective Boundaries

Some of the most challenging situations are the ones for which there is no obvious lesson, solution, or teacher. Facing the same problem in different forms is disheartening when you are in the midst of it but nothing short of exhilarating when you finally recognize the pattern. What makes the revelation I am about to share so powerful is the fact that the pattern started thirty years ago and impacted at least two areas of my life. If this doesn't make sense as you read it, fear not. It didn't make sense to me at first either, but it will at the end.

In late 1979, when I was 13 years old, the price of silver skyrocketed over a five-month period before hitting an all-time high of $48 per ounce in January of 1980. Like many naïve, wide-eyed investors, I decided it was a great time to invest and started buying silver by the ounce with my dog walking money. At the same time, my grandfather, a professional trader, sold silver coins with a face value of $50 for $1,000. I never told him what I bought because I couldn't understand why he was selling. But I do now. He understood something I didn't. The market was technically overbought and the spike in price was destined to retreat. As I write this, more than 40 years later, silver is trading at $25 per ounce, well under the 1980 highs. The silver trading experience was memorable, but since my investment lost less than a few hundred dollars in value, it was nothing more than a minor personal embarrassment I never shared with anyone until now.

The next identifiable phase of this lesson started in the late 1990s when a family friend recommended an investment in the Initial Public Offering (IPO) of Illinois Superconductor. Several members of my family and I purchased 1,000 shares each and hoped for the best. After a few years with little to show in the way of results, the market took an interest in superconductor stocks. By 2000, I had money in almost all of the superconductor companies and watched with excitement as the stock prices skyrocketed during a relatively brief period, not unlike the spike in the silver market 20 years earlier.

Apparently, the lesson wasn't painful enough the first time because my elation turned to horror as I watched well over $100,000 in paper profits disappear almost overnight. What made this situation worse was my emotional attachment to superconductor stocks in general and Illinois Superconductor in particular. As a result, I continued to buy more on the way down. Sadly, Illinois Superconductor is no longer a going concern so we lost the entire investment.

Viewed in isolation, the lesson in these trading experiences would seem to be about unwarranted optimism or an excessive focus on getting rich quick. But it took another ten years and a series of frustrating experiences in a different area of my life to discover the deeper lesson.

My parents would often say, "bad things happen in threes" when tragedy struck. They pointed out the pattern so often I started to believe it was true. Looking at it objectively, my intuition tells me this only seems to be the case because we make it so. In other words, single tragic events happen all the time without being followed by two subsequent events. But when two happen in relative proximity, people who believe "bad things happen in threes" start looking or waiting for the third. Once the third event is identified, the tendency would then be to stop looking so a fourth event might not even be noticed. Like anything related to the Law of Attraction, if you give "bad things happen in threes" consistent attention, energy, and focus, it will eventually become part of your reality.

In my case, the fact that it took three consecutive and progressively more negative events for me to gain clarity is not evidence of my parents' belief that bad things happen in threes. More likely, it is a result of the resistance I had to grasping the lesson that had been playing out for three decades.

The third scenario started in January of 2005 with my accountant at the time. For simplicity, we'll call him Accountant 1. At that point, my dislike for anything tax-related had prompted me to keep good records and get them turned over to my account by the third week of January. In 2005, Accountant 1 moved to Israel and was concerned that some clients might not continue to work with him even though he'd be making relatively frequent trips back to the States. When he told me about his plans, I assured him that we could continue to work together — even though there might be an adjustment period that required filing extensions. Since I didn't expect to owe any taxes for fiscal year 2004, I didn't have an issue with the extension but hoped my returns wouldn't be delayed too long. In August or September, Accountant 1 finished the returns, acknowledged me for my patience, and promised to be more prompt when the 2005 returns were due.

The following year, Accountant 1's mother died. I can't even begin to imagine how hard that must have been. Even though I had all the necessary paperwork completed in January, I gave Accountant 1 extra time and understanding when he asked to file another extension. Months later, in late summer or early fall, the returns were sent to me along with another promise that it would never happen again. In 2006, Accountant 1 filed extensions for the third year in a row. In August, the returns still hadn't been completed, so despite his last-minute pleas and apologies, I started looking for another accountant. Based on an endorsement from my attorney, I hired Accountant 2. I liked his energy and outdoorsy spirit, but was especially excited about the possibility of a yearly business trip to meet with him in the mountains of Colorado. From our earliest conversations, Accountant 2 knew my greatest frustration with Accountant 1 was the uncertainty and stress of not knowing where I stood from a tax standpoint. Upon hearing this, Accountant 2 assured me that he would not put me through that again.

Two weeks after I fired Accountant 1 and hired Accountant 2, I had a session with PsychicDave Tillman, a gifted reader. The very first thing he said was, "Rob, I see you've got some accounting issues you need to address." I replied, "I know. I just fired my accountant and hired someone else. Is there a problem with the new guy?" Hearing that this had all taken place in the past two weeks, PsychicDave said it was difficult to know if the issue he saw related to Accountant 1 or Accountant 2. Nevertheless, he cautioned me, "Watch this guy and check your returns, I have a bad feeling he is missing something big."

Preliminary conversations with Accountant 2 pointed to the possibility that I wouldn't owe any additional taxes for 2006. Given his confidence, and knowing how busy he was, I decided to be patient. Even though it bugged me that Accountant 2 wasn't especially responsive, I waited. Once again, weeks turned into months. Near the end of the year, he encouraged me to send my 2007 info with a promise he would get everything done at once. But that didn't happen either. In the interim, we had a few conversations in which he assured me that there was nothing to worry about for 2007 and encouraged me to be patient.

In late 2008, Accountant 2 sent my returns for 2006 and 2007. Remembering PsychicDave's cautionary words, I looked over the returns even more carefully than I otherwise would have. To my extreme displeasure, I noticed that Accountant 2 missed thousands of dollars in business airfare deductions. Trusting my gut that he wouldn't respond to pressure, I was careful to approach the situation as casually and non-confrontationally as possible, but that didn't work because Accountant 2 was neither apologetic nor responsive.

Had he sent updated returns along with an invoice, the whole matter would have been resolved. Instead, Accountant 2, when he finally called, responded defensively and used the opportunity to tell me I "obviously need more hand-holding than other clients." I would be lying if I didn't admit how hurt I was by his efforts to shift the blame to me — especially when I had gone out of my way to not pressure him. He never was able to explain how the three conversations we had in the year we worked together made me a needy client. It also wasn't believable because Accountant 1 often acknowledged me for being so easy to work with and so prepared. The result of this unpleasant conversation was a promise from Accountant 2 to send the revised returns.

That never happened. No revised returns. No invoice. And no returned phone calls. I briefly considered reporting Accountant 2 for negligence, but decided against it for two reasons. First, I'm not a vindictive person. Second, he was a relative of the good friend and attorney who recommended him. With that in mind, I let it go and began the search for another accountant. Enter Accountant 3, the last and worst of the bunch.

Accountant 3 and I met when we were young, but hadn't seen each other in years. When I put the word out to my network that I was looking for an accountant, he responded. The situation seemed like a perfect fit because he had time available and was looking for project work. Even if it took him a couple of weeks to get to my returns, I appreciated his reasonable rates and felt good about helping a childhood friend.

In early 2009, I sent Accountant 3 the incomplete returns from 2006 and 2007 as well as my 2008 information. Despite a slew of broken promises and meetings that never seemed to happen, I remained patient and hopeful. Later, tragedy struck when Accountant 3's younger sibling died unexpectedly. Having three brothers and two sisters myself, I could only imagine a death like that would be devastating. Letting the frustration I'd been keeping to myself transform into compassion, I gave him the space he needed to grieve. Several months later, I saw Accountant 3 at a party. We talked about the fact that the 2009 returns would now have to be part of the mix. He looked me in the eye and said he would have everything done by the end of January, 2010.

In mid-February, nothing had been done so I called Accountant 3 who explained that he needed access to special accounting software to do multi-year returns. He thought he'd be working part-time at an accounting firm, but ended up taking on a different project that left him without any extra time. He said he'd be willing to help me find a different accountant, but if I didn't mind waiting a month or so, he could still do it and save me a lot in the process. In yet another example of exceptionally poor judgment on my part, I gave him another chance.

What made the experience especially maddening was the fact that Accountant 3 posted multiple daily status updates on Facebook talking about spirituality and integrity. Every time I saw one, I became more furious. How could someone publicly talk about the importance of integrity yet not demonstrate it? This was important to me because I was raised by parents who stressed the importance of keeping our deals no matter what. I don't recall a single scenario in which it would have ever been deemed appropriate to make promises like Accountants 1, 2, and 3 and not keep them. In my last email to Accountant 3, I made it clear I wanted all the returns completed by April 15. Six weeks later, when I hadn't heard from Accountant 3, I called. I would have left a message, but instead heard the emotionless computer message telling me "The mailbox is full."

Hearing this recording was disconcerting because I firmly believe that serious, emotionally-charged conversations should never be communicated via text or email. Since talking by phone didn't appear to be an option, I sent a neutral, but direct text message requesting a conversation that same day. Accountant 3 replied a few hours later to let me know he'd call that night. I shouldn't have been surprised when that didn't happen either.

Early the next morning I received a text with an apology and a promise to call later in the day. When we finally talked, Accountant 3 confessed that he'd done nothing. Historically, I have had issues expressing my feelings and have avoided confrontation whenever possible. But more recently, I had seen and read a lot about how unexpressed anger and unspoken feelings often lead to illness and disease. For this reason, I had made a consistent effort to be a better communicator and protect my boundaries when people violate them. I had also learned the distinction between legitimate anger and temper.

I knew it wasn't going to be easy or pretty, but I openly expressed the hurt and disappointment I felt at the fact that another year hand gone by and he, Accountant 3, had done exactly nothing. At this point, I was feeling some serious stress knowing I now had four years of unfiled tax returns. Accountant 3 acknowledged he was "out of integrity", but his apology sounded as insincere and hollow as any I'd ever heard.

The conversation, which lasted almost 40 minutes, quickly turned into a heated argument. When I expressed my anger and disappointment at the long list of broken promises he and the other two accountants made, he inexplicably tried to turn the tables by suggesting that I was the "common denominator" in the situation. In other words, the broken promises of Accountants 1, 2, and 3 were somehow my fault. In a strange sense, Accountant 3 was right. But not the way he might have expected.

During the four years this drama played itself out, I often wondered what I was supposed to be learning. I firmly believed there was a lesson, but I had no idea what it was. Our argument ended with Accountant 3's promise to overnight the files for 10:30 am delivery. Even though his apology still felt hollow, I accepted it and apologized for losing my cool on the phone.

The next day, I went to the gym early so I would be home before FedEx arrived with my files. Much like the day before, our conversation continued to replay in my mind — especially the "common denominator" comment. Directing my energy and frustration in my workout felt liberating and inspiring at the same time. Weight training always has a way of helping me see life more clearly. With each successive repetition, I gained a deeper sense of peace that led to two critical insights. First, I realized why Accountant 3's apology sounded insincere. In Randy Pausch's book *The Last Lecture*, he described the three parts of an apology:

1. I'm sorry.

2. It's my fault. It won't happen again.

3. How can I make it right? (This is what makes it sincere.)

Accountant 3 said, "I'm sorry" and he did admit fault by acknowledging his lack of integrity. But, rather than move on to part 3, he chose instead to find a way to blame me. In other words, "It's my fault, but here's why it's your fault too." In our conversation the day before, I had suggested that the right thing to do under the circumstances might have been to take the initiative and find a way to get access to the appropriate software. My accountant's less-than-helpful response: "You're not God. You can't tell me the right thing to do." Knowing why Accountant 3's apology didn't work reinforced my commitment to include all three critical ingredients in my own apologies. But I still couldn't figure out the lesson.

Perhaps it was a brief moment of peace and clarity, or maybe the Universe was tired of watching me struggle, but as I prayed to understand the drama, I received a flash of insight or imparted wisdom that clarified the lesson that started 30 years before. The phrases "flash of insight" and "imparted wisdom" both describe the experience well because I literally understood in a moment what will take several paragraphs to explain.

Unlike some of my other life's lessons, this one proved more complicated because it involved integrity, boundaries, decision-making habits, feelings, and what I'll call the time value of emotional attachment.

Let's start with integrity and boundaries. First, each of us has to establish clear boundaries with regards to what we are willing to accept, especially as it relates to the behavior of others. The challenge is to set and maintain these boundaries without attachment. In other words, it is important to let people be who they are rather than impose our expectations on them. Trying to change someone else's behavior is, by far, the most futile exercise. You'd have better luck changing the tides.

In both cases, the accounting debacle and my trading mishaps, I was swimming upstream. A clear pattern had emerged that I chose to ignore. Traders often talk about the idea that "the trend is your friend." In other words, no matter how much you like an investment, if the market drives the price down, chances are excellent it is not as good as you think it is.

In the case of the accountants, the trend I ignored was the persistent inability to keep promises. Recognizing that everyone makes mistakes, I do my best to give people a second chance. Many people are worthy of the initial leniency and use the opportunity to regain trust. Other people aren't. I'm not saying this is universally true by any means, but everyone who has violated my trust twice went on to do it a third time.

Unfortunately, this is the boundary I failed to set with my accountants. In each case, more broken promises followed the first two. Rather than acknowledge the lack of integrity and make a calm, rational decision to cut my losses and move on, I stayed in the game. Each passing day and each broken promise increased my emotional investment to the process.

Not coincidentally, this was the same scenario that played out in the silver and superconductor markets. The only difference was my decision to ignore a rapidly declining price. The more it dropped, the more invested I became in sticking with the position hoping the market would reverse. In other words, I lost my objectivity and became emotionally attached to being right. Under those circumstances, the shift from trader to long-term investor is almost always disastrous. Good traders are able to set limits, admit when they are wrong, and get out of the position as quickly as possible. I didn't do that because I hadn't fully learned the lesson. Before he died, my grandfather enthusiastically talked about the time value of money and how the value increased exponentially when you resisted the urge to spend it or move it from investment to investment. In negative situations, the time value of emotional attachment has the opposite effect.

Throughout the accounting drama, I failed to set clear expectations and I failed to establish a rational exit point. The longer the process dragged out, the more emotionally draining it became. What should have been a logical, straightforward business transaction deteriorated into a disappointing and frustrating emotional experience simply because I allowed the situation to spiral. This realization about the need to set and maintain boundaries does not absolve the accountants of their misdeeds. I firmly believe they are each guilty of negligence and malpractice. But at the same time, I clearly recognize that I was a common denominator because I tolerated their lack of integrity far too long.

Looking at the situation from a more spiritual level, I am actually grateful for the experience. In the children's book, *Little Soul and the Sun*, Neale Donald Walsch does a wonderful job of illustrating the agreements we make on a soul level and the role we play in each other's lives. The premise of the book is that many, if not all, of the people we encounter are souls with whom we have made agreements to help us learn certain lessons or practice a particular way of being. For example, in the book, the main character, the Little Soul, wants to experience himself as forgiveness. But naturally, in order to demonstrate or practice a quality like that, we have to have someone to forgive. That's where the "angels" in our life come into play. These angels, as strange as it might sound, are far more likely to have horns than halos.

The awareness and insight I've gained have already helped immeasurably because I am more rational and decisive when people break promises. Rather than get emotionally attached to changing the person's behavior or doing what I can to influence them to do something they obviously don't want to do, I simply move on. And we are all happier for it.

Putting It into Practice

Thinking back to Shen Robinson's quote at the beginning of the chapter, this is a great time to reflect on those challenges that have us feeling like we are swimming upstream. It could be a medical issue. Perhaps it is the frustration you feel at work. It could be a relationship. Whatever the case, identify anywhere you feel stuck. What is keeping you there? It is easy to play the victim and blame outside forces or other people for our struggles. For the purpose of this exercise, imagine the possibility that you are 100% in control of your situation. What do you need to let go? Where do you need the most faith to take a step into uncertainty?

While it certainly isn't true in all cases, there are people who define themselves by their struggle, whatever it happens to be. While some struggles, like certain types of depression, have a biochemical basis, there are other struggles that appear quite real but may be more in our control that we want to admit. To what degree has your struggle become a defining part of who you are? What do you get out of your struggle? For some people, the caring, compassion, attention, and love they receive because of their struggle may be what they crave. Whatever the case, it's a challenging question that deserves an honest answer.

In the spirit of complete transparency, I have never felt more love and was never happier — on a consistent basis — than when I went through chemo. If I had an unhealthy attachment to that feeling, I'd be trying to find a way to go through it again. I can assure you I have no intention of doing that. Instead, I remind myself of the love in the world and challenge myself to find other ways to live a happy and meaningful life that don't involve people pouring love out because of a particular challenge. Loving myself more is a much better place to start.

CHAPTER 6:

Synchronicities

Chance is always powerful. Let your hook always be cast.
In the pool where you least expect it, there will be fish.
-- Ovid (43 BC – 17AD)

Carl Jung, a Swiss psychologist, was fascinated with the concept of synchronicities, the term he used to describe what others like Frank Joseph, author of the book *Synchronicity & You*, call meaningful coincidence. Synchronicities are defined as unrelated events that occur together and have particular meaning for the person who experiences the connection.

Some people insist that synchronicities are not signs from the Universe, but rather are two or more events that happened at the same time by chance. Einstein had a different take on it when he described synchronicities as God's way of remaining anonymous. People like Jung and Joseph have dedicated significant time and energy to studying the phenomena and offer insights for those willing to consider the possibility of a deeper meaning.

For simplicity, I will use the term "signs" to refer to the various forms of meaningful coincidence as I understand and have experienced them. What strikes me, as I look back on my life, is the way in which the signs

I received became more meaningful as I became more spiritually aware. But even today, although the signs come more frequently, they are not necessarily a daily occurrence. That adds to the impact when they do occur.

Synchronicities and signs from the Universe come in different forms for different people. For many people, myself included, signs often come in the form of repeating numbers that show up far more often than can be attributed to coincidence. The belief in a divine, mystical relationship between numbers and coinciding events is known as numerology. Having had a few experiences in which numbers have played a role, I am somewhat familiar with the interpretations connected with various repeating numbers.

Six months or so before I discovered the first tumor in my neck, I began to notice the number 555. Over the next few months, 555 appeared with greater frequency, and before long, I saw 555 multiple times a day: on license plates, addresses, receipts, clocks, everywhere.

Why is this significant? According to numerologists, 555 means "major life change is upon you." Accepting the first full-time position in 15 years and getting diagnosed with lymphoma certainly qualifies as a major life change. But to be honest, it was not exactly what I envisioned when I thought the angels were alerting me to upcoming life changes. Falling passionately in love with the woman of my dreams or winning the lottery would have been a bit closer to my ideal.

Following the diagnosis, I continued to see 555 a few times a week, but not as much as I had previously. I still remember Lauren, one of my colleagues, was more than a little skeptical about my story until I started pointing it out to her whenever it appeared. One of the most striking examples was a restaurant advertising large pizzas for $5.55. I can't speak for your neighborhood, but $5.55 is not a typical pizza price in Chicago.

Once again, the appearance of 555 built to a crescendo through the end of the year and into the following one. When I ended up leaving a company after a particularly challenging few months, the 555 sightings stopped and did not pick up again until almost one year later.

My experience with 555 reminded me of one of the first signs that spoke to me powerfully. Not long after college graduation, word spread quickly that Cassie Champion, a high school classmate I remembered but never formally met, was in desperate need of a bone marrow transplant. I headed to the National Marrow Donor Center (along with many of the 1,200 people in our graduating class) to see if

I might be a match. Despite our collective efforts, the doctors were unable to find a match in time to save Cassie.

Over the next few years, I often thought it would be wonderful to be able to donate bone marrow to someone and was genuinely disappointed I had not been contacted by the National Bone Marrow Registry. After the initial postcard thanking me for registering, there were no requests for money, no newsletters – no contact whatsoever. Worse yet, I was never notified of any potential matches. I often wondered if they had lost my information completely.

One night, when I was feeling particularly depressed about the future and my desperate need to leave the Chicago Board of Trade, I went up to the roof of my apartment building. Walking aimlessly, dodging the skylights and chimneys, I had what felt like a one-sided conversation with God:

"God, I could really use your help right about now. I have no idea what it is that I am supposed to be doing career-wise, but I know trading is not it. Also, while I know being an organ donor is not my life's purpose, it is something I would really like to do. That seems like such an incredible way to help someone else."

The following day, when I opened my mailbox and saw a letter from the National Bone Marrow Registry, a chill went up my spine. The chill was immediately followed by a feeling of peace and the certainty that God had somehow reached out to say, "I heard you. Don't worry. Everything is going to be fine."

The letter, which promoted an upcoming registration effort, probably went to everyone on the National Bone Marrow Registry's list, but it was meaningful to me because it was the first contact they had made in several years and it so closely coincided with my prayer.

There is a lot more going on in the Universe than we could ever know. It would be easy to ignore the signs and let our rational, questioning minds talk us out of following our feelings and intuition, but life would be a lot less interesting and fulfilling. I am amazed at the number of books and CDs I have searched for and eventually found trusting my gut feelings. By learning to pay attention to the small stuff, I am building my intuition to trust it for more important issues and opportunities. Start paying attention. It does not work every time, but it works more often than chance would predict. And either way, it is always good for a smile.

Escalating Synchronicities

Jennifer is one person who knows the power of synchronicity and the feeling of being watched over in the best of all possible ways. Through a series of fascinating, seemingly predestined events, she and her young children were given five additional years with Rich, their husband and father before he succumbed to cancer. Jennifer summed it up beautifully when she said, "Those cards were laid out before I knew they were coming my way."

The first milestone on the journey occurred shortly after Jennifer and Rich moved to Charleston, South Carolina. Jennifer was pregnant with their second child and Rich had recently left a position to pursue a more entrepreneurial opportunity. A few months after Sam, the second baby, was born, Rich's health insurance from the previous employer expired. Reflecting on the fact that they were young and neither was in a high-risk category, Jennifer and Rich weighed the option of going without insurance until they made more money. Around this time, they received an expected call from Rich's former secretary who was adamant about the need to extend their health coverage through Cobra. At first Jennifer resisted, but the secretary insisted they not "mess around" when it came to health coverage. Heeding her warning, Jennifer purchased the Cobra insurance despite the additional expense. This proved to be the first of several gifts they experienced.

Two days after Jennifer signed the family up for Cobra, Rich found a lump on his abdomen in the same location where he once had a hernia. The doctor who examined the lump wasn't concerned because it looked exactly like a hernia so he didn't order any tests.

Two weeks later, synchronicity number two occurred when the doctor Rich was seeing for reflux called to say they had an opening in a study on gastroesophageal reflux disease (GERD) and invited Rich to participate. All of the study-related treatments would be covered and he would have access to cutting edge care. The first step was a complete physical.

The doctor who did the physical thought the lump was a cyst, rather than a hernia and the decision was made to remove it two weeks later in what was predicted to be a relatively short 30-minute procedure. As Jennifer and her mother-in-law waited, the hours ticked by. Three hours. Four hours. Five hours. At one point, Jennifer joked, "If they were taking a kidney out, they'd tell me, right?"

Seven hours. Ten hours. Twelve hours passed.

Finally, the doctors came out and said, "There are some complications. We are getting the pathology done now."

At last, Jennifer and her family met with the surgeons who explained what happened. What was supposed to be a relatively simple procedure turned out to be the most complicated surgical case the hospital had seen in over two years. The cyst wasn't a cyst at all, but a football-sized tumor. Had the surgeon who was scheduled to do the procedure been available, they would have closed Rich up right away and sent him to a specialist at a better equipped hospital. Thanks to the third synchronicity, that wasn't necessary. The substitute surgeon covering the case happened to be the best surgeon in the South Eastern U.S. and the only one in the area capable of doing what needed to done – a Whipple procedure, which effectively rerouted his entire GI system, and the removal of one of his kidneys – something Jennifer joked about without knowing it was actually happening.

The tumor, which engulfed Rich's pancreas, intestines, kidney, liver and other organs, was so aggressive he would have died in a few months without the procedure. Even with the procedure his odds weren't considered good. When the surgeons first started describing the case, many of the terms were completely unfamiliar except for what Jennifer described as "oncology, pathology, and every 'ology' you could think of."

In response to one of the surgeon's overly technical explanations, Jennifer said, "I deal with the facts best. I need to know I'm dealing with and what's ahead of me." Hearing this, the surgeon replied simply, "His goose is cooked."

Fortunately for Jennifer and her daughters, the Universe had slightly different plans. The fourth, in an escalating series of synchronicities involved Rich's brother Bob, who lived in Boston and was dating a doctor. At Bob's girlfriend's request, a second sample of the tumor was sent to Boston for evaluation by one of her colleagues. Meanwhile, the pathologists in South Carolina diagnosed the tumor as a particular category of gastrointestinal cancer and recommended chemotherapy.

The doctors in Boston reached a completely different conclusion. They had recently discovered that this cancer had two distinct types only one of which could be treated with chemo. Rich, as it happened, had the much rarer tumor, the one that wouldn't respond to chemo and the one very few researchers studied — few researchers other than the colleague of Rich's brother's girlfriend.

The fifth, and most life-giving synchronicity, was the FDA's approval of a Gleevec, a treatment originally intended for leukemia that proved to be effective on gastrointestinal stromal tumors like Rich's. Had Rich not had access to the experts in Boston, he would have had a miserable few months on chemo followed by an untimely death not long after his youngest child turned one. Instead, Rich lived for another five years — two and a half of which proved to be relatively healthy with a high quality of life.

A number of years have passed since Rich's death, yet Jennifer still looks back with awe at the remarkable series of synchronicities that defied the odds and gave her and her daughters five extra years with Rich. For the rest of us, Jennifer's challenging journey is a heartwarming and inspiring reminder of the many synchronicities and miracles that happen, even in the midst of heartbreak and loss.

Synchronicities in Dreams

Another category of meaningful coincidence described in *Synchronicity & You* is dreams. If you are fortunate enough to remember them, dreams provide a fascinating look at our inner emotions and how we feel about life in general. At times, they do even more than that.

After almost a year working at the Chicago Board of Trade, I began growing more uncertain about my future as a trader. Nine months into the job, I had what remains one of the most powerful and vivid dreams of my life. Unlike my ordinary dreams, in which I am an active participant in the action, this was more like a movie with a spirit guide walking me through different scenes.

The dream started with the message that I needed to write two books. At one point, I was genuinely surprised to watch the background imagery disappear and a black, book-shaped void appear. As I struggled to understand what the image meant, I received a clear message: "You are not ready to know what this is yet."

Stunned by what I had been shown, I awoke instantly. Although the dream got my attention, I wrote it off as a curiosity in much the same way I ignored the people through the years who told me I needed to write books.

When I left the Chicago Board of Trade three months after the dream, I did not do so with the intention of writing a book; that didn't happen until a few months later when my mother made the insightful suggestion I mentioned earlier.

Not long after writing my first book, Asa Baber, a former columnist for *Playboy*, contacted me following an interview I did on *The Stock Market Observer,* a show that aired on WCIU Channel 26 in Chicago. A few days later we met for lunch, at which point he asked me to work with a close friend of his who was struggling with her job search. At lunch, he also encouraged me to reach out to Jane Jordan Browne, a Chicago-based literary agent who ended up successfully placing my book. Except for a few follow-up phone conversations, that lunch was the only time I spoke with Asa in person. Unbeknownst to me, he died a few years later at age 66 from amyotrophic lateral sclerosis (ALS), otherwise known as Lou Gehrig's disease.

It often amazes me how different people impact the trajectory of our lives. In more than one way, Asa was one of those people. Before he died, I had a dream about visiting Asa in the hospital. In the dream, Asa and I talked about two different titles for my book and his preference for the first title. What was noteworthy was not the topic of conversation, but the fact that Asa was in the hospital. Unfortunately, I did not piece any of this together until a long time after the fact, when I heard about his illness and death. Months later, I found the entry in my dream journal describing the dream about Asa. Given the date of his passing and the nature of the disease, he would almost certainly have been in the hospital or hospice the night I had the dream. My only regret is that I missed the message in the dream that he was ill – had I been more in tune, I would almost certainly have contacted him.

Although there may not be a foolproof method for catching all the signs, there is a definite power in being appreciative and finding faith in the signs we do see. What I love about signs from the Universe is that you do not have to wait for them to appear at random times. You can ask and they will appear. It is a case of "when you believe it, you will see it."

When my sister's dog, Joey, was dying, our other sister, suggested they ask for signs from the Universe. After a day of Joey not being able to use his hind legs, ML, my sister, and her boyfriend decided it was time to put the dog to sleep. Joey surprised everyone by walking proudly from the front yard, up the stairs and through the house one last time. Knowing how scared Joey had always been about visits to the vet, they asked permission to bring Joey in through the back door. But Joey had other plans: he walked calmly from the car right up to the front door of the vet's office and back to the examining room. A little while later, ML held Joey in her arms and said goodbye as the medicine took effect. The moment his heart stopped, ML heard a voice come over the intercom: "Paging Joey. Paging Joey." The timing was so uncanny ML knew immediately Joey was fine. My other sister, Clare, received her own sign about Joey in the form of the Beatles' song "Golden Slumbers" which began playing on a hard rock station she was listening to when Joey made his transition – a song totally out of character for the station.

What I love most about signs is the fact that the Universe has so many ways other than dreams and songs to reach us. Some people even get messages from license plates. As Gwen discovered, when we have trouble believing or asking for additional confirmation, we get even more messages:

I'm a very spiritual person; I believe in the powers of the Universe, Law of Attraction, meditation, energy healing, and I listen to spiritual gurus almost daily. I'm already tuned into messages from the Universe, and receiving them. With that in mind, maybe I wouldn't have taken notice of these signs when they occurred, had I not been such a spiritual person.

A year ago, I had come to pivotal time in my life, where I was trying to make a decision about whether I would stay in LA, or take the leap of faith and move to Chicago. I was raised there, but I'd been living on the west coast for 20 years. I have an enormous amount of extended family in Chicago, and a few friends, so I came back regularly for visits and the holidays. I've always loved the city and felt a deep connection to it, which is why it was on my radar to potentially move back.

I'd been in the same career in LA as an agent, for about 17 years. My career was 7 days week, 24 hours a day. I was deeply entrenched in the celebrity world, so day in and day out, I was talking to some of the world's worst individuals. As an agent, I had to be aggressive, strong-willed, and fight for money, every single day. Needless to say, after 17 years, I'd HAD IT. This was no way to live.

Given my level of spirituality, it became obvious I wasn't living my authentic life. I had two personas – the aggressive, hardcore agent persona and then, outside of the office, I had my softer, more feminine, fun and loving persona. This had to change; I didn't want to split my identity anymore, so to speak.

*This is when I started heavily considering coming to Chicago. My anxiety was through the roof. I literally asked the Universe to give me a sign. I arrived at my apartment building on a Friday afternoon, and dead center, parked in front of my building, was a car I'd never seen before. The license plate read **312 KG**. I stopped in my tracks. Some may think I might be grasping at straws here, but I was struck by "312" because it is the Chicago area code right next to my initials (but backwards). Since I'd lived in that building for 7 years, and never seen that car, even in the neighborhood, I couldn't quite chalk it up to coincidence. That car stayed in that spot the entire weekend. By Monday, it was gone and I never saw it in the neighborhood again.*

Ten days later, I still couldn't get it out of my mind so I asked the Universe again, "If that was a legitimate message you were sending me, can you please send me one more message to affirm it?" That very night, I was stuck in traffic on the way *home from work. I suddenly took notice of two cars in front of me. The first car's license plate read, **7BYE312** and the car next to it read **7UGK029**, The "BYE312" and "GK" side by side made by jaw drop. I took at as my affirmed sign that it was time to say goodbye to LA (at least for now), and go to Chicago. I ended up giving my notice a few days later.*

Although Gwen did not mention it, there are a few other aspects to the license plates worth noting. First, her request for confirmation basically communicated to the Universe, "I would like to believe the message in the license plate, but I am not 100% convinced you were talking to me." To emphasize the point, the Universe flipped the initials from KG to GK and added a "you" as if to say, "Yes, you. We are talking to U, Gwen K." I can almost hear the teasing, semi-exasperated tone. It is also noteworthy that the two plates were on cars that were side-by-side, as if to say "You can't miss this." In addition, both started with the number seven. In numerology, the number seven communicates "keep up the good work and know your wish is coming true." For this reason, the message is even more positive than the way Gwen initially interpreted it. The Universe basically said, "Yes, Gwen, this message is for you. Your plan is a good one. And your dreams are manifesting."

Nature signs are also quite common. For example, more than a few people have reported seeing butterflies or certain types of birds following the death of a loved one. But the signs aren't limited to insects nor are the subjects limited to death. As Willow Star discovered, sometimes the signs come with a different message.

Willow, a gifted photographer who was healing Stage 4 metastatic breast cancer, experienced one such sign in her search for alternative treatments. Willow was gifted a prayer bracelet from Peru. Her friend said someone had gifted it to him when he was at Standing Rock and wanted her to have it. The next week, she heard about a treatment using the venom of the Kambo frog from Peru. That same morning on her hike, she heard frogs everywhere.

Intrigued by the sudden appearance of these frogs, she started to Google information when she realized that "Monkey Frog" was her best friend's Instagram username. Without knowing any of this was going on, Willow's mother emailed her a frog-themed photo. Later, she did a sound meditation only to discover it was, you guessed it, frog sounds. When Willow looked into the meaning of frogs as spirit animals it said that "the frog as an Animal Spirit Guide may be coaxing you toward a physical or emotional cleansing." The more she read, the more it all made sense. Willow interpreted the sudden emergence of frogs as a sign that she was on a path of transformation and exactly where she needed to be.

As we talked about this particular sign and the fact that the frog, like the butterfly, is a spirit animal and a symbol of radical transformation, Willow laughed and said, "Has the Universe always been speaking this loudly to me? I actually knew it was but I wasn't listening. Now I am." Willow now finds this connection with the Universe to be a beautiful way to move through her journey.

Putting It into Practice

Here are a few suggestions for opening yourself to the signs and meaningful coincidences in your life. First, get a journal and start paying attention to the meaningful coincidences.

- If you think of someone you haven't heard from in ages and the person contacts you, write it down.
- What repeating numbers do you frequently see?

By learning to pay attention to the small stuff, you will build your intuition and be able to trust it for more important issues and opportunities. Start paying attention. It does not work every time, but it works more often than chance would predict. Either way, synchronicities are almost always good for a smile.

CHAPTER 7:

Dreams and Their Messages

Last call, all aboard, come along now all ye ghosts
And the conductors before me
Are in the bar giving a toast,
We have miles to go before we sleep
And there are bridges we need to cross
The woods are lovely, dark and deep
*-- from the song **"Dreams About Trains"** by Michael McDermott*
Reprinted with permission: Michael McDermott/Pauper Sky Songs (ASCAP)

What fascinates me most about dreams is that they seem to play so many different roles in our lives — not many of which are particularly well-understood.

Problem-Solving Dreams

There are many people who have consciously and unconsciously tapped into the creative problem-solving abilities of dreams. Thomas Edison is a famous example of someone who attempted to do so consciously. He reportedly would nap sitting up in a chair with small ball bearings in his hands. When he drifted off to sleep, the balls would drop into a metal tin and wake him up. At that point, he would make a note of whatever he was thinking or dreaming about at that moment, thus giving him access to thoughts most of us never remember simply because they get lost amongst the dreams that happen later in our sleep.

Another famous example took place in 1953 when Dr. James Watson awoke from a dream in which he supposedly saw two serpents intertwined in an ascending helix. This image gave him the insight to finally understand the shape and structure of DNA, something that had eluded people until that point.

Elias Howe experienced a similar insight that led to the invention of the sewing machine. While he was working on the problem, Howe had a dream he was being attacked by natives with spears. Later, when he thought about the dream, he realized that the spears had holes near the point. Until that moment, Howe and other would-be inventors had been unable to mechanize the process because sewing was done by hand with needles that had holes on the opposite end – a design that didn't lend itself to machine stitching.

Creative Inspiration

For some lucky souls, dreams do a lot more than help solve problems. Perhaps the most amazing and aspirational are those dreams that bestow on the dreamer what might be considered otherworldly inspiration. My favorite, by far, is a story the wonderful songwriter, Arlo Guthrie, shared about a dream he had in 1967 that led to his classic song "Darkest Hour". Here is how he introduced the song when I saw him at City Winery in Chicago on Oct. 2, 2017: *"I don't usually write songs in my sleep. There was one time, though, I was sleeping and in my sleep I was dreaming, and in my dream somebody was singin' this song. When I woke up, I wrote it down. And then I went back to sleep. And when I woke up again the next morning, there was this song sitting' there. I didn't know if it was my song, or what. But then I thought, what the heck; it's my dream."*

I'd like to learn how to write songs that way. Or books for that matter.

Paul McCartney of The Beatles and Keith Richards of The Rolling Stones had similar experiences, but neither awoke with a completed song like Guthrie. Instead, McCartney awoke with the tune for "Yesterday" but thought it must have been someone else's song he heard before falling asleep. Only upon further investigation did he realize the tune was original. In a way, Richards was even luckier because he had a guitar and a Philips cassette recorder next to his bed. In early May of 1965, Richards awoke sometime during the night and recorded the guitar riff that later became the hook for "(I Can't Get No) Satisfaction". Strangely, he didn't remember doing it. In the morning, he listened to the tape and heard the now famous riff played on his acoustic guitar followed by the sounds of him snoring. Three days later, the band began recording the song at Chess Records in Chicago.

Prophetic Dreams

As it happens, the power of dreams extends well beyond problem-solving and creative inspiration. Some have been known to give insight into our emotions, accurately foretell the future, and even provide warnings.

There are many examples of people who had prophetic dreams before disasters that, in many cases, saved their lives. Some fortunate people, including my friend Defne Gül, don't have to be hours away from boarding the Titanic to experience prophetic, even life-changing, dreams.

Defne Gül, who is very spiritual and in tune with signs and dreams, shared how two prophetic dreams helped guide her though a difficult career transition:

> *Six-and-a-half years ago, I was working in one of the best internet companies in Turkey but had the strong feeling I needed to change companies in favor of a more traditional work schedule, better benefits, and the opportunity for career advancement.*

> *Although I had great qualifications and had applied to a number of companies, three sad and frustrating months went by without a single interview. That's when one of the top telecommunications companies called me directly to ask me to interview for a position. This came as a huge surprise because the company had a reputation for being extremely selective and I hadn't applied for a job with them. Better still, the open position met all of the requirements I had listed as priorities.*

> *Two days after the initial phone interview and three days before the company invited me for the second phase of interviews, I had a dream in which I walked into company headquarters for the first time. In the lobby, I was directed to follow a circular staircase to the floor below. At that point, a*

representative from HR directed me to a meeting room, where I was given an exam. Once I finished, the HR person apologized for bringing me to the wrong room and directed me to a different room called PD. The name struck me because I had never heard of a meeting room with that name.

A few minutes later, two people entered the room and apologized for the absence of a third person who was also scheduled to join the group interview. This dream ended with the message that I would be offered a job, and that I would need to be trusting and patient because, although I would eventually love working at the company, my first month would be extremely difficult.

When I awoke from the dream, I remembered the details vividly but didn't think much about it until the actual interview three days later. When the big day arrived, I walked into the building and was directed to take the spiral staircase to the floor below. I immediately remembered the dream and realized why it seemed so familiar. From there, everything happened exactly the way it occurred in the dream. When the HR person moved the interview to a different conference room and I saw the name "PD," I realized that everything in my dream was real. I had literally seen the future.

After making it through the first three interviews, I found myself face-to-face with one of the most senior people at the company. The experience was quite odd because he almost never looked me in the eye, and to my surprise, he ended the interview asking me what I though the sales target should be for the new division of the company. I started to explain that I didn't have any of the data on which I could make a solid estimate, but I heard a voice inside say "10.2 million." Given how much guidance and support I'd received up to that point, I had no reason not to trust the number so I confidently shared it with him. At that moment, he ended the interview with no discernible expression on his face. I was a bit confused until the next day when the HR people called to ask what happened in that interview. Even they were surprised to hear the decision had been made to hire me immediately following my interview with the senior executive. It wasn't until my first day of work that I discovered the sales target for the year really was 10.2 million.

The first month with the company, as predicted by the dream, proved to be incredibly difficult and personally challenging. If I hadn't been given the message "Wait one month for all difficulties pass" in my dream, there is almost no question I would have left. Fortunately, four weeks later, negative people were dismissed and my happy days started in the company.

What I love most about Defne Gül's dream is the fact that it contained more than a simple glimpse into the future; it also carried a warning and message to prevent her from quitting the job when almost anyone else would have left in disappointment and frustration. With stories like Defne Gül's, it is difficult not to believe in guides who are there to help us. As she puts it, "Never give up following your messages in your dreams; they sometimes guide you in your life."

For Nadia, who went on to become the most accurate psychic I have ever encountered, the first prophetic dream she remembers wasn't a warning as much as it was a sign that helped her realize she had a gift.

"I first realized I was different as a young girl when I began dreaming about events that later happened. It was very weird. For example, I remember being seven years old and dreaming I was at a birthday party, but it was raining. I vividly remember being in the garden with a clown, a big group of kids, and a black and white bunny rabbit that was hopping around in the rain in my next-door neighbor's garden. Three weeks later, I received an invitation to my next-door neighbor's birthday party where I saw exactly the same clown who appeared in my dream. He wore long, yellow trousers with red patches. I still remember those. I also remember that my neighbor got a white and black rabbit as a birthday present. At first the weather was fine, but the moment it starting pouring, I remember thinking, 'That's weird. I had a dream the other day that this happened.'"

Recurring Dreams

A dream series that I began to notice in my life involved springboard diving, a sport I began at nine years old. In high school, I was a decent diver but far from a great one. With my history of club feet, I was not destined to challenge Olympic legend Greg Louganis, or anyone else for that matter. There just is not much room at the top for a diver who cannot point his toes. Go figure.

The diving dreams first started when I was in my twenties. Unlike recurring dreams in which people report having the exact dream repeatedly, the diving dreams change every time. What remains the same is the frustration I often feel in not being able to go off board and dive into the water. In many dreams, my efforts are thwarted by a diving board that curves downward at such a steep angle there is no way to jump without either falling or launching myself to the shallow end of the pool, where I would risk breaking my neck. In other dreams, the issues have included water that is too shallow, lane markers, nearby swimmers, or other hindrances that make it unsafe to dive. But most of the time, the board itself is somehow the obstacle. No matter what the issue, I awaken feeling frustrated about not being able to experience the excitement of flying through the air and doing a full twisting one-and-a-half or any of my other favorite dives.

The first person I remember mentioning these dreams to was Dr. Jan Nussbaum, a psychologist I saw once a week during a particularly stressful time at Leo Burnett. When I described the dreams to Dr. Nussbaum, he suggested I treat the diving board as an animate object and ask it why it would not let me off. Surprised by his suggestion, I asked how I would have the awareness to do that in the middle of a dream. He said, "Trust yourself. Set the intention so the next time you feel the frustration, you will, in that moment, remember to stop and ask the board why it is preventing you from diving."

Taking Dr. Nussbaum's advice, I set the intention and waited. A few weeks later, I dreamed I was standing on a low, one-meter board getting ready for my first dive. Unlike other diving boards in my dreams, everything about this board was normal – except for the sharp blades all around the edge of the board that looked like widely-spaced shark's teeth. To my surprise, I remembered my intention, took a deep breath, and followed Dr. Nussbaum's suggestion. As non-confrontationally as possible I asked, "Why are you doing this to me? Why won't you let me dive?"

There was no verbal response, but at that moment, everything changed and the environment became even more inhospitable. The lights in the pool area dimmed, the water level rose to a few inches below the board, and flames appeared around the perimeter of the pool. I immediately found myself swimming in the middle of the pool with no recollection of how I got there. I knew it was important for me to get to the shallow end of the pool, but I was not particularly fearful. Even though the rapid changes surprised me, I was more confused than scared. Unfortunately, I still did not understand what the dreams meant. I did find it odd, though, that I would be more interested in getting to the shallow end, the part of the pool divers avoid because of the hazards of slamming into the bottom of the pool and the catastrophic injuries that could result.

Knowing I could consciously alter the trajectory of my dreams was fascinating. It was even more amazing to see how doing so could lead to completely unexpected outcomes. I had not thought about it much before that, but I suppose if I had been asked, I might have made the case that dreams were often little more than midnight fantasies that played out in our minds.

This particular diving dream changed all that: I made a conscious decision to alter the action in a dream and was met with a completely unpredictable outcome. This is just one reason it is hard for me to view dreams as simple fantasy or wish fulfillment; instead, dreams seem to point to another level of consciousness, one that was not ready to reveal itself to me for another 17 years.

The person who helped more than anyone in my understanding of my recurring dreams is a woman from Michigan named Judy Crookes, who channels a spirit group whom I will call Jake. When I asked Jake what the diving dreams meant, the insights shared were quite helpful. Jake, who agreed with the generally accepted premise that water in the dreams represents emotions, went on to make the connections that had escaped me. Jake interpreted the diving dreams somewhat literally: *"You are not diving into your emotions. You are not allowing yourself to feel them."*

The idea of viewing the water as a metaphor for emotion was something I had heard before, but I never considered that I was the one preventing myself from experiencing the full range of emotions. This was new to me, and it would take some effort to process.

At first, I thought about the Dalai Lama and other more spiritually evolved people who seem to handle difficult situations with compassion and ease. I still aspire to be more like that, but I also know intuitively that I am more than 12 steps and a few interventions away from that ideal. My slowly expanding awareness has helped me be more compassionate with myself, but it did not explain why emotions like anger surface in the first place.

In some moments, I began to ask myself, "Why am I angry?" I eventually realized I was asking the wrong question. Anger was not the primary emotion; it was a mask for something deeper. In other words, on the surface, the anger and frustration seemed to be directed at the behavior of someone else. However, when I finally acknowledged that my anger or frustration was often out of proportion to a given situation, I had to ask myself the deeper question: "If this is not about the other person, what is this really about?"

I soon discovered that in some cases, anger and frustration at others simply masked the anger and frustration I felt toward myself. In other cases, the anger hid deeper feelings of unworthiness or insecurity. Identifying the raw, underlying feelings helped, but if my dreams are any indication, this will be an ongoing process.

Fortunately, some dreams come with messages that don't take so long to understand or interpret – like the one that literally saved my life.

The Telepathic Lifeguard

Although this happened in 2019, there are only a handful of people I have ever shared this with including my siblings, who, for reasons that will become obvious, needed to know. I originally shared the story on Facebook and wrote it as if it happened to my friend, Allison, from the gym because I wasn't ready to be public about it. Now, I am.

On the morning of December 30, 2019, I awoke from a vivid dream in which I found myself standing on the shores of an unfamiliar ocean. The surrounding area included a number of difference places where people hung out depending on the tides. In the early part of the dream, the day felt somewhat ominous even though the waves weren't particularly big. In the next scene, I was standing next to a lifeguard in the middle of the beach, not far from shore. About 100 yards behind us and away from the water, a large cliff-like wall, at least 50 feet high, served to protect the street and the area beyond the beach from storm surge. The wall itself was constructed of huge, gray, rectangular, boulder-like rocks stacked on top of each other with seaweed and other plants visible at the seams where the rocks came together.

Seeing how much the seas had calmed since the morning, I let my guard down somewhat thinking the danger had passed. The lifeguard, however, telepathically communicated that exactly the opposite was true and that we needed to get out of there fast because the next surge would be significantly more severe. At that moment, he turned around and began running at top speed through a shallow pool leading away from the shore. Alarmed by the lifeguard's quick retreat and the telepathic way in which he communicated, I turned around and ran as fast I could in the same direction. I managed to reach the wall and looked to my left at the same moment a huge wave crashed into it. The wall stopped 90% of the water, but the remaining 10% or so poured through the cracks between the rocks pushing the long strands of seaweed on the opposite side of the wall. Looking across the island, it was clear I must have been on a peninsula because I could see waves crashing on the other side of the island as well.

When I awoke, I wrote the dream in my dream journal but couldn't shake the disconcerting feeling it created. Unlike many dreams that I quickly forget, this one stayed on the forefront of my mind most of the day.

After leaving the gym that morning, I noticed a very slight discomfort in the muscle near my left collar bone but didn't pay much attention except to massage it briefly. When I went to get a cortisone injection in my left ankle later that morning, I asked Dr. Kelikian why the pain was not in my ankle, but a few inches above in my calf. He said, "That's referral pain – the same way you'd get it if you were having a heart attack." (Referral pain is a feeling you get when the pain you are experiencing is in a place that isn't where you would logically think it would be based on an injury or sensitivity.)

That same afternoon, I had an appointment with an oral surgeon to see if one of my top teeth was cracked. When he asked if it hurt, I said, "No, but one below it sometimes does."

The oral surgeon replied, "Oh, that's referral pain."

Although I was struck by the second mention of referral pain in less than three hours, I didn't think much about it and headed home for an appointment with one of my coaching clients.

At this point, it was almost dinner and I was craving shrimp tacos from Gringos, a restaurant up the street from my townhouse. As I walked up Grand Ave., the weird sensation near my collarbone returned.

The feeling, which was more of a dull ache or throb than a pain, was the kind of thing I would typically have ignored and written off as a possible pulled muscle had it not been for the dream. Alarmed by the fact that the intensity increased after a period of calm — exactly like the dream — I literally stopped in my tracks at the corner of Grand Ave. and Ogden. Trusting my intuition, I took an incredibly important step. Rather than rationalize the experience away, I silently asked my intuition the question, "Is this something I need to get checked right now or can I go get shrimp tacos?"

The unmistakable response came immediately: "You need to get this checked. Now."

After a Google search to find the closest Immediate Care facility, I called an Uber. The physician on duty did an immediate EKG, determined that my heart was not getting enough oxygen, and encouraged me to get to the emergency room as fast as possible. For the next few hours, my resting heart rate remained above 120, more than double my normal rate. After tests, medication, and what seemed like an extraordinarily long wait under the circumstances, I was sent to the cardiac cath lab where the doctors found that all of my arteries looked perfect except for one on the outside left wall of the heart. That artery was 90% blocked so they put in a stent to reopen it. The cardiologists were genuinely surprised because of what seemed like an almost complete absence of risk factors. At one point, they mentioned that "broken heart syndrome" is very real and asked if I had recently experienced a relationship trauma. I hadn't.

Looking back, I clearly see that the lifeguard in the dream was a Spirit Guide warning me about what was to come so I didn't ignore it. The period of calm was the afternoon I spent free of any discomfort before the referral pain near my collar bone – the only noticeable symptom of the heart issue – returned. Likewise, the sea wall to my left in the dream that blocked 90% of the water represented the artery on the left wall of my heart that was 90% blocked. At one point, the technicians in the cath lab thought they saw a slight tear in the artery — not unlike the seams of the wall.

People sometimes ask if I think the lifeguard in the dream was my dad who died of heart failure six months earlier. Even though I know he is watching over me, I am quite sure it wasn't him; he didn't run that fast.

While I am not at all happy about labels like "coronary artery disease" and "heart attack" which don't seem to fit my mainly healthy lifestyle, I focus primarily on my gratitude for the dream, my Spirit Guide, and the intuition that literally saved my life.

A year or so later, in yet another example of our remarkable ability to heal, the cardiologist, Dr. Kannan Mutharasan, said that my heart seems to have found a way to compensate for the small amount of damage it sustained. Also, to his credit, he and his team of medical students listened with fascination as I shared the dream and intuitive voice that saved my life. I loved the fact that they were so open. My dad, who probably had a hand in picking my care team in the first place, would have been proud.

As much as I don't like people thinking of me as having had a heart issue, I share this with the sincere hope that anyone else who considers themselves too young and too fit to experience a life-threatening blocked artery will pay attention to their dreams and check in with their intuition when they experience even mild, unexplainable symptoms.

Putting It into Practice

As you think about your own dreams, be open to the many wonderful messages and possibilities they may contain. You may not get the melody for a new song, the script for next year's Oscar winning movie, or valuable information for an upcoming interview, but then again, you might. One thing is certain though: if you don't recall and record your dreams, the magic definitely will not happen.

Keep a blank journal by your bed to record dreams. Or use the Notes or voice memo feature on your phone.

- What reoccurring dreams have you had?
- How do you feel in the dreams?

Part of the fun of keeping a dream journal is finding unexpected synchronicities. For example, one night I had a dream in which I saw my friend, Angie, at what seemed to be a book signing. Shortly after I awoke, Angie sent me a text. Hearing from her that early in the day was, by itself, unusual, but the real surprise was the fact that she wrote to tell me she had just signed up for a children's book writing class.

Another interesting result of keeping a dream journal is that you will begin to remember more dreams because you will be training yourself to remember. After I had kept a journal for a few months, there were nights I could remember up to seven different dreams. Unfortunately, when I got out of the habit of writing every morning, that recall dropped significantly.

PART II

APPLYING WHAT YOU HAVE LEARNED:

EMBARKING ON YOUR JOURNEY

CHAPTER 8:

Expect Positive, Experience Positive

Nothing is so wretched or foolish as to anticipate misfortunes.
What madness is it to be expecting evil before it comes.
-- *Lucius Annaeus Seneca*

chieving a consistent, positive, approachable mental state is all about reminding myself daily of a lesson from Albert Einstein:

"The most important question facing humanity is, 'Is the universe a friendly place?' This is the first and most basic question all people must answer for themselves."

This is one of the most profound and accessible examples of Einstein's brilliance. It is also a question I ask myself almost every day — especially when I get in the car or ride my mountain bike through the streets of the city. When I don't think to ask myself this question, I find myself in a defensive stance expecting people to cut me off, open car doors in front of me, or take other actions to inconvenience, upset, or injure me. If you accept the Law of Attraction and the idea that our thoughts create our experience, you already know how unhealthy negative thoughts are. That's why it is so important to view the universe as a friendly place.

Perhaps the best example of living this way was Nelson Mandela, the inspiring South African leader who helped his country emerge from the horrors of apartheid. After reading Mandela's autobiography, *Long Walk to Freedom*, it is clear how much optimism and positive expectations played a role in his success. Throughout his life, he related to everyone in a welcoming way — even the captors who kept him imprisoned for decades. As John Carlin, author of *Playing the Enemy* (which was made into the movie *Invictus*) put it:

> *"His (Mandela's) secret weapon was that he assumed not only that he would like the people he met, he assumed also that they would like him."*

Considering the oppression faced by the black people of South Africa, the fact that Mandela was able to maintain such a positive expectation about all his interactions is both astounding and inspiring.

Johnny Clegg, the South African musician who inspired Paul Simon's *Graceland* album, describes the impact Mandela had on people as transformative. At one point, Mandela invited the elderly wife of the architect of apartheid to tea. Had Mandela felt resentment toward this woman for what her husband created, no one could have faulted him. But Mandela chose a different and more difficult path — kindness and compassion. Truly inspiring.

Mandela may not always have seen the Universe as a friendly place, but his positive expectations must have kept whatever doubt he had in check.

In the same way positive energy and optimism seem to emanate from people like Nelson Mandela, there are people on the opposite end of the continuum. These are the complainers who aren't happy unless everyone around them is equally unhappy. I strongly suspect that people who are absorbed in their own negative energy are unaware of the impact they have on others in the same way I was oblivious to my own scarcity mentality.

For many of us, it may be as simple as checking in with our feelings and being more aware of how people are responding. Have friends stopped making plans with you? Do you catch yourself feeling angry and frustrated more often than usual? Pay attention. I remember one yoga studio with a sign at the entrance that read:

Please be aware of the energy you bring into this space.

What a great reminder of the responsibility we all have to be accountable for the energetic ripples we create. After all, the driver we flipped off this morning may have taken her anger out on an assistant who, in turn, may have yelled at their child. It doesn't take much to create an avalanche of negative energy. We've all done it. With a little awareness and a stronger sense of accountability, we can either stop the cycle or not start it in the first place.

During the summer when I was in sixth or seventh grade, my friend Bryan Nelson and I went to a sports camp on the University of Notre

Dame campus in South Bend, Indiana. For a week or two, he and I shared a dorm room. One night, when we weren't quite ready to go to sleep, Bryan and I got into a conversation about the other people in our class at Ogden, our grade school in downtown Chicago. We had one classmate I'll call Mitch who used to drive me crazy. Mitch and I always had fun when it was just the two of us, but when other people were around, he made it a point to find ways to aggravate me. This had been going on since at least second grade when our class performed "We Three Kings" in the Christmas assembly. I was picked to sing solo as one of the kings. During what should have been my solo, I could clearly hear Mitch standing directly behind me singing along. The teacher told him repeatedly to stop, but he never did.

As Bryan and I talked that night at camp, I shared example after example of Mitch's annoying behavior. I honestly didn't realize how negative I sounded until Bryan brought it to my attention. I don't remember his exact words, but I distinctly remember the sudden awareness that I was coming across in a way that was at least as immature and annoying as Mitch, if not more so. I can still see myself lying on my back, staring up from the bottom bunk, grateful that Bryan couldn't see my face. Feeling like an insecure slug was all the embarrassment I could handle in the moment.

It didn't occur to me until years later that Mitch's insecurities grated on my nerves because they so closely mirrored some of my own. But thanks to Bryan I did see, for the first time in my life, how I was coming across as insecure as well. My only regret is that I never thanked Bryan for doing what he did. He could easily have rolled his eyes and let me continue whining. But he didn't. Unfortunately, Bryan is one of those people who disappeared after we graduated from 8th grade. No one seems to have any idea what happened to him. Nevertheless, Bryan was the first person I remember who helped me grow by making me aware of the way I can come across to others. Fortunately, he wasn't the last.

In an effort to teach me what was socially acceptable and what wasn't, my mother pointed out that a boy I'll call Ahmed, who was a year ahead of me in school, frequently practiced one-upmanship. Like many behaviors that come to annoy us, I might never have paid any attention to Ahmed's antics had it not been brought to my attention. But once it entered my conscious awareness, it started to annoy me as well. Later, at the end of my freshman year of high school, I joined my classmates from St. Ignatius College Prep on a canoe trip to Quetico, the boundary waters between Minnesota and Canada. After rowing all day, our group would stand by the fire and tell stories. I don't remember any of the specifics, but I must have talked a lot about Ahmed because it quickly came back to haunt me.

Fr. Menke, one of our guides, quietly watched and listened to our stories night after night until he had heard enough. Here we were in a pristine part of the country, surrounded by clear waters, gorgeous greenery, and an immense variety of wildlife, and we weren't paying attention to any of it. Fr. Menke was so at home in the wilderness that I might have completely forgotten he had been on the trip if it weren't for the night he finally exploded.

In hindsight, a big part of Fr. Menke's frustration stemmed from the fact that our unrelenting noise kept him from enjoying the beauty of our surroundings. When Fr. Menke finally spoke up, he talked about the loons we would never hear because we wouldn't shut up. As the tirade continued, his voice shook with anger and his words took on the shape of daggers as he directed his attention to the people who caused him the most disgust. To my horror, I was one of those people.

I stared uncomfortably at the dirt and debris at my feet as Fr. Menke's searing gaze pierced me from the other side of the fire. Each word felt like a punch as my stomach twisted in my gut. I could almost feel myself doubling over in pain when I heard the brutal truth:

"Robert, for someone who claims to hate one-upmanship, you sure practice a hell of a lot of it."

Having made his point, Fr. Menke quickly shifted his attention to other people and other grievances. It took less than five seconds for him to shine the bright light of awareness on a behavior, which, left unchecked, would have become socially debilitating. But in that brief moment, he spoke the truth and changed my life for the better. It isn't an exaggeration to say I will always be grateful to Fr. Menke for saying what many other people standing around that campfire no doubt thought.

On more than a couple of occasions I have been struck by how few people like Bryan Nelson and Fr. Menke there are in the world. That's unfortunate because the people who have the courage and conviction to tell me when I'm screwing up will always have a special place in my heart. There is nothing more revealing and helpful than the candid observations of people who care enough to say what others are thinking but lack the presence, courage, or ability to communicate effectively.

My Turning Point

One night, my friend Stacy Minks and I went to see Wayne Dyer at the Rosemont Convention Center in Chicago. That evening, Dyer shared Albert Einstein's quote about seeing the Universe as a friendly place. I had heard it before, but never internalized it the way I did that night.

Upon hearing those words, I suddenly realized how I had taken the frustration I had been experiencing at different aspects of my life and allowed it to color my expectations. The more I objectively looked at my thoughts, the more I realized I was treating the Universe as a hostile place in dozens of ways every day. Acknowledging my negative worldview was especially embarrassing because I often remind friends and clients about the Law of Attraction and how what we give our attention, energy, and focus comes into our experience. In that moment, I made the decision to shift my focus and consistently view the world as a friendly place, a decision that must be reaffirmed multiple times a day, because there are so many opportunities to be distracted by people and circumstances I otherwise might find frustrating.

Over the next few days, I noticed my mostly positive disposition become even brighter. Four days after Wayne Dyer's session, I awoke in the middle of the night from a thought-provoking dream: I was back at the Holy Cross campus watching people move the desk of the magistrate to make room for the person who was taking over. The school was changing its name to Villanova. At first, that was a bit confusing since there already is a school named Villanova. While I was still asleep, or at least very groggy, I started thinking more about the name and the dream. At first, I mistranslated Villanova as "new ground" or "new territory," but that did not make sense until I realized the Latin word for that would have been "Terranova." It was not until I translated "Villanova" correctly as "new house" that I understood the meaning behind the dream.

In this case, the college campus – higher education – represents my higher self. The renaming and the new magistrate is symbolic of the new attitude I am taking on: my conscious decision to remind myself that the world is, indeed, a friendly abundant place.

It was all part of my realization that the way I had been thinking and living — ready to attack at every turn — was not working for me. I have no interest in being an angry man or an angry old man. Instead, my desire is to be an approachable, happy guy who is blessed by the abundance of financial prosperity, a loving wife, great kids, wonderful friends, trips, and experiences.

That is the choice I decided to make. It was a new house and the new owners were moving in. It was an exciting moment indeed.

Lesson 1: Reframing

I love the fact that we can achieve a different perspective and change the way we interpret our own unhealthy stories simply by gaining additional experience. The best part is that the experience does not necessarily have to be our own. I would not have thought it possible to release negative energy through someone else's story, but that is exactly what I experienced through a conversation I had with my good friend Tim Cunningham. Tim and I met in an on-camera acting class at The Green Room in Chicago, but we did not become friends until after the eight-week class ended. Tim was an inspiration to a lot of us because, while many actors work temporary or part-time jobs so they have the freedom to go on auditions, Tim worked full-time as a compliance officer for one of the largest securities firms in the country.

A few months before *Getting Your Foot in the Door When You Don't Have a Leg to Stand On* was published, Scott Mendel, my agent, called and said the publishing company that purchased the rights to my book had just been acquired McGraw-Hill. I still remember the excitement in his voice when he said, "The stars are aligning for you."

The thrill I felt was short-lived because I quickly began to see a growing list of missed opportunities that had a profound, negative impact on book sales. For example, I received a letter from a school that had stopped using the best-selling book *What Color is Your Parachute?* in their career development classes because the students and instructors had found my book more helpful. I forwarded this good news to the editors and marketing team, but was told, "We don't see your book as a textbook" — despite the fact that at least seven schools were already doing so.

I began feeling neglected, lost, and without an internal advocate. It was not long before the stellar alignment looked more like a perfect storm, and for most of the next nine years, my frustration ebbed and flowed. Back then, every few months, Tim and I would meet to share stories about acting and modeling or our shared passion for speaking and training. One afternoon, Tim told me his modeling agent had encouraged him to find a different agent to represent him for on-camera work. The firm, which had been acquired by one of the top modeling agencies, was still willing to represent him as a model, but felt he would have a better chance being represented by someone else for on-camera opportunities.

In a situation where other people might have been discouraged or devastated, Tim remained positive and hopeful as he talked about the future. I was even more impressed by Tim's gratitude to the firm and his agent not only for their honesty, but also for having represented him as long as they had when he had not "earned the spot on their wall."

Until that moment, I am embarrassed to say, I never stopped to realize that I had not earned my place on the McGraw-Hill wall either. After the acquisition, they could easily have cancelled my project, but they didn't. Thinking about the impact that might have had on my career trajectory, especially given the many opportunities that have come to pass because of that book, was enough to make me shudder. Simply put, being a published author with a recognizable publishing house creates a level of credibility that would be difficult to replicate any other way.

The timing of my conversation with Tim was remarkable for another reason. That very day, I was coming to terms with the decision that the publisher was cancelling my book after four printings. Through Tim's story, I gained the perspective I needed to finally release the negative feelings I had. I was finally ready to admit the cancellation wasn't personal; it was a business decision. When I thought about Tim's insight in rational terms, I was reminded of a great book by Martin Seligman, Ph.D. called *Learned Optimism*. Seligman describes the process of changing our thoughts about a situation as reframing. In this case, I was able to change my interpretation of the story by considering additional facts.

I once used a similar technique to help employees of one of the top global companies deal with a potential outsourcing. Six months before the company made a final decision regarding whether to outsource the entire information services department, management decided to let the employees know the options being considered, as well as the impact it might have on their jobs. From an objective point-of-view, the company's willingness to provide so much advance notice clearly demonstrated its commitment to employees. But not everyone saw it that way.

In the first stress management workshop the company hired me to lead, people expressed hurt and anger, even though the likelihood that jobs would be lost was relatively small. The real concern was which company would be signing their paycheck – their current employer or the outsourcing firm. Despite the company's openness, suspicion and distrust abounded. Recognizing this, I started the workshop with a group exercise in which we divided a flipchart into two columns. On the left side, we listed all of the reasons people had to be upset with the company. This included the fears, disappointments, and factors that caused people to distrust what they were hearing from management. Once we could think of nothing else to add to the list, I asked the group to share any evidence that the company really did care about its employees. At first, people were relatively quiet. However, as the team considered the question, they spoke up with various examples. The more evidence they uncovered, the more the tension in the room dissipated. The same people whose voices had cracked with fear a few minutes before when they had shared their distrust of management were now surprised to find evidence that the company truly did care. Most of the items on the right side of the flip chart were facts they had either dismissed or not previously considered. For example, the company's management:

- had no obligation to provide advance notice and did so at considerable risk (valuable employees, after all, might have left);

- was acting differently than executives at other companies who make decisions and lay employees off at will;

- continued to invest in workshops like stress management to help employees;

- invested in career development by holding résumé writing workshops and one-on-one coaching to help employees in case their positions were eliminated or they decided to leave voluntarily; and

- created a separate newsletter to address employee concerns and keep people up-to-date.

When the facts on both sides were viewed together, a different picture emerged. Most people began to see that the company, despite changing economic conditions, had taken steps to communicate as much as possible and as early as possible. Unlike companies that do not factor employees into the equation, this company incurred considerable expense to make sure everyone either had a job or was well-prepared to find another.

Predictably, some employees found the prospect of change disruptive and believed they would have been better off not knowing anything until the decision had been made. But most people emerged from the workshop with a more objective view of the situation. They had every right to be disappointed and to experience grief at the prospect of transitioning to a different employer, but at the same time, they gained a deeper appreciation of the steps the company was taking to make the transition as seamless as possible.

Lesson 2: You cannot change others

I learned this lesson after reading *The Vortex* by Esther and Jerry Hicks. A similar theme can be found in their other books, such as *The Law of Attraction: The Basics of the Teachings of Abraham* and *The Amazing Power of Deliberate Intent: Living the Art of Allowing*. Regardless, the concept is simple but powerful:

Most of the unhappiness on this planet is caused by trying to change the behavior of someone else.

Take a moment and think deeply about that. How many times do we get frustrated because someone else is not doing what we expect or believe they should?

The desire to change the behavior of others is not limited to people we know. I notice it with strangers as well — especially when I am driving. This might seem like a trite example, but the life skills we most need to master can be practiced anywhere.

Although I am getting better, I still slip into moments of intense frustration when people take unexpected or stupid actions behind the wheel. For example, I am a firm believer in the need for a separate license for driving in major cities like Chicago. It is horrifying how many people drive in from out of town and are oblivious to the fact that when executing a left turn, drivers need to pull up halfway into the intersection to wait for the oncoming traffic to pass. I do not know who taught people to wait behind the crosswalk, but there is no way anyone could ever successfully make a left turn from there. Traffic does not work that way in congested areas without a left turn light.

Psychologically speaking, the car itself creates a false sense of protection. Somehow, doors and windows make it seem safe to let anger escalate to a point it might never reach in a typical face-to-face interaction. Knowing that one of the life skills I need to master in this lifetime is patience, I have been working hard to exercise more compassion behind the wheel. One of the strategies I use is to imagine the person in the other car not as a faceless annoying driver, but an otherwise kind person having a bad day.

Thoughts That Make Us Sick

Our thoughts have the power to heal our bodies, but they can also make us sick. Given this, it's no surprise that reminders of this are not always pleasant.

The point of the following story is not who was right or wrong – after all, that is a matter of perspective and not particularly relevant. Truth be told, everyone involved could probably have handled this situation better. In this case, what is most important is the dramatic positive impact of changing perspective, especially in moments of conflict and misunderstanding.

A few years back, I had begun to develop a close friendship with Pete (not his real name) based on our shared passion for music. The last time we were out, he had asked me about an attractive mutual friend, Heidi (also not her real name). Later in the evening, Pete asked if Heidi and I were dating. I could tell Pete was interested in her so I assured him that we were not. Heidi and I had dated a few times, but remained friends when it became apparent there was no long-term chemistry. Since I knew she was interested in Pete, I encouraged him to ask her out.

A few weeks after my conversation with Pete, I called Heidi to ask the exact date for Pete's rapidly approaching birthday. I knew Heidi would be able to tell me the date because I had heard through mutual friends that she and Pete had begun dating.

Shortly after Heidi answered the phone, I said, "I know Pete has a big birthday coming up, and I don't want to forget it, but I haven't heard from him in a while." After an uncomfortable pause, Heidi replied, "And you won't be hearing from him either."

Shocked, I asked why. Heidi proceeded to tell me Pete was "very hurt" that I had lied to him about my relationship with her. When I asked her to clarify, Heidi told me that Pete asked me about my relationship with her because he has a "rule" that he will not date anyone his friends have dated.

Putting aside the fact that I found Pete's rule to be odd, I expressed surprise, as I had the impression Pete already knew that Heidi and I had dated a few months before. I had no intention of lying to Pete or misleading him in any way; I thought his concern was that he did not want to pursue Heidi if she and I were still dating.

Even though miscommunication requires two people, I decided it would be far easier to accept 100% of the blame for the situation. In a sincere attempt to re-establish connection, I called Pete and left a message accepting full responsibility and apologizing for any difficulty it may have caused. I closed by asking him to get in touch so we could talk.

Ordinarily I would not leave a message like that on a voicemail, but since it was an apology, and I already knew intuitively it was unlikely he would call me back, I made an exception.

I never heard from Pete. With each passing day, I became progressively more hurt and disappointed. Although I started out feeling badly that I had somehow hurt him, the hurt was replaced with frustration when it became clear I wouldn't be hearing from him.

Well aware of the connection between my mental/emotional well-being and my physical health, it did not surprise me when I developed a sore throat and congestion. I remembered reading that sore throats and congestion are often a physical manifestation of something we are not saying but should be.

By the time my sadness and disappointment had fully transformed to anger, I had worked myself up to the point where I was immobile on the sofa with a rising fever. When I described my symptoms to my dad, he told me I probably had the same severe flu many of his patients had been experiencing. At his suggestion, I dragged myself off the couch and headed upstairs to bed. Before going to sleep, I took a deep breath and said an urgent prayer: I asked God to help me find another way to view the situation so I could let go of the anger and disappointment I felt toward Pete.

The moment I uttered that prayer, I had a 3D-like vision of my young friend, Steele, who was three-and-a-half at the time. The image presented was of Steele in a hologram-like circle that looked exactly like the famous Da Vinci drawing of the human anatomy. Steele's image overlapped with an image of Pete that took up the exact same amount of space within the circle; it was as if they were the same size. This was particularly strange because Pete was almost 47 years older, 5 feet taller, and 300 pounds heavier than Steele.

I immediately laughed and prayed again, "That's an interesting picture but I don't get it. Please be more specific." My prayer for clarification was answered instantly with the sound of a voice that was neither male nor female: *Pete's emotional development is at the level of a young child. That is not his fault. Be more compassionate.*

Pete's developmental level was not right, wrong, good, or bad; it simply was. Therefore, it was not fair or appropriate to be mad at him for something he could not control. After all, I wouldn't be mad at Steele either. The message was brilliant in its simplicity, directness, and ability to get me to view the situation from a healthier perspective.

As I recognized the wisdom in this, I felt my body let go of all the anger, frustration, sadness, and disappointment. I immediately fell into a sound sleep. Twice over the next few hours, I awoke drenched from sweat as my body released all of the negative emotions I had accumulated over the week. The following morning, I felt fine, with almost no trace of illness and no residual anger toward Pete. Through prayer, perspective, and the power of shifting my emotions from anger to compassion, I moved from sickness to health in an instant. Better still, the anger never returned.

A more humorous example of changing one's perspective comes from my friend Becky. Whenever she is driving and hears someone honk, rather than get defensive or upset, which is typically my first reaction, Becky smiles and waves. The first time I saw her do it, I looked at her incredulously and asked, "What are you doing?" Becky replied with a mischievous grin, "Oh, I just assume it's someone who recognizes me and wants to say hi." Brilliant! I love her approach even more when I think about how maddening that must be for drivers who are honking because they are angry and being jerks.

To bring this back to the idea about the root cause of unhappiness, I cannot think of a single instance in which I was upset with someone that did not involve the perception they were behaving differently than I thought they should. Even if I could see the other person's point-of-view perfectly and understand at a deep level the factors involved in their behavior, it would not necessarily change my disappointment and frustration in the moment.

This is especially true when the other person makes a decision that impacts us without involving us in the process. Either way, we can be left feeling hurt and disappointed. Whether their behavior is caused by different values, conflicting priorities, thoughtlessness, or even just blatant disregard for our feelings, it does not change the fact that our negative feelings are caused by an underlying desire to alter their behavior.

In those moments, I am reminded of one particular inspirational message I frequently see posted on Facebook:

> *How people treat you is their karma.*

> *How you respond is yours.*

From a spiritual development standpoint, the choices we make play a pivotal role not only in our happiness in any given moment, but also in our experience going forward.

The Power of Compassion

I firmly believe our thoughts and expectations determine our experiences. When I lead sales training workshops, I remind participants how this can play out in meetings or conversations we expect will be challenging or unpleasant. In these situations, it is helpful to shift our expectations. When I catch myself thinking, "This is not going to be fun. I am not looking forward to this," I stop myself. Then, I consciously shift and say to myself, "I don't know how, but my commitment is that this conversation will go better than I would ever expect."

This works because it trains the mind to think differently. If you go into a potentially difficult situation with a more positive thought, your mind begins looking, both consciously and unconsciously, for evidence that it will go well. This increases the possibility of a positive outcome simply because you stop your mind from seeking evidence to the contrary. In other words, you avoid a self-fulfilling prophecy.

The key is to remember to shift your thinking *before* the conversation takes place. The same strategy can also work miracles when interactions take a quick, unexpected turn for the worse. Making a mental shift under such circumstances is especially challenging, but it can also be incredibly rewarding.

One summer, I was scheduled to fly to Sioux Falls, South Dakota to lead a training workshop. When I arrived at Chicago's O'Hare International Airport, I received a boarding pass that required me to check in with the gate agent for a seat assignment. The gate representative assured me of a seat, but cautioned that I would probably be the last person on the plane. Happy to have encountered a gate agent who clearly knew how to instill confidence in passengers, I expressed my gratitude. Then I waited patiently – something I do not always do well.

After the other passengers boarded the plane, the agent smiled warmly, told me how much she appreciated my patience, and handed me a boarding pass for aisle seat 3B. When I got on the plane, I discovered that seat 3B was occupied, but 2B was not. Pretty sure that no one else would be getting on board, I decided to take 2B rather than ask the man in 3B to move. I sat down only to discover someone else's carry-on bag under the seat in front of me.

Since the flight was moments from taking off, I grabbed the bag that was under the seat and attempted to find a space in the overhead compartment. I would have put my own backpack in the overhead bin, but I needed access to the workbooks inside. Besides, I felt confident that the storage space under the seat in front of me was designated for me, not some other passenger. After I grabbed the other person's bag, I reached to open the overhead bin in search of an open space. At that moment, the flight attendant, who must have been frustrated already, directed her aggression at me when she snapped, "What are you doing?"

I explained the situation, but flight attendant raised her voice and exclaimed, "Oh, no you don't. That person was here first." Before I could even reply, she continued by saying, "If you don't stop being rude to the other passengers, I'm going to kick you off this flight."

This entire interaction took place less than one minute from the time I set foot in the plane. Partially because I knew there were no other flights to Sioux Falls, and partially because I was too stunned to react, I sat down quietly. Inside I was burning but I did my best to hide it. To my surprise, the middle-aged woman in the seat next to me leaned over and whispered, "Wow. Did she ever overreact!"

Still shaking with adrenaline, I quietly replied, "Thank you for saying that. It's nice to know I'm not the only one who thinks that."

Faced with even a mild, non-life-threatening attack, we are biologically wired for one of three primary responses: fight, flight, or freeze. Since my goal was to remain on the flight, the only reasonable response was to freeze – even though, I am not proud to say, my typical reaction to a verbal attack is to defend myself or fight back.

With my heart and mind racing, I sat back in the seat, shut my eyes, and began to craft the angry letter I planned to send to the airline. Those thoughts continued for a few minutes until I realized I was only making myself more upset. Besides, anyone who has ever contacted airline customer service knows it is not an optimal strategy for feeling acknowledged or understood. I decided a better approach would be to use the techniques I often share with others.

First, I reflected on the previous few minutes in an attempt to process and understand why the situation spiralled so quickly out of control. As I prayed for help, I had a strong feeling the situation could be healed with compassion. I would work hard to summon up compassion for the flight attendant, myself, and even for the guy in the 3B who no doubt changed seats when he saw there was no storage space to go with his assigned seat.

This was not an easy process. Part of me desperately wanted to be right, educate the flight attendant on baggage etiquette, and receive an apology. Without knowing about my interaction with the gate agent, the flight attendant probably saw me as just another inconsiderate passenger who did not feel the need to board on time. Perhaps she felt justified in being angry with me for being late and screwing up what she saw as a reasonable solution to the limited luggage space.

Whatever the case, I spent the next hour or so of the short flight struggling to replace waves of anger with those of compassion. With my eyes shut, I visualized my Higher Self communicating a message of forgiveness to the flight attendant. Throughout the process, I kept slipping back into my angry-defensive mode every time I thought about how embarrassed I had been. I found it uncomfortable to think a plane full of strangers had a bad impression of me.

When I finally managed to calm my mind, two astounding things happened. First, the flight attendant began to playfully tease me by smiling and asking the woman next to me in a joking tone, "He's not bothering you, is he?" By the time we landed, I was in a much more peaceful place but was genuinely and pleasantly surprised when the flight attendant gave me a big, sincere hug as I walked toward the jet bridge. Anyone on the cramped commuter flight who noticed our initial interaction would have been more stunned by our affectionate hug than by my near-miss ejection from the plane.

What made this transformation even more remarkable is that the flight attendant and I had not spoken at any point during the flight. There is no question in my mind it was the meditation, the letting go of anger, and the active practicing of compassion and forgiveness that made this change of heart possible. If I had maintained my stubborn and self-righteous stance, there would have been no reconciling hug at the end of the flight. Worse yet, the memory of the experience would have continued to upset me to this day.

This misunderstanding reinforced the power that compassion, understanding, and forgiveness have to defuse anger. I simply need to practice it more often.

It is difficult to overstate the importance of the link between our thoughts and our experiences. When we direct our attention, energy, and focus to particular feelings, it has a direct impact on our experience. As I discovered the hard way with Pete and with the lymphoma (more about this later), we can think ourselves sick, but we can also use focused thought and attention to restore health. Thanks to free will, we can choose whatever we want. We can think positively or we can focus our attention on negativity – we always have a choice. At times, we may need professional help to make better choices, but even that is a choice. The choices we make every moment of every day determine the degree to which we experience health, abundance, and positivity.

Keeping yourself healthy by monitoring your emotions demonstrates why trusting your internal compass so important. Think about the word "disease". The word is literally created by adding the negating preface "dis" to the word "ease". In other words, we experience disease when we are no longer at an energetic or emotional place of ease or balance. It doesn't get much more direct than that.

Pandemic-Inspired Questions to Consider

As I reflected on the events at the start of the Covid pandemic and watched previously scheduled workshops get postponed indefinitely, it would have been easy to panic and worry about finances moving forward. To be completely transparent, I will be the first one to admit that my thoughts immediately went to discretionary expenses that could be cut and steps I could take to stretch what I had until that situation became another distant memory. But then I realized I was asking myself the wrong questions. I am embarrassed to say that my approach was firmly rooted in a scarcity mentality.

As mentioned earlier, I have worked hard in my adult life to cure myself of this disease — and make no mistake, a scarcity mentality is a disease. It changes our behavior. It changes the way we view the world. Worst of all, it has a direct, negative impact on our happiness. Even when you think you have adopted an abundance mentality, scarcity thinking can re-emerge unexpectedly as it did for me at the beginning of the pandemic.

While contingency plans are certainly important, there is a far more challenging question I started asking myself. Believe it or not, the answer came more quickly than I expected.

The question is simple to state but, at times, requires a high degree of creativity, introspection, and openness to answer:

What is the gift in this experience?

In asking this question, I am in no way minimizing the trauma, pain, and even death experienced by the most susceptible among us. Instead, my question is intended for those us who experienced minimal physical impact. The question itself was inspired by the recognition that in many cases our most traumatizing challenges come with a gift. In some cases, many gifts.

Five years ago, the lymphoma diagnosis that my dad once told me would have been a death sentence when he was in medical school, brought enormous gifts I never expected. The love and connection I experienced as a result of my walk with the tumors opened my heart in a way that otherwise would never have happened. Without question, the tumors, as scary as they were, brought the biggest gifts I've ever experienced.

A few years ago, when I had the courage to leave a position that was not a fit for a wide range of personal and professional reasons, part of me was terrified because I had no idea how or when my next paycheck would arrive. However, once I had the courage to leave, the speed at which abundance showed up stunned me. I gave notice at 6:15pm on a Thursday. At 6am Friday morning, less than 12 hours later, a client I hadn't talked to in several years sent an email and hired me for a project that covered my expenses for the next six months. It literally left me feeling as if I had spent the previous few months leaning against the door of abundance trying to keep it shut.

I could share many more examples, but the point is not about the past. The point is about our future. We have an important choice to make in times of difficulty. Are we going to focus on fear or are we going to focus on possibility? Are we going to focus on scarcity or abundance? So, when you discover the gifts in challenging experiences — and you will when you remain open — please share them. Few things would make me happier than hearing about positive outcomes from challenging situations.

#MeTooButNotMeToo

I am closing this chapter with a breathtakingly beautiful piece of writing by someone very special to me. Elli, not her real name, gave me permission to share this as yet another example of the power we often have to decide how we will respond to the challenges we face on our individual journeys.

I am going to tell you something about my life.

Spoiler: At first, you will probably be shocked. Then, you may focus all of your thoughts on what happened to me, what I went through, and what I had to deal with as a result. But I ask you not to do that.

That might sound strange, so let me explain.

What happened to me doesn't define me. I am so much more than a girl who was raped.

Of course, it did change me. It made me the person I am today. So yes, I am one of those #metoo girls. But it's more like #metoobutnotmetoo.

Why?

First, I decided to accept what happened (because it's not like you would ever forget something like that). However, experiencing rape is one very, very small part of the entire puzzle that makes me, me.

If I had a few minutes to tell you about my life, I probably wouldn't even mention the rape - not because I am in denial or feel the need to hide it, but simply because it isn't a defining characteristic. Instead, I would tell you about where I grew up and what I love to do in my free time. I would tell you about the trips I have taken and the mountains I have climbed. I would for sure mention some of the fantastic food I've experienced. I'd probably even tell you a few of the funny and embarrassing moments in my life. If there is time, we might get to the part about where I went to university, with whom I fell in love, and how I made it through my heartbreaks. If we were having this conversation 10, 20, or 30 years from now, I would also be telling you about a few of the lives for whom I made a difference. That's my commitment. That is so much closer to how I want to be remembered.

Is what happened terrible? Absolutely. Did I somehow wish for it? Most definitely not.

Actually, I never thought this could happen to me. Rape. That's something you see in movies, read in newspapers, and hear about on the news next to stories about violent crime and kidnapping. The possibility that it could happen to me seemed so incredibly unreal.

I will never forget the last dinner I had with my dad after my graduation. For some reason, we started talking about experiences that would be so unbearable that we would seriously question our ability to survive and carry on with life. At the time, I was so sure that rape would destroy my life to the point where it wasn't worth living anymore. As the words came out of my mouth, I had no doubt; I was absolutely certain.

Well, life is what happens when you plan something else - right?

Two months later, with a few remaining boxes still unpacked in my room, I was raped. Yet, despite my earlier pronouncement, I am still here six years later and even happier than I was back then. I am more myself, much less insecure, and far more eager to achieve something, change something, and live my life to the fullest.

To be clear, I did not suddenly become spiritual—although I certainly wouldn't judge people who did. I didn't start believing in angels, God, or miracles. But still, I found a way to deal with what happened. I found a way to become an even better, happier, and more peaceful version of myself.

That's what I want you to focus on.

It's not what happened to me, but what I did afterwards--all the wonderful things that occurred after that particular day. There are so many little things in life that make living so much more than just bearable. As Charles R. Swindoll said: Life is 10% what happens to you and 90% how you react to it.

So how is someone who just turned eighteen supposed to react to rape?

I can begin with telling you about the reactions of a few of my closest friends and relatives.

Because if you think that everyone will be all understanding and compassionate about what just happened to you, something that may change your life completely – well that's definitely something that just happens in movies.

Real life is different.

Of course, I have a bunch of people for whom I am completely and all-heartedly grateful!

There were a few friends who were simply there for me. Even if it meant sitting next to my bed, watching me sobbing into the 98th tissue, not wanting to leave the house even if it was the perfect weather to go outside and enjoy the sun and the nature. They were those kinds of friends who cycled back to the house from school in their short break in order to bring me some chocolate croissants and coffee in bed. The kind of friends who at one point rang my doorbell twenty times to take me out to the cinema. Oh yes, I will never forget them.

But if there is one lesson I definitely learned in that time, then it's the following:

No matter what happens, no matter how you feel or what you wish for, the world will keep turning. And life will just keep going on. And people will go back to work or to school every morning and come back in the evening and have supper and talk about their day. And if you had a job or a teacher, they will ask you when you think you will be coming back. With a kind, somehow ashamed, somehow shy voice. But they want to know when they can start to count on you again. That is life. Sorry for maybe bursting the bubble.

Life is also what happens when your dad tells you after finding out what happened that you shouldn't look at it in such an emotional way, because that won't help. And life is also what happens when people actually stop talking to you for a time, because they "just didn't know how to react". There are those people who tell you "Everything will be okay" and then again others that advise you to keep it a secret, cause "You don't know what people will think...".

C'est la vie.

So it's simple math: you can either quit, stay in bed, deny that life is happening outside.

Or you can – after taking yourself the time to moan, be sad and angry and frustrated and think that life is unfair – stand up, tidy up your room, make your bed, open the curtains, and face the world outside.

And this I can promise: It's definitely the better choice.

Taking all the cheekiness away and taking into account what I have said earlier, it's not like you have much of a choice. You can't not work forever, you can't stay in your room forever and expect everyone to understand you. And guess what – there are pretty amazing things out there.

So that actually is the story of my life. Those are the things worth remembering, worth telling. It's – as most of the things in life – a thing of perspective.

The question you have to ask yourself is: which path do you want to walk?

The man or the woman, or maybe even a couple of awful people, took away your control over you own life in those minutes and hours. They took away your feeling of safety. You definitely were a victim at that point, there is no doubt in that.

But what are you now? What do you want to be after that?

Don't get me wrong. I am definitely not in favor of keeping "that" a secret. What do people keep a secret? Lies, decisions taken the wrong way, things they feel sorry for or ashamed of – right?

But this wasn't your fault. You didn't ask for it. You couldn't have done any better than what you did. Trust me, it took me a time to realize that.

But one thing is to let it be a part of your story (which sadly, from that point on it will always be) and the other, is to make it your story.

I myself, decided not to be a victim (anymore). It wasn't easy.

Actually, it was pretty hard. My rapist was a doctor. Believe it or not. And that's horrible. It felt like a double abuse. Abuse of my private space and abuse of my trust. The kind of trust you always give to a teacher or a parent or, well, a doctor.

But again — a thing of perspective. 60% of the people who have been raped, were victims of family members abusing them. Nevertheless, it's not a battle.

That's another thing I always tell the people who are sorry for talking about their problems, as if they would be ashamed about them. They shouldn't!

It's like the poem one of my favorite German authors wrote, in which he says that it doesn't matter if your doll breaks when you are a child, or you later on lose a friend.

Maybe my worst and scariest moment was that time with that person in that doctor's room. And when I think back, I can still feel his touch, still feel a shiver, get sweaty palms.

But you may as well react the same way when you think about the loss of a family member or pet, or about that moment in class when you were mobbed by this lonely, seemingly mean little kid.

It's how you react to that that makes the difference and that is of most relevance. So yes, indeed. #metoobutnotmetoo.

Putting It into Practice

Starting now, check your thoughts and expectations. Catch yourself before you go into a meeting or conversation. What are you thinking? What are you expecting?

If you think to yourself, "This meeting is going to be a complete disaster" or "I'm not going to get anywhere with this conversation", you may as well not go. You've already told yourself it won't work. The Universe will be more than happy to deliver that outcome. If, on the other hand, you choose a different thought, there is a high likelihood you'll experience a different outcome. The good news is that all you have to do is say to yourself, "I don't know how, but my commitment is that this meeting go better than I could have ever expected." Hold and believe that thought. Then, watch in amazement as miracles unfold.

As you begin to catch yourself and change your expectations, some of you reading this will find yourself with wonderful success stories. If you like the idea of inspiring others, please share your stories on www.atrekwithin.com.

CHAPTER 9:

Mindfulness, Meditation, and Other Mind-Numbingly Difficult Challenges

If it weren't for my mind, my meditation would be excellent.
– Pema Chodron

"Quiet your mind."

"Let your thoughts go."

"Quiet the voice in your head."

"Imagine your thoughts floating away like clouds."

"Stay present."

"Focus on your breathing."

These are just a few of instructions I have been given during meditation and yoga classes over the years. Not once did I find any of them helpful – there was never a moment when I stopped thinking, experienced ecstatic emptiness, and emerged blissful and fully present.

If your mind is anything like mine, you can appreciate the utter impossibility of shutting your eyes and turning off the running commentary. Sure, I can focus on my breathing – for about 20 seconds.

Then I start thinking about something else. If there were thought bubbles above my head while listening to the instructors, this is what you would have seen:

"Simply observe your mind." Excuse me?

"Now, empty your mind." Wait. What does that mean?

"Acknowledge your thoughts and let them go."

Acknowledge them? How? "Hi, Thought. Go away, I'm trying to meditate."

"Let your thoughts float away as if they are clouds."

"What? Now you've got me thinking about clouds. I thought my mind was supposed to be empty. Sitting upright like this is uncomfortable. There is no way I'm going to make it for 20 minutes."

"Turn off your mind."

"How am I supposed to do this without thinking? I work with a few people who never seem to think. I bet they would be really good at this."

Inevitably during these classes, a chi gong or bell would sound and we would "return to our bodies" (the one I never successfully left) and listen as a few blissed-out people described their experiences in glowing, aspirational terms. The best I ever did was to fall asleep, something I can do pretty much anywhere, turning the experience into little more than an expensive nap.

People meditate for different reasons. Some seek spiritual and other-worldly connections, but many others are focused on the more practical aspects like relaxation and lower blood pressure. Somewhere in between the two extremes is a place where we create an openness to new experiences and access the abundance we may be unintentionally keeping at bay. As often happens, I found the right approach when I wasn't looking, and I would have given up on the promise of meditation completely had it not been, strangely enough, for two intuitives and a wilderness survival course.

Five Sense Visualization

During one of several sessions I had with PsychicDave Tillman, he offered what turned out to be a life-changing suggestion in helping me attract my first corporate speaking client. At the time, I was leading workshops for an outplacement firm as an independent contractor. Although I made very little money, the professional development was phenomenal because I was on my feet speaking up to 40 hours a week.

Eventually, I reached the point where I knew I was ready and on the verge of finding my own clients, but I needed to take the first step. More importantly, I needed to release any self-doubt or limiting beliefs that might be energetically shutting the door to abundance. To create that opening energetically, PsychicDave recommended the "5-Sense Visualization." The idea is to spend 15 minutes activating all five senses at the same time. Learning the technique described below was easy; experiencing how quickly it worked was shocking.

Start with an intention or goal: In my case, to attract my own corporate clients.

SIGHT: Visualize the goal. Picture yourself doing whatever it is you would like to create. I simply visualized myself in large auditoriums and conference rooms leading workshops.

TOUCH: Hold something that makes you feel strong and confident. I held a copy of my book, *Getting Your Foot in the Door.When You Don't Have a Leg to Stand On*.

SMELL: Given that my ultimate goal was financial abundance, PsychicDave suggested holding paper money near my nose because dollar bills have a distinctive smell.

TASTE: Activating the taste sensation is easy. Find something that has a strong taste you like and hold it in your mouth. If memory serves, I chose Altoid Mints for the strong peppermint flavor. If I were doing it today, I would use Listerine Breath Strips.

SOUND: Find music that makes you happy. Be sure to pick a song that does not have distracting lyrics that will derail your thoughts. I chose "Catch a Wave" by the Beach Boys and listened to it on repeat for the entire 15 minutes. It is one of those songs that always make me smile because it reminds me of singing Beach Boys songs with my friends in grade school on the playground, fantasizing about being older and riding surfboards. This song also worked because the lyrics "Catch a wave and you're sitting on top of the world" captured exactly the feeling I was after.

I don't remember if it was recommended or not, but I did the entire visualization dancing around my room. With the door shut, of course. I'm sure it was quite a sight. There I was holding my book in one hand, stuffing Altoids in my mouth, holding a billfold to my nose, and dancing around the room with headphones on for 15 minutes. I don't care how it looked though because it worked. Immediately. And I'm not even slightly exaggerating.

When the song ended for the sixth or seventh time, I sat down on my bed with a huge smile on my face. I took the headphones off, put my book on the table, slid the billfold back in my pocket and walked across the room to my computer. To my amazement, the email at the top of my inbox was from McDonald's corporate headquarters. A woman from their training department who had seen me speak almost a year earlier had written to ask if I would be interested in leading a few stress management workshops for their Information Services Department. Although neither of us had been in contact in the interim, she remembered me, liked my style, and hoped I would be able to help. Within a few short weeks, I found myself at McDonald's Hamburger U training facility leading the first of many McDonald's workshops over the next year or so.

With success like that, you would think I'd be dancing like a maniac around my room several times a day. But the truth is, the experience freaked me out a little – not in a bad way, but enough that it felt greedy to do the visualization more often. It was as if I had gotten the energetic jumpstart I had hoped for and did not want to come across as spiritually needy or greedy. No doubt it is also related to my often fiercely independent nature and a misguided desire to do everything without any help.

Chakra Alignment Visualization

I met Gwynne Montgomery a few years ago when she was traveling through Chicago. Even though the technique she shared is closer to traditional meditation, I love it because it is easier to visualize than other meditation exercises.

Start by picturing an energetic cord coming from far above your head and extending deep into the earth. Once you have that visual, imagine a glowing ball of light moving down the chord and through your crown chakra at the top of your head. Picture each of your chakras like discs: as the glowing ball of healing energy moves through your chakras, imagine the discs shifting into perfect alignment so the ball moves effortlessly downward. Notice where the light gets stuck. Once the ball has travelled the entire length of the chord, imagine it looping back up to the top for what should be a faster journey through your chakras.

It only takes a few minutes to do this, but I definitely feel more balanced and centered afterwards. What I like best about this particular meditation is that it doesn't take long and provides an immediate sense of accomplishment. It's become my go-to practice when I am sitting in the sauna at the gym. I always find it interesting to note where the energetic ball of light gets stuck momentarily. The longer it takes to align my chakras, the more important it is to run the visualization a few times to makes sure I'm back in alignment. This practice isn't as fun as the next meditation, but it's great when you only have a few minutes to center yourself. If this does not work for you, it helps to remind yourself that you haven't failed. Nothing works for everyone and nothing works all the time. Instead, focus on discovering a menu of meditation options and always be ready to move on to the next one.

Lessons from Wilderness Survival School

Wide Angle Vision

In addition to running the tracking, nature, and wilderness survival school he founded in 1978 at the age of 28, Tom Brown, Jr., is driven by a strong passion to share the many lessons he learned from his teacher and mentor, Stalking Wolf, an 83-year Lipan Apache, also known as Grandfather.

Tom met Grandfather when he was seven years old and collecting fossils by a riverbed in the Pine Barons of New Jersey. Grandfather, a shaman, medicine man, and scout who never lived in civilization, recognized Tom from a vision he had been given over 70 years earlier, long before Grandfather had ever seen a white person.

Through the 10 years or so that Grandfather trained Tom in the ways of the Native Americans, he shared two particularly powerful forms of meditation, both of which I continue to use. Although he practiced multiple forms of meditation, Grandfather felt strongly about the need for moving meditation – in other words, for meditation to be truly useful, you have to be able to do it while you are walking. The gateway to this practice is wide-angle vision.

As it stands, we spend most of our lives shifting our focus from one object to the next. The problem is that this focus causes us to miss a lot. To practice wide-angle vision, sit in a park or natural setting and identify two objects in front of you that are different distances. For example, you might see a park bench and a tree beyond it in the distance. Focus on one briefly, then focus on the other. Shift your gaze between the two until you are no longer focusing on either but instead seeing and noticing everything in your field of vision – that is wide-angle vision.

When I first practiced this, it was amazing to sit in the park across from my house and see squirrels running in front of me, birds chirping on a tree branch, kids playing on swings, a couple walking by, a car turning the corner, and an airplane flying high overhead, all at the same time. As I watched everything happening at once, I noticed something incredible: I was not thinking about anything else. At last, I was fully present and my mind was quiet. In a way, it makes sense that this would be easier with my eyes open. When my eyes are shut, my mind thinks and visualizes on its own. When they are open, my mind can observe without adding its own thoughts.

For Native Americans, wide-angle vision was more than a way to meditate while walking through the forest; it was a prerequisite for hunting. In the same way people sense when you are staring at them, even when their backs are turned, our focus has an energy and an intensity animals can sense.

If you stare at a wild animal like a deer, unless it is sick or rabid, it is not going to come anywhere near you because they sense the threat; wide-angle vision changes that. For example, one afternoon I walked to the forest preserve across from my parents' house to practice this technique. In the distance, I saw an opossum sauntering through the woods. I continued looking in its general direction and followed its progress without moving or looking directly at it. Within five minutes, the opossum walked all the way up to me and sniffed my shoe. Unable to maintain wide-angle vision, I shifted my focus and immediately saw it jump with a start. At that point, the opossum must have realized I was not a threat, but it did walk away slightly faster than it had approached. Had I been focusing on the opossum the whole time, whether I remained still or not, there is no way the animal would have come anywhere near me.

The only other times I have come close to that degree of physical and mental presence is while playing guitar or piano for long periods or while I am scuba diving. With scuba in particular, it is easy to get into the natural rhythm of the breathing because you hear it so clearly with the regulator. But the truly wonderful part is the opportunity to take in the breathtaking scenery of the coral reefs. It is not a place where you are likely to swim among the fish and think, "When I get back, I really need to do laundry."

The Medicine Place

Two of my favorite books by Tom Brown, Jr., the founder of the wilderness survival school mentioned above, are *Awakening Spirits* and *The Way of the Scout*. Of all of the wisdom I have gained from reading these, the most powerful and long-lasting lesson concerns what Native Americans call the Medicine Place.

Unlike silent, eyes-shut meditation in which you quiet your mind, creating a Medicine Place is an active visualization method in which you create a permanent place in your mind to go for healing, relaxation, and alone time.

Following Tom's instructions, I created my Medicine Place over a series of visualizations. There is no set number; you might be able to do it in two or three sessions, or you might decide to add more features and use more sessions to do it. There is no right or wrong approach. The key is to create an area with only natural surroundings – it could be trees and a forest, a beach, a river, a lake, an ocean, or a rocky desert with stone caves like central Turkey. It could be the surface of the Moon. It does not matter. All you have to do is imagine a place that inspires peace and joy and does not contain artificial structures like parking lots or roller coasters.

After sharing the basics of what to visualize, Tom says, "You know your Medicine Place is complete when you don't need to add anything else to it; you know it's real when you can take other people there." This is a bit mind-blowing – you can literally do a meditation with someone else, take them to your Medicine Place without telling them anything at all about what you have created, and have them come back and accurately describe what they saw and experienced.

The first time I took anyone to my Medicine Place, it was not one person, but my entire acting class. David Murphy, a gifted improv teacher and casting director in Chicago, created a class on the more spiritual and energetic side of acting called Acting Through Meditation. When we did the meditation in class, I was amazed how many people had shockingly accurate observations and experiences. It worked so well, we did it again a year or so later with another class.

When we did the meditation in class, we sat in a large circle and held hands. Before we began, I explained that once we shut our eyes, we were to imagine a path with an enormous field of flowers on the left and a mountain in the distance. After we spent a few minutes getting settled and taking in the surroundings, I would squeeze the hands of the people on either side of me. They, in turn, would squeeze the hands of the people sitting next to them. That was the signal indicating that they should look for a stairway on the right-hand side descending into the Medicine Place. From there, they were to pay particular attention to the stairs as well as what they saw when they reached the bottom and turned right to see the Medicine Place. We spent the next 10 minutes exploring before another hand squeeze signalled it was time to go back up the stairs and slowly open our eyes.

At times, I have also shared my Medicine Place with a few of my more open-minded friends. What fascinates me most when I do the visualization with only one other person is the fact that they sometimes show up with more than just themselves. When I did the meditation with Alissa, for example, I was shocked to see a female African lion walk peacefully through my space. After the meditation, I described the animal and asked Alissa what her connection was with female lions. With a surprised look, she proceeded to tell me that she has always felt a powerful connection with that particular animal – I had the strong sense it was her spirit animal.

During a recent trip to Europe, I reconnected with my friend Josseline and had another memorable experience sharing my Medicine Place. We had talked about visiting my Medicine Place for fun, but decided to do it with more of a purpose because her stomach was bothering her. The only information I gave her beyond what anyone else knew is that one part of the area is dedicated for healing work. With that, we started the meditation. Almost immediately, I felt what can only be described as a soul-level understanding or agreement in which Josseline separated into two distinct spirits. One stayed with me for the healing while "Little Josie", the much younger version of Josseline playfully explored the surroundings. Although I had never seen anything like that happen before, it made me happy because it meant Josseline could get the healing and explore at the same time; I never dreamt it would be simultaneous.

Was it real? Read Josseline's account and judge for yourself:

I wasn't sure what would happen, even more, how it would feel. Now I can only say: Don't miss out on this experience! Breath in the somewhat different air and just let yourself be carried away. Just for this moment.

Rob had explained a bit and told me he would take me to his healing place. I was feeling a bit of a stomach pain, so it seemed appropriate. The only thing he told me was that it was built only with natural things, and he described the path that we have to walk on, till we will take a right turn and walk down a few steps until we get to the "healing place." And that was everything I knew when I closed my eyes.

We started breathing more calmly, relaxing and focusing on the feeling of our hands holding on to each other, trying to picture this path... it happened faster than what I would have ever dared to imagine. Within only a few seconds (or maybe minutes), I saw myself walking along a narrow path in between a forest with only a few trees and a huge grass plane. Further in the back I could see grey enormous mountains and a bright blue sky. It was, already, a beautiful place.

But what made my heart skip a beat was the sight of, well... myself. There I was, a younger version of myself. Skipping and jumping around, laughing a lot, giggling even more. Strange enough, but then there was the "adult" version of me as well, holding onto Rob's hand. I could see myself from the eyes of the young girl. I was able to turn around, and see little "me" tripping stones, smiling and waving at us. It was such a crazy and undeniably wonderful feeling. It actually made me feel at home in an instant and knowing myself, my concerns and my personality (always trying to control and organise the next ten steps I will take), this was probably the "pause," the "healing" I needed from "reality." I had been so stressed out about work, having to write my thesis and moving to another city that I had completely lost track of the small things in life that make you happy. All the somewhat wonderful things you cherish as a child, but forget once you grow up.

It didn't take us long to get to the stairs Rob had told me about, and then we arrived at our destiny. Even though – of course – I couldn't be sure that this was Rob's healing place, I felt that we had arrived. The place reminded me of a children's book I read when I was younger: I saw a hut covered with fungus and mud with a chimney and a table made out of stone, a small river, trees and flowers. In general, everything was extremely green, colourful and bright. As if someone had sat there for days, sprinkling watercolours all over. The sight reminded me of summer and lemonade; I could nearly taste it.

I was watching "little Me" running around, trying to catch butterflies, when suddenly we were all on this wooden boat (or let's say a wooden something letting us float on top of the water surface). I could reach out and touch the branches of the trees while we were floating down the river. It was extremely peaceful.

The images kept changing at a high speed, and further away I could hear a waterfall. And then suddenly I was right there, seeing dolphins playing with each other, jumping in and out of the water. I couldn't believe that all of this was only happening in my head and yet again, I was just filled with plain curiosity and joyfulness. I somehow got the feeling I should just enjoy every little thing I saw and felt. I decided to lay down on the ground, feeling the dampness of the grass, the sun shining on my face, blinding me. I couldn't see myself anymore, but after some time, I woke up, seeing myself from the eyes of the child, lying on the stone table, while Rob was healing me with Reiki. Seeing me lying there made me feel warmth wherever Rob's hands were gently moving over my body without touching me – I could feel the energy running through my legs and arms, the warmth of the sun on my skin.

I could have stayed there forever, but Rob pressed my fingers, the sign for us to slowly walk back, so I opened my eyes and still feeling a bit sleepy, walked back towards the stairs and down the path.

Nothing had changed. Our suitcases where still lying at the same spot, we could still hear the humming of the mini bar in the hotel room. And yet I was already so sure that something had changed. A tiny door had been opened inside of me. Maybe my inner child was the one that had to be there in order to heal me, to show me how life doesn't always have to be complicated and can't always be explained and understood, scrutinised and analysed.

It is worth noting that the greenery, the hut, the dolphins, and the waterfall Josseline described above matches my Medicine Place perfectly.

Whether your goal is to reduce stress levels, lower blood pressure, improve your sleep, visualize healing, or access your inner wisdom, higher self, or spirit guides, meditation can be a great tool. The challenge is to find a comfortable, natural way to achieve it – sitting cross-legged in lotus position listening to meditation gongs did not do it for me, but it might be perfect for you. Even if that does work for you, I would encourage you to experiment with the more active variations described in this chapter. Despite what I first thought, there is no one right way to meditate.

Putting It into Practice

The easiest of the meditations described above is the 5-Sense Visualization. Your task is simple. Think about a goal and do the visualization. It may be the easiest and most effective visualization you've ever done. Then, visit www.atrekwithin.com and share your stories. I would love to hear what magic you create.

Later, when you have more time, create a medicine place for yourself. It's so peaceful. For even more information on this, read Tom Brown, Jr.'s book *Awakening Spirits*.

CHAPTER 10:

Hands of Heat and Healing

Reiki is love,
Love is wholeness,
Wholeness is balance,
Balance is well-being,
Well-being is freedom from disease
-- Dr. Mikao Usui, founder of Reiki

Reiki is a hands-on Japanese energy healing technique based on the belief that we are surrounded by a life force energy that flows through every living thing. When a person's energy is low, stress and disease are more likely to develop. Treatments involve placing the hands on or near the body in an effort to restore balance. When receiving a treatment, what most people notice first is the heat that comes from the Reiki practitioner's hands. It's not unusual for a Reiki Master's hands to be substantially warmer than the person's normal body temperature.

Though my dad specialized in internal medicine, his abilities went well beyond what is typically thought of as Western medicine. After I became interested in Reiki, dad shared one of his favorite techniques for diagnosis challenging cases: "If I'm not sure what's wrong with someone, I'll run the back of my hand a few inches above their body and slowly scan for the source of the problem." I am quite sure that is not something he learned at Northwestern University's Feinberg School of Medicine. I am equally certain Northwestern didn't offer a class in recognizing the smell of certain types of cancer, but that was another one of my dad's fascinating abilities.

My dad's heightened sense of awareness was also attuned to detecting pregnancies, often before a woman was aware herself. I learned about this ability when I was in college. My parents had been at a party when my dad noticed that a family friend was pregnant. To confirm his suspicion, he turned to another friend and quietly asked when the baby was due. The second woman insisted that, as the other woman's best friend, she would know if the first woman was pregnant. The second woman assured him her friend was not. Two weeks later, both women were surprised to discover he was right.

I asked dad what he was seeing in those cases, and he described a "glow" that women get as a result of the hormonal changes that take place upon fertilization. Here again, if this were obvious to everyone, there would not be a need for pregnancy tests.

My dad has often said that one of the best approaches to diagnosing difficult cases is to simply ask the patient what is wrong. I can vouch for the validity of asking patients to diagnose themselves with a personal, much less serious example. A few years ago, I fell, and as I hit the railing on a flight of stairs, my elbow absorbed the blow.

My elbow hurt a lot at the time, but it did not seem too serious, so I never had it examined. However, during the following few years, it hurt from time to time. Even though I did not feel anything out of the ordinary, I had a strong feeling I had chipped the bone. I asked Shen Robinson to look at my elbow because it had been bothering me quite a bit, especially when lifting weights. Shen took one look at my arm and said, "You chipped the bone and you have a hairline fracture. It's in a bad place though, and there isn't much you can do about it."

I did not need an x-ray to confirm the diagnosis because we both knew she was correct. What she was not correct about was the prognosis.

Not wanting to deal with the pain, I sought out the assistance of the late Jei (pronounced Jay) Atacama, a Japanese doctor in New York who had a reputation as a powerful hands-on healer. Jei, who came from a family of nine generations of healers and practitioners of Japan's own traditional medicine, became a Doctor of Oriental Medicine and a Licensed Acupuncturist in his youth. The Atacama Healing Method (www.atacama.org), pioneered by Jei's late father, Dr. Masahilo Nakazono and practiced by his son, Chiro, is a form of Faith Healing that involves regulating biological and spiritual energies through healing meditation and some light touching on different areas of the body. It can also be done remotely. Although Jei was 1,000 miles away, his apprentice, Gail, lived in Chicago not far from me. Gail decided to train with Jei after he cured her mother of rheumatoid arthritis. Before she went to Jei, Gail's mom had difficulty even walking across a room. After meeting Jei, she led an active life that included playing tennis.

Jei treated me with a combination of what he calls life-ings, reportings, and healing water. The life-ings are longer, more focused sessions in which Jei tunes in to a person energetically and works to rebalance the energy. The reportings are shorter, more focused treatments to address particular symptoms. The healing water is spiritually infused. By taking a few tiny drops people can focus their attention and align with Jei's energy. After a series of life-ings, my arm, which had hurt on and off for five years, improved by about 90%. After a few minor relapses, the pain disappeared completely.

My Introduction to Reiki

Amy introduced me to Reiki shortly after we started dating when she was working on my back, but the first noticeable results I had from my own efforts to do Reiki occurred during a Memorial Day group scuba trip to Cozumel, Mexico. On our second day, as the bright Mexican sun approached its high point in the sky, the afternoon temperature climbed well above 90 degrees Fahrenheit. The island heat must have been getting to me because I decided it was a great time to go for a run. Afterwards, I noticed a huge, painful blister had developed between the third and fourth toe of my right foot. I had experienced enough blisters on my feet to know how painful this one would be when the skin burst and the fluid drained to reveal the raw, dark pink skin underneath. Since I was already hobbling around, I knew the discomfort was about to get worse.

That night, I sat at the foot of the bed in my hotel room with the intention of quieting my mind in meditation. Moments later, however, I received a strong impression that I should use my meditation time to direct Reiki energy to my foot. I cupped both hands over my right foot and visualized healing energy surrounding and penetrating the skin. Fifteen minutes later, I turned off the lights and fell asleep.

The next morning, I looked at my foot and was amazed to discover that there was no longer a large blister. I immediately reached down to touch the skin, but there was no blister, no tenderness, and no trace that a blister had ever been there.

[Note: all of the names in the following story have been changed.]

Another time, I travelled with my friend Barb and her baby, Emma, to the Mayo Clinic in Rochester. While there, we met Afet, a seven-year-old girl from the United Arab Emirates, who was staying in the adjoining room.

It Is a bit difficult to describe Afet. When she was out of bed, Afet had a wild, uninhibited energy and would frequently run up and down the halls. I suspect that cognitively she was closer to two or three years old. To complicate matters, she seemed to have a difficult time communicating. When we first met Afet, she did not speak at all, and instead would grunt, yell, and make all sorts of indecipherable noises. Afet was fascinated by Emma and liked to touch the top of her head. These encounters usually happened after one of Afet's marathons around the floor, so she was generally out of breath. With the energy still surging through her body, we often had to encourage Afet to be gentle because she had little awareness of her own strength. You could see the terror in Emma's eyes when Afet's hands flew toward her with intensity.

Afet's parents spoke limited English but seemed to appreciate the time we spent with their daughter. In those rare moments Barb and I were able to calm Afet, we worked with her on being more gentle and saying

Emma's name. Afet clearly appreciated the attention and worked hard to say "Emma." The process was fascinating to watch because whenever Afet said "Emma," the veins and tendons in her neck bulged as she leaned forward and loudly forced out each syllable: "EMM – aa" Afet's guttural style made it seem as if each syllable was somehow trapped in the depths of her diaphragm. After repeated attempts, Afet had less difficulty, but still struggled to verbalize Emma's name.

A day or so after Afet first pronounced Emma's name successfully, I saw Afet sitting up in bed. At first, I was amazed to see Afet sitting relatively still and motioning for me to come closer. Despite her calm appearance, I knew her well enough at this point to sense an underlying urgency. The moment I reached her side, Afet grabbed my right hand and placed it firmly on the lower left side of her back on top of her kidney.

Based on what I had learned from my friend, Christopher Brown, who spent years living in the United Arab Emirates, I knew that Afet's culture had strict boundaries about interactions between males and females, especially when it involved Westerners. I started to pull my hand away, hoping her parents would see that I was not the one who had initiated the physical contact, but Afet was determined. She grabbed my hand even more firmly and placed it over the same exact spot. Not sure what to do, I looked over at Afet's mother who shrugged her shoulders as if to say, "If that's what makes Afet happy, it's fine with me." Relieved, I stood next to Afet and marvelled at how this girl, who clearly had a number of impairments, intuited that I practiced Reiki. Even after sitting quietly for five or ten minutes – an eternity for many children her age – she was reluctant to let me leave. From that point on, whenever Afet was in bed and I was nearby, she would motion for me, and we would start the process again.

A few days later, upon hearing Afet's guttural exclamations of "EMM – aa, EMM – aa," a somewhat perplexed nurse walked by and said, "Wow! It really sounds like she's saying 'Emma.'"

Barb replied, "That's exactly what she's saying." But the nurse shook her head and said, "That's impossible. She's deaf."

Barb and I were too taken aback to respond. Having spent quite a bit of time with Afet, we were certain she could hear. After all, how else would she have been able to repeat Emma's name? The exact situation played out the following day with one of Afet's doctors. This time, I was thinking more quickly. "Afet is NOT deaf," I said. "The fact that she chooses not to acknowledge or listen to you does not make her deaf."

Letting my words sink in, I paused for a moment before continuing, "By the way, here's something else I learned from Afet. I know you can't confirm this because of patient confidentiality laws, but I happen to know that whatever else may be going on, she is here at least partly because of an issue with her left kidney."

The stunned doctor did not say a word. He didn't have to. When I told him about Afet's left kidney, his jaw dropped. Knowing he was legally prevented from discussing her case with me, he turned around, looked at Afet with a very confused expression, and walked away as slowly as I have seen any able-bodied person walk.

Other than acupuncture, Reiki is one of the most popular of the alternative healing methods. At one point, the children's hospital even had volunteer Reiki practitioners working with patients. While some people like me get tuned for Reiki and dabble casually, others, like Ardath Berliant, use their gifts to do Reiki as a profession. One of her more impressive testimonials came from a woman named Jodi:

> I had a double mastectomy after being diagnosed with a recurrence of breast cancer. After my surgery, I developed a massive post-operative infection, and was placed on IV antibiotics at home for weeks. I ran a fever every day for a month. The infection kept morphing, so the antibiotics were changed several times, and they all came with severe side effects. I was very, very ill - weak, feverish, unable to eat.

> A dear friend suggested I see Ardath. I was willing to do almost anything to feel better, and I know that traditional western medicine is not the only path to health. Ardath was kind enough to come to my house and treat me there. The treatment was powerful – I felt the energy in my body move with her movements. That was the last day of my month-long fever. The next day, I woke up without the fever, pains, and chills that had been plaguing me for a month. The infection began to dissipate, and my road to recovery began.

Unlike acupuncture and other healing modalities, you do not have to be a fully-certified Reiki Master to use the skills. For example, Marni, a nurse who has considerable spiritual connections, had this to share:

I am not Reiki-trained at all but was encouraged by a Reiki friend to "try it out." I healed my husband's runner's back in two sessions (his neurosurgeon did nothing for him). I shocked myself — I think most people assume that they do not have gifts. I used to assume that everyone sees auras; I found out they do not. The gifts we are given and the signs and synchronicities that show up are so subtle sometimes that we can miss them unless we have an open mind.

Marni not only sees auras, but she is so in tune with her family members that she knew the instant her 18-month-old son fell into a pond even though she was not with him at the time. She also knew the exact moment her father went into cardiac arrest and was able to independently confirm it with the nurse on duty. She even has a son who, when he was three-year-old, frequently talked of his past life "when he used to be a woman."

Doctors and Healers – Insights from West and East

By profession and personality, my dad was a healer. As a child, I can't begin to guess how many times strangers approached my siblings and me on the street and said, "You are Dr. Sullivan's children, aren't you? I recognize you from the pictures in his office." Then, they'd go on to tell us how wonderful he was and how he'd cured them of ailments that had, in some cases, troubled them for years. It happened so often all we could think to do was listen politely, say thank you, and watch them walk away smiling. It wasn't until years later that it occurred to me how unusual these encounters were. Had we lived in a small town, it might have been more understandable. But we didn't. We grew up on the corner where Michigan Avenue meets Lake Shore Drive in the heart of downtown Chicago. Even though there weren't many children who grew up in our neighborhood at that point, the chance of such random and repeated encounters seems astronomically low.

The fierce loyalty my dad inspired is at least partly due to his bedside manner, his generosity, his diagnostic abilities, and his genuine interest in treating everyone with a high level of care and attention. He also treated everyone with equal respect. I'll never forget the afternoon one of his colleagues called to ask if he had time to see Mick Jagger, the lead singer of The Rolling Stones, who was in town for a concert. My dad was appreciative of the referral but politely declined because his schedule was already jammed with regular patients.

A born teacher with an uncanny ability to uncover simple solutions others might miss, my dad occasionally shared insights from interesting cases while being careful to respect patient confidentiality. Whenever he spoke about a problem he solved or a diagnosis he made, we could hear the unmistakable pride in his voice and passion for his work.

Most of these stories were shared over dinner, a sacred time in our house. Even when he was in law school, dad came home for dinner every night unless he had class. It was the one time of day we were all together.

One of my dad's favorite stories was about a new patient who came in for a routine physical. At some point in the conversation, the patient offhandedly mentioned how he had been plagued by back pain for years but had reached the point at which he had given up hope of finding a remedy. Intrigued, dad began asking questions and learned the man had invested an enormous amount of time and many thousands of dollars flying all over the country to see various experts with no success. After an unfruitful visit to the Mayo Clinic in Rochester, Minnesota, the man gave up and accepted his back pain as a permanent condition. For that reason, he almost didn't mention it to my dad.

Trusting his intuition, my dad immediately measured the man's legs, discovered they were noticeably different lengths, and prescribed a lift for the shoe on the shorter leg. The patient left the office, walked directly to a shoe repair shop, and had the lift put on while he waited. That same afternoon, the man called back to share his appreciation for his first pain-free day in years. In many respects, the diagnosis seems simple, and to some degree it was, but why did so many other doctors miss it? Were they looking for the exotic cause when they should have been seeking the simple truth? Whatever the case, I suspect it was gratitude like this that led so many of his patients to stop us on the street so we'd be sure to know how wonderful he was.

Furthermore, it made me wonder how often we seek grand, complex solutions for seemingly big problems when small changes can make all of the difference. Take door stoppers for example. So small, especially if you compare them to relatively big doors, and yet – by putting them in the right place – they create all the impact necessary to prevent the door from shutting. In the end, it is not the size that is important; it is looking at things from the right angle. My dad was an expert at it.

Finding the common threads with other stories my dad shared over the years leaves me convinced that an intuition bordering on psychic is what made him such a great doctor. He also possessed a finely tuned awareness. And he was a fantastic listener. When it comes to making a diagnosis, that proved to be a terrific combination.

Healing and Alternative Medicine

Starting around the time I was in college, I often found myself struggling to keep my eyes open and stay awake. Considering the odd hours my classmates and I kept, nothing about the experience struck me as out of the ordinary. If I was sleepy on Tuesday, it was probably from having a few too many beers at Monday Night Madness. If I was sleepy on Sunday, it probably had something to do with a midnight trip across town for Buffalo wings after finishing my gig as DJ in the campus pub. Since there was always a likely cause I could point to, I didn't think much about the countless afternoons and evenings I'd fall asleep in the library when I should have been studying. Sometimes, I'd lift my head from between my crossed arms, wait for my eyes to readjust to the light, and go back to work. But if enough time had passed or if I still felt groggy, I'd simply give up and head back to the dorm.

One dark, fall night during first semester of our freshman year, my roommate, Mark, and I went to the Dinand Library at Holy Cross in Worcester, Massachusetts to study. He was pre-med and often carried massive textbooks about organic chemistry and other arcane and difficult classes I was happy not to take. At the time, my major was undeclared so I was plodding along through classes like calculus and composition. I had trekked to the library that evening to pick of a reserve copy of a play for American Drama: 1920s to the Present, a class taught by Pr. Steve Vineberg, one of my all-time favorite teachers. Pr. Vineberg put the plays on reserve either because they were hard to find or he didn't want us to have to buy a lot of extra books. Either way, this was one of those nights I was forced to study in the library because no one was allowed to check out reserve material. This wasn't ideal from a studying perspective because it only took a week or so to realize the Dinand Library was a far better place to talk and people watch than it was to study.

On this particular night, I chose a deep red, cushiony chair that seemed more appropriate for a sitting room than a library. With my left leg hanging over the side, I leaned back, started reading, and promptly fell asleep. When I awoke an hour later, Mark and I decided to hang it up for the night and head back to the dorm. Knowing I'd have time to finish my assignments later, I wasn't particularly concerned. I was, however, a bit confused by the strange looks people seemed to be giving me as I walked back toward the main entrance of the library.

As soon as we stepped onto the dark, lamp-lit street to hike across the hill to the Clark dorm, I turned to Mark and said, "Maybe it was my imagination, but I got some pretty strange looks just now. What was that all about?"

Mark replied, "Yeah, you snored pretty loudly for the past 45 minutes. I didn't want to wake you up, though, because I thought you'd be mad."

As we walked among the towering pines and other trees that lined the path back to the dorm, I was both embarrassed and mystified. I still don't fully understand why a roomful of students would rather sit there and be bothered than get a staff member, or take it upon themselves, to wake me up. Nevertheless, from that time on, I made it a point to find a desk in the depths of the library where I could put my head down and bother fewer people. While my need for naps didn't interrupt my life, it did impact my course selection and my choice of a major. Even though I've always enjoyed writing, I knew I would never survive as an English major because I found it so difficult to stay awake while reading. As a result, I consciously avoided reading-intensive courses.

Inspired by my high school psychology teacher, Mr. Charles Provow, I decided to become a psychology major. I remembered watching a hilarious video in high school psych class about narcoleptic dogs. Narcolepsy was fascinating to me, and the more I learned about the excessive sleepiness associated with condition, the more familiar it seemed. However, I also remembered Mr. Provow's adamant warnings to avoid the temptation to diagnose ourselves. At the time, it was relatively easy to dismiss the similarities to my own experience because fortunately, unlike the dogs I had watched the year before, I did not fall asleep midstride while chasing rabbits or crash into things when I fell asleep.

I honestly do not remember giving the sleep issue another thought beyond the occasional frustration of waking up in a study room with drool on my cheek when I should have been reading. I instead chose to view my ability to sleep anywhere at any time as a gift. In a way, it was.

After I graduated from college in 1989, I continued to need naps, but again I didn't think much of it because I was working at Chicago advertising giant Leo Burnett and kept a highly irregular schedule. Some nights I'd get to bed by 10 p.m. Other nights I'd be up through the early hours of the morning. I didn't get up at any set time either, so I thought being constantly tired was simply the price people paid for keeping odd hours. Besides, being the resourceful type, whenever I needed a nap, I'd take two or three of the massive 3' x 4' pouches we received daily, line them up in front of the table in my cubicle, crawl underneath, and fall asleep. The pouches, which were used to carry advertising comps and proofs back and forth between Burnett and Philip Morris, were the perfect cover. The people from the mailroom would stack them in front of my desk whenever they arrived. When I did the same, it didn't look out of place; it just looked like I hadn't been there in a while.

In 1994, everything changed. I took a job working with Cooper Neff, a proprietary options trading firm, trading bond options and futures at the Chicago Board of Trade. Trading in the pits at the Chicago Board of Trade started promptly every day at 7:20 a.m. and ended at 2 p.m. For the first time in my adult life, I had a predictable schedule. As soon as I noticed myself getting tired during the day, I made immediate adjustments. The first was to use all of my breaks to sit outside and take a quick nap. When other traders saw me sitting on the sidewalk leaning up against the building with my knees tucked into my chest and my head down, they'd joke that they wanted to put a cup in my hand for donations. It was the perfect look for a trader who was down on his luck.

When I realized how hard I found it to stay awake on the trading floor with thousands of screaming, adrenaline-driven traders, I started going to bed even earlier. That got old pretty fast when I realized there were seven-year-olds who got to stay up later than I did. Nocturnal by nature and not wanting to miss out on all the fun that seems to happen after sunset, I did what I always do when I have a medical question — I called my dad.

After a blood test revealed my thyroid functioning was on the low end of the normal range, my dad prescribed Synthroid, a synthetic version of a chemical secreted by the thyroid. At the same time, he told me to avoid sweets because there was a good chance I also had low glucose tolerance — a condition that makes people sleepy after consuming food with a high sugar content.

Unfortunately, the Synthroid had almost no effect. I continued to have difficulty waking up in the morning, and still felt the uncontrollable urge to sleep during the day. At that point, my dad referred me to Dr. Phyllis Zee, a prominent neurologist who specialized in sleep disorders.

After taking my medical history, Dr. Zee recommended a sleep study in which I'd spend the night at the hospital hooked up to a wide range of monitors under the watchful eye of a technician and a video camera. By the time the technician finished, there were wires attached to my head, chest, arms, and legs. Only my teeth were spared. Thanks to what seemed like a radical experimental treatment, I felt like I was on the verge of a rapid transition from the inability to stay awake to an inability to get to sleep.

As I pulled up the sheets and shut my eyes, my last thought was a strong desire not to do anything embarrassing while the video camera was recording. I also said a short prayer for the sanctity of patient confidentiality.

When I awoke the following morning from what seemed, under the circumstances, like a reasonably restful sleep, the technician surprised me by asking, "Were you in pain? It didn't seem like you slept all night."

The question caught me off-guard because I thought I had slept relatively well. For a brief moment I felt like a nut case, but quickly smiled thinking, "Well, that's good news. If I seemed like I was in pain, the far more embarrassing alternatives are almost certainly not on that video."

I left the hospital that morning more confused than ever. A week later, when I went back to see Dr. Zee, the results surprised us both. First, the study revealed that I snored "loudly and continuously all night." At times, I snored so loudly I even woke myself up. The more serious problem was the uncontrollable muscle twitching that woke me up an average of eight times per hour. Although I wasn't conscious of it, the twitching was more than enough to disrupt my sleep cycle — thereby causing daytime drowsiness.

Armed with the diagnosis of nocturnal myoclonus (a.k.a., periodic limb movement disorder), Dr. Zee prescribed Klonopin, a drug frequently used to treat the twitching associated with Parkinson's. While I was on it, Klonopin made me more aware of my twitching and led to unpleasant withdrawal symptoms when we discontinued the treatment. We experimented with a variety of other drugs, several of which resulted in even more unpleasant withdrawal symptoms when we phased them out in favor of other potentially promising medicines. I don't remember all of the drugs we tested, but I do remember our collective frustration at the lack of a solution and my own growing distaste for life as a lab rat.

In the course of the treatment, Dr. Zee ordered genetic testing to see if I had any genes associated with other known sleep disorders. When Collette Johnson, Dr. Zee's nursing assistant, gave me the results, she said, "Rob, I almost fell off the chair. You've got all the genetic markers for narcolepsy."

Having a firm diagnosis was both a relief and a challenge. In the moment I learned about the genetic component, I became aware of another aspect of my internal wiring — that part of me that had no interest in being held hostage by a condition that, although not deadly, had no adequate treatment.

As it became apparent that there was more to my condition than anyone thought, Dr. Zee and the other neurologists involved in the case prescribed a combination of Ritalin and Prozac and sent me for a daytime sleep study, known as a Multiple Sleep Latency Test (MSLT). In my case, the MSLT was used to answer two questions. First, did I go right into REM or dream sleep — an accepted diagnostic indicator of narcolepsy — or did I start out with the normal sleep stages? Second, was I so drowsy that I could fall asleep for five consecutive naps? The answer to the first question was inconclusive although I would have to say yes considering that I fell asleep and started dreaming waiting for the technician. The answer to the second question was affirmative.

Over the next few months, the doctors gradually increased my dosage of Ritalin and Prozac. I loved Prozac because it helped me wake up feeling completely alert and rested. I wasn't so fond of Ritalin because my tolerance grew quickly. I started taking a five to ten milligram dose and eventually found myself taking it on an "as needed" basis. Although the drug is commonly used to reduce hyperactivity in children, it's actually a very powerful stimulant. It didn't help me much though. Before long, I was taking up to 150 mg. a day and still needed naps.

With the diagnosis, my professional life changed as well. Almost overnight I became a huge liability. Under the circumstances, I wouldn't have felt comfortable trading my own money; I certainly didn't want to trade anyone else's. After taking all of these factors into consideration, and against the advice of almost everyone, I left Cooper Neff at the end of 1994 without a job or direction. My only goal was to find a cure or, at the very least, a better treatment than Ritalin.

When the doctors considered switching me to a different stimulant, I decided to give up the life of a lab rat and pursue other treatments. I had done everything I was supposed to do – sought out specialists, submitted to tests, played Russian roulette with medication – and nothing seemed to help. I was exhausted, and desperate for a new perspective. My first stop was Chicago's Chinatown to visit the late Dr. Pak Lau, a well-known herbalist and doctor of Chinese medicine.

I never told Dr. Lau my problem because I didn't have to. All he wanted to know was my name and age. Then, after checking my pulse and looking at my tongue, he asked through a translator, "Have you been feeling overly tired lately?" Astounded, I listened as he prescribed an herbal tea and a diet that avoided certain foods. I stayed on the diet for a few months and spent over an hour every night boiling herbs for the tea. However, the tea, which looked and smelled like rotting forest debris, didn't have a significant impact beyond driving my roommates crazy.

It was around this time that I first met Shen Robinson, a shaman, healer, and medical intuitive. Like Dr. Lau, Shen knew nothing about me when we first met. However, ever since she was a child, Shen has been able to see chakras and energy fields. She also has the amazing ability to diagnose medical problems. Within seconds of seeing me, Shen said, "You have the most profound food allergies of anyone I've ever seen." Over the next two hours, she continued to shock me with a long list of highly accurate physical, mental, and spiritual observations.

I didn't provide Shen with any confirmation or feedback until the end of the session when I diplomatically shared that I had never had much of an issue with food allergies, unlike my sister. My sister had major food allergies and frequently awoke with hives all over her body. Shen replied, "That's because it doesn't affect you the same way. In your case, the foods you are allergic to alter your brain chemistry and make you feel tired." Shen's comment really surprised me: I had not told her about the sleep disorder and, until that moment, she had not included anything related to it in her observations.

Shen went on to say that my thyroid was "functioning on the low side of normal." Surprised by her accuracy, I replied, "That's definitely true. That's why I've been taking Synthroid." Shen proceeded to tell me that Armour Thyroid was a better treatment because it contains all three of the chemicals secreted by the thyroid while Synthroid only has one.

When Shen told me which foods to avoid, I was horrified to see all bovine dairy products, wheat, citrus fruits, mushrooms, nuts, and shellfish at the top of the list. Considering what a staple pizza is in my diet, I knew I'd never be able to stick to her recommendations. I followed the guidelines for a few weeks, but eventually found it too difficult. Not willing to be a slave to medicine or restrictive diets, I continued my search for a cure.

It wasn't long after meeting Shen that I first learned about Jei Atacama. When I heard Gail talk about her mother's miraculous recovery from rheumatoid arthritis, I knew immediately that Jei and Gail would be the ones to heal me.

After consulting with Jei, Gail recommended that we begin with three treatments per week. The treatments, which at the time cost $60 each, often consisted of little more than Gail putting her hand on my shoulder for 10 or 15 minutes. If I let my rational mind take over, I would have questioned the wisdom of paying $180 a week to have someone put her hand on my shoulder, chest, or abdomen for a few minutes at a time. Had there been any doubts, they would have been completely erased about two weeks into the treatment when I had an experience I'll never forget.

As I sat in a chair in small room usually used for massage, Gail put her right hand in the middle of my chest. The heel of her hand rested on my sternum and her fingers pointed up toward my chin. Within seconds, every cell in my body felt as if it were on fire. The unbelievably intense heat pulsated like a ball of energy extending from my heart and lungs to every corner of my body. Sweat instantly poured out of my forehead and I became so dizzy I thought I'd pass out.

After the longest five or ten minutes of my life, Gail pulled her hand away and the feeling instantly subsided. With what little energy I had left, I looked at Gail in amazement and asked, "What just happened?" In her quiet, understated way, Gail said, "I noticed that too." Her tone was casual, as if she were commenting about a breeze that had just blown through the room. When I pressed her for more, she said, "The area I was treating is your soul center. I'm not really sure I know how to explain it but I can tell you this — when Jei treated my mother, she had almost the same experience and it was the turning point in her therapy."

The experience proved to be a turning point for me as well. Over the next few weeks, I gradually felt more alert and needed fewer naps. I continued to receive three treatments per week but didn't experience anything like that again. After seven or eight weeks of Gail's hands on healing, we cut the treatments down to twice a week at her recommendation.

About three months after our first appointment, Gail put her hand on my shoulder as she often did, but the treatment seemed shorter than usual. As Gail lifted her hand, she looked at me and quietly said, "That's it. You're back in balance. You don't have to come back here anymore. But always remember, *you* did this!" That was more that 30 years ago.

Thanks to Gail Katz and Jei Atacama, I am healed. I no longer take Ritalin, Prozac, or unplanned naps. Where the drugs, tests, and experiments of traditional western medicine failed to make an impact, the hands of a healer restored balance and health in my life. And for that, I am eternally grateful.

An Unsolicited Affirmation

By the time I saw James Van Praagh speak at the now defunct Transitions Bookstore in Chicago, I had been doing Reiki for a few years, but I had only completed two of the three steps required to become a Reiki Master. I remember the night vividly because I had been looking forward to it for weeks. James Van Praagh was in town to promote his book, *Ghosts Among Us*. In hindsight, I'm not sure why attending the event was so important to me, but I arrived early enough to earn the second spot in line.

The many fans present who had read James Van Praagh's books knew that he often did spontaneous readings for audience members at book signings and other public events. However, at the start of the talk, he said he was sorry to disappoint, but that he wouldn't be doing any readings because he was exhausted from his travels. I wasn't too disappointed though because, unlike some of the other attendees, I wasn't there hoping he would channel a message from one of my loved one's on the other side. But that's also why the unexpected reading I received was even more special.

After his talk, James and the staff at Transitions invited attendees to wait in line for the book signing. However, to accommodate all 300 people, they requested we be respectful and not ask questions while James signed our books. To maintain order among the people waiting for autographs, only one person was allowed at the table where he sat at a time. The rest of us waited about 20 feet away near the front of the room.

The line moved quickly through the first dozen people when the assistant motioned for me to come forward. I stepped forward in silence as James shut the previous book and said goodbye to the person in front of me. When James looked up at me, his face brightened with excitement as he said, "You do this [psychic] work. You are very intuitive." Although I don't remember everything he said, I was even more surprised when he added, "Reiki! Yes. It's all around you. You need to do more of it. You need to bring it more into your work."

I was not sure what James meant because my work at that point focused in two primary areas: sales training and career transition. Neither of those groups was a likely candidate for Reiki. Now as I piece together my own life purpose, I realize that James may have been referring to my decision to share the more personal and spiritual aspects of myself as a way to help people on their own journeys. Writing this book is a step in that process. Completing my Reiki training, which I did a year or so later at his encouragement, was another.

I am heartened to see how many more people are opening up to the power of Reiki, but it intrigues me how many people remain skeptical. The skepticism is even harder to understand when it comes from Christians because the miracles of Jesus described in the Bible involved hands-on healing. Jesus also made it clear that others could and would have the same abilities or greater:

> "I tell you the truth, anyone who has faith in me, can do the same miracles I have done, and even greater things than these will you do." (John 14-12)

Then again, the Bible also mentions angels, yet many still do not believe.

Those of us who have experienced the healing power of hands know the heat, healing, and relaxation that happens as a result of Reiki is real. The Reiki practitioners themselves are almost always quick to point out that the energy does not come from them, but rather *through* them. Wherever it comes from, it is a unique and, at times, powerful healing option for those who are open.

Another person who uses Reiki to heal herself is Veronica Rae Cowen.

> In 2007 about seven months after I committed to consciously be on a path of spiritual growth (albeit it was a half-assed commitment), I shattered my ankle one day at summer camp. I had had an intuitive feeling not to order an inflatable water slide which my business partner was set on having the last week of camp at a celebration. I just had a feeling someone was going to get seriously injured. I think in an attempt to

prove myself right, and to protect the kids - I took the injury on. I slipped while draining water from the slide at the end of the party, my ankle slid outwards and snapped. "Oh, hell no!" was my initial response and I grabbed my ankle and popped it back into what looked like alignment, I then began giving myself an energy healing - a technique I had learned a few months prior.

Although I didn't fully heal the injury, the surgeon said I had re-located the ankle, and the following week (once the swelling had gone down) I needed urgent surgery. I had seven screws, a metal plate, and a "basket of wire" put into the ankle to rebuild it. The surgeon said I could not have physically done more damage. This, however, was exactly what I needed to kick my butt and get me onto the aligned path!

Over the next six months I found my level of commitment to my spiritual growth increase immensely. Everyday, I gave myself healings and somehow through the process, the energy healing work I was doing became socially acceptable within my community. Often when we encounter a major life-changing experience, others give us permission to have transformation beyond that related to the injury - and in this case - my energy work, meditation and healing techniques became known among my peers. Now being in my mid-twenties the name of the game at the time was "party, party, party" and as I experienced more depth of healing, my desire to go to clubs and bars diminished at a rapid rate. Although my friends couldn't understand what was happening to me on a spirit level, they could write it off to the injury. In retrospect, I can see clearly how I manifested that broken ankle to justify and commit to my spiritual growth. In life when we are veering down the wrong path, or a path that is not aligned with our purpose, we will often unconsciously create some type of trauma or ailment to get us back into alignment. The more we can see and understand this - the less painful, or traumatic it has to be. The more we resist it - the harder it becomes to process and learn from the injury, sickness, ailment or disease.

Although the break was an extremely severe one, I experienced very little pain through the healing process. So little pain in fact, the doctors and physical therapists were blown away with my healing progress. Little did they know every time I felt pain I would imagine a ball of white light around my ankle and leg and the pain would dissipate immediately. Through my healing journey I recognized that I did need the pain to slow me down, I was willing and committed to learn what I needed to learn - how to surrender, how to let others help me, and even harder yet - how to ask for help. (I also failed to mention that in the years prior to this break I sprained both ankles a total of five times - and did not learn what I needed from those experiences, which is why I created the dramatic ankle shatter.)

In 2006, about six months before the water slide experience, I had been, for the first time, introduced to my Spirit Guides. One of them, who was called Bob, appeared to me as a man sitting in a meditative position. Although I had met Bob a few times prior to the injury, and had shared brief conversations with him, I had not yet developed a trusting relationship with him.

One day, while sitting with one of my spiritual teachers, Bob appeared. My teacher told me very clearly he saw I had a guide named Bob who could help my body heal. I was shocked, and excited to tell him I did in fact have a guide named Bob – who was there! That evening I went home and asked Bob to show up in my bedroom. And there he was - sitting on the end of my bed. His presence gave me a warm feeling and the chills. I knew I was safe, and he was here to help me.

Because the surgeon had cut such a large incision to insert the metal plate into my ankle some nerves had been cut, and the feeling around the scars on either side of my ankle was gone. It was numb to touch. With humility in my heart, I asked Bob to heal me, not knowing what to expect. Again, I felt washed with warmth, and I lay back on my bed in his presence to receive whatever healing might come through, and I fell asleep. When I awoke in the morning all the feeling in my ankle had been returned. The numbness was completely gone.

Over the next few months, I called on Bob daily for healing, counsel and support. And through my relationship with Bob, my openness and receptivity to all my guides and the spirit world expanded.

One day, the book "Autobiography of a Yogi" by Parmahansa Yogananda was given to me. I began reading it only to learn about Yogananda's teacher's teacher – a man named Lahiri Mahasaya. "Turn to page such and such..." Yogananda explained, "to see a photo of Lahiri Mahasaya." I did as I was told – and there was Bob! I was so happy to see my friend I was moved to tears. I got on my crutches and hobbled down the hall to show the image to my father (who knew I had been quietly receiving healings from Bob). He was surprised and grateful, and asked me if Bob could possibly give him a healing too? To which I replied, "You have to ask him."

Our guides are always here for us, as is healing energy and presence – it is, however, up to us to call on it. I have never yet met someone who did not have spirit guides. We all have a network of support just waiting to help, to heal and to guide. Our guides are so neutral though – they will not impede on our free will – and will not get involved until we ask.

Other Healing Modalities

Although my eyes were first opened to alternative medicine in general and Reiki in particular by my former girlfriend, Amy, I gained a deeper appreciation of the value of these approaches when I saw them succeed where Western medicine had failed. As Asli discovered, it isn't about having a narrow, misguided allegiance to a particular approach, but a willingness to explore and never give up, no matter how dark the world may seem.

For three years, Asli suffered in pain. unable to walk and unable to find relief from local doctors in Istanbul who had no idea what was causing her issues. Not surprisingly, this proved difficult to handle emotionally.

> *For years, I didn't want anyone to help me. I was trying to solve everything myself, but experienced more and more pain. I did my best to understand life, but found myself baffled by problems that appeared again and again. At one point, I was so depressed about not being able to walk and in so much pain, I attempted suicide as a way to quiet the voice inside me. Fortunately, my lovely neighbor, sensing something was wrong, appeared at my door with other concerned neighbors at the precise moment I was preparing to end my life. Realizing the mistake I almost made, I decided to address my problems by asking the Universe to restore my health, happiness, and ability to walk.*

> *After a short time, the answer arrived; I met with a doctor and she directed me to a gifted healer. When we met, I felt an instant connection with her and knew she'd help.*

> *Although doctors believed I had a tumor in my leg, the healer knew that wasn't the case. I had two options; continue believing the doctors who, for over four years, had been*

unable to heal me, or have the faith to accept her help even though it would be time-consuming and I wouldn't necessarily understand what she was doing.

The healer diagnosed my issue as ankylosing spondylitis, a disease that was later confirmed in a blood test. During the year-and-a-half it took her to cure me, one of the key lessons I learned was about the importance of asking for help.

When I first started struggling emotionally, I didn't want anyone to help me. That continued for years until the pain, frustration, and uncertainty became too much. That's when I realized how much I desperately needed someone to help me so I wouldn't be alone. Asking for help is the key. Nothing happens until you allow yourself to be vulnerable enough to be helped by someone else. Through that process, I regained my health, inner peace, and beauty. The decision to be alone is a choice. But it isn't a healthy choice. We are all connected.

One reason I love Asli's story is the way it demonstrates how alternative medicine can work in conjunction with Western Medicine.

Putting It into Practice

Having had so many wonderful experiences with Reiki, hands-on healing, and other forms of energetic healing, I am a huge believer in its effectiveness. It is interesting to note that some hospitals have begun to accept it as well. There is so much healing to be had from energetic and hands-on practitioners, I strongly encourage everyone to try it. It's non-invasive so you won't have to worry about it interfering with anything else you might be doing. Better still, it's very relaxing so you might find yourself drifting pleasantly off to sleep.

Be sure to share your experiences on www.atrekwithin.com

CHAPTER 11:

Signposts Through Time and Space: Understanding the Present Through a Glimpse into Past Lives

I don't really understand that process called reincarnation, but if there is such a thing, I'd like to come back as my daughter's dog.
-- Leonard Cohen

My first exposure to the concept of reincarnation came through the aforementioned George Harrison song "Give Me Love (Give Me Peace on Earth)." However, when reincarnation was first explained to me, I understood the concept as it related to the caste system in India. At the time, I found the whole idea of suffering through incarnations of poverty and disease in an attempt to work your way to a higher class completely distasteful. But the bigger horror was my conclusion that if we constantly reincarnated, we would never get to heaven to see the friends and relatives we knew and loved. It was a disturbing possibility, so I chose not to believe it. I was relieved to learn the Catholic Church did not seem to accept the possibility either. To my young mind, it was a nice black and white proposition, and I knew where I stood.

Later, my beliefs were challenged. I never set out to read about reincarnation, but found it was one of the many themes that came up repeatedly in the books I was reading. By this point, I was more open to the idea because so many authors provided similar stories and evidence not explainable in any other way. As a result, I began to see reincarnation as a learning opportunity rather than a punishment. That was a possibility I could easily see being offered by a loving Creator. I cannot pretend to fully grasp how each incarnation contributes to the evolution of every individual soul, but I find it comforting that we get so many opportunities to practice, resolve challenges, and experience different aspects of ourselves. It is a lot more positive than my original understanding that saw reincarnation strictly as a punishment.

Of the books that discussed reincarnation, the most fascinating was *Many Lives, Many Masters* by Brian Weiss, M.D. In the book, Weiss, a Yale-trained psychiatrist, describes how one of his patients, while under hypnosis, began detailing past-life experiences. Weiss was intrigued to witness how the revelations actually relieved the anxiety his patient had been experiencing. In reading the many accounts of past lives Weiss uncovered through regression therapy, I no longer saw reincarnation as some nasty fate that kept people from ever getting to heaven. Instead, I began to understand how people shared multiple lifetimes and often reincarnated together to help each other gain new experiences and learn new lessons. Until that point, my faith was based on three primary beliefs:

- God is loving, forgiving, and infinitely compassionate;

- Life is a gift; and

- You only live once.

These three beliefs fit nicely during the first two decades of my life because I gave my attention, energy, and focus to the events and circumstances that confirmed them. But the more I saw at the children's hospital, the more I could no longer reconcile the inconsistencies; the three pieces no longer fit. After all, if life is a gift, God is loving, and we only live once, it made no sense at all that some children had the opportunity to live only a few short hours, weeks, or years.

By replacing the third belief, "you only live once," with a new belief, based on a revised understanding of our human/spiritual experience, I was able to expand my thinking without abandoning my two most important core beliefs about the existence of a loving God and the gift of life:

- God is loving, forgiving, and infinitely compassionate;

- Life is a gift; and

- We choose to reincarnate to help ourselves and our loved ones learn and grow through different lessons and experiences.

Loved ones, in this case, are not limited to immediate family. A loved one is any person with whom we have a strong soul connection. Accepting the possibility of reincarnation proved helpful not only in expanding my understanding of the Universe and our place within it, but also in gaining wisdom and insight from situations that previously brought only pain. It was liberating and inspiring to see spiritual beings with a mission and a purpose where I once saw only needless suffering and death. It made so much more sense than anything I learned in religion class. Better still, the physical shift I felt when the realization finally dawned on me confirmed what I knew to be true at a soul level.

Guided Regression

An experiencer by nature, it was not enough for me to read about hypnosis as a way to access insights or information about past lives – I felt a growing need to experience it myself. So, I called Dr. Weiss' office and asked for a referral in the Chicago area. One of his assistants gave me the contact information for Dr. John Houck, a psychologist who worked in Hyde Park. My goal in doing a past life regression was to see what connections existed between the challenges I faced in this lifetime and experiences I may have had previously. In traditional hypnosis, a psychologist may guide the patient to certain periods of their current life to uncover memories or traumas that may be the source of anxiety they are dealing with now. In some cases, our minds may have buried certain memories if they were too painful. By accessing the memories and dealing with them in a safe, guided environment, it is often possible to release whatever grip they have on us.

With past life regression, the goal is the same: to uncover memories that help explain the themes and challenges that may be consistent from one life to the next. The major difference is that the memories uncovered are from another lifetime. Having never done a guided regression, other than a few unsuccessful solo attempts during meditation, I honestly wondered if it would work. Since many of the people I read about uncovered recurring themes that helped them to better understand and work through challenges in their present lifetimes, I hoped for similar insights. However, because I had not had any overwhelming crises or traumatizing personal experiences, curiosity, more than anything else, fueled my interest.

The hypnosis began with me sitting in a relaxed position on a comfortable sofa in Dr. Houck's office. There was no swinging watch or finger snapping. Instead, I sat upright on his sofa with my eyes shut. He sat across the room and, using words alone, instructed me to relax different muscles in my body. Within a few minutes, I felt strangely disconnected from my body as my arms and legs began to feel heavier and heavier. I was not sleepy and remained aware the entire time. In less than five or ten minutes, I found myself in a year I knew immediately was 1857.

The first part of the memory was disturbingly real. My arms felt incredibly heavy, like cement blocks, and my body felt as if I were in shackles. I was alone in a wheelchair, feeling very old and unable to keep my head up. As I took in the scene, I saw myself in a white gown, far out in the country, and surrounded by other patients who were walking around talking to themselves. As I sat in the chair, I began to feel heavier and heavier, until I fell over and died. It seems odd to phrase it like that, but in the hypnosis, I was both participant and observer, so I knew exactly what was happening. At that point, I did not identify with the person in the other lifetime, so I did not have a feeling one way or the other about the death except that it seemed very lonely.

Based on the surroundings, the white gowns, and the presence of other patients, Dr. Houck and I pieced together that this lifetime had ended in a mental hospital out in the country. Once we made that determination, he said something like, "Take me back to the day you were sent to the hospital." At that moment, I began to describe a life as an angry, misunderstood, complaining mother. I was hunched over with a tumor, tuberculosis, osteoporosis, or some other disease that was causing pain in my lower back. Two people grabbed me and took me away, while my children, a young boy and a two-year-old girl, watched helplessly.

When I looked into the little girl's eyes, I realized immediately it was Amy, the ex-girlfriend I was still grieving over. I do not remember the facial features of the girl, or those of her brother, but the recognition at a soul level, driven almost entirely by her ocean blue eyes, was unmistakable. The scene continued with me lying in a horse-drawn wagon, on my side and with my hands tied in front of me. I was in so much physical pain that I could not even begin to think about my children. Sadly, I never saw them again; I had a strong sense that the little girl in particular had subsequent issues with abandonment, later bouncing through relationships like a pinball.

Dr. Houck closed the regression by giving me the opportunity to summon Jesus, Buddha, or any spiritual guide to whom I felt a connection. I chose Jesus. With loving, sad eyes Jesus put His right hand on my left cheek, knelt down beside me and said, *"Remember that I love you; you have a tendency to forget that."* When I asked if Amy and

I would be together again, He replied, *"This or something better. It's not for you to know. Just know you are loved."*

When I think back to this regression, I am struck by the fact that the messages did not even come close to what might have been considered wishful thinking. If it had, I would have encountered a Jesus who was willing to tell me what I wanted to hear in that moment – namely that Amy and I would get back together – and I certainly would not have chosen to spend the last half of a past life in a mental hospital.

Knowing of my interest in the spiritual, my dear friend Jackie Hart, the former director of volunteer services at the children's hospital, told me about Stacey Gorman and suggested I get a reading (or soul session, as she called it). At the time, Stacey was living in Scottsdale, Arizona and was doing sessions by phone. Jackie was amazed at Stacey's ability to understand and communicate important life themes and events from a broader perspective by channeling a collection of souls that refers to itself as "Jacob." My first session with Stacey took place more than five years after I had last seen or heard from Amy. Unlike a psychic who translates the images and communications they receive, a channel communicates the message directly because they are somehow able to allow the spirit to bypass their conscious mind. In addition, there are two key differences between the session I had with Stacey and a session with a typical psychic. First, after the opening prayer, Stacey's voice changed completely as she allowed Jacob to come through. The transformation was amazing, because Stacey went from sounding like a typical middle-aged Caucasian woman to a somewhat heavily-accented, elderly Asian woman. Additionally, unlike psychics who may share an impression or two before they start asking questions, Jacob did not ask any questions at all for the first 45 minutes. Instead, Jacob started talking and spent almost the entire session sharing insights and observations. Even though my next two sessions with Stacey took place several years apart, Jacob picked up right where we left off and referred to many of the same themes.

As open as I am, I am also a bit of a skeptic about people with whom I have not worked. For this reason, I went to great lengths to make sure Stacey knew nothing about me. I even sent the first check to her as a money order so she would not be able to look up my address. In the first session with Stacey, Jacob surprised me by talking about numerous lifetimes in which I was a speaker, writer, or poet. In one lifetime in particular, I was an English writer who wrote and cared deeply about the working class and employment-related issues. Considering my interest in career coaching and professional development, I found that fascinating. What I enjoyed most about the first session in particular was Jacob's ability to answer questions I had not yet asked. For example, I have always wondered about my neck-related fears like choking and vomiting and the discomfort I experience when anything touches my neck. Here is how Jacob addressed that issue and the unspoken question:

> Another lifetime you were a poet in England. You also were a
> poet in Italy. So, you have written many times about what
> human beings go through when you open your heart to open
> your mind to write about it. One of your last lifetimes that you

affected the Earth greatly is one we want to speak about now. It is because you did not finish that experience to a full circle.

Everything in Earth is you and God simply having an experience. That it goes out from you based on choice and returns to you in teaching you do you want to do it again or not. So, everything is like a circle. It go[es] out from you and must return to you as co-creator to see what you have created.

So, in this particular lifetime you were a male. You have been both male and female many times, but in this lifetime you were male. It was from 1547-1619. Your name Johan von Olden Bar Nevelt...you were Dutch. And you began as you got older to again want to serve humanity...so you chose to be religious reformer and...go against the ones that were in power. And they did not like that. So, guess what happened to you? You were taken and you were imprisoned and you were brought up on charges of religious subversion. They believed you to be subversive. You were loosening the beliefs of their religion. And they didn't like that. And you were beheaded.

As neck-related issues go, that's fairly serious.

Jacob's comment "you did not finish that experience to a full circle," and the fact that I had been beheaded, support the idea that whatever went unresolved would manifest in another lifetime, this time in the form of neck-related issues. Weiss talks about this phenomenon in his book *Through Time Into Healing*. Many of his patients who had lifelong weight issues successfully resolved them once they uncovered and understood the connections to past lives in which they had been sexually abused. They convinced themselves on a soul level to make themselves so unattractive that they would never experience that trauma again. Once they made the connection and came to terms with it spiritually and emotionally, they were able to lose the weight. Weiss is one of the first to point out that you do not need to believe in past lives to appreciate the effectiveness of the treatment. Whether the past life occurred or not makes no difference.

Weiss also talks about how his patients often had birthmarks at the site of a past-life mortal injury. To my surprise, I have what looks like a faded, crescent-moon-shaped scar at the base of my neck that extends from the far edge of one collar bone to the other. When I showed it to a physical therapist and asked if she could think of an anatomical explanation for such a perfectly curved line under my neck, she couldn't explain it. Neither can I.

Equally fascinating was Jacob's observations about the ongoing need for me to speak out about what I see. This is something I have literally built my career around, especially when it comes to delivering sometimes difficult feedback in executive coaching sessions. It also makes sense given the calling I have felt to write this book. Jacob put it this way:

> *You are one who helps others to expand the way they see something. It does not mean they are going to see it your way. It does not always mean they are going to see it the way you would prefer. But you help them to walk away saying, "What*

does this mean to me? Does it make me see a little bit more my own truth?" And if it does, you have served them well. So even if they go home and say, "I didn't like that at all. I don't like that painting that one showed me. I don't like what he showed me. I don't like what he say[s]." It still make [sic] them go away asking what do they like. And that is part of your purpose. Though sometimes others will disagree with you vehemently, but it is just for you to speak it anyway. If it is an opinion and your truth, it is meant to be said.

For some people, like the patients of Dr. Weiss, past-life regression is helpful in healing current traumas related to past life issues. For others, the knowledge is helpful and reaffirming on a slightly less profound scale. In David's case, a past-life regression helped him understand, appreciate, and develop his talents in his current lifetime. The regression revealed a lifetime in the 5th Century during which he was well-known for his ability to diagnose and heal people using only his hands. Despite his many successes, he felt immense guilt when someone he thought he healed later died. On a personal level, this provided valuable insight about the importance of forgiving himself. On a professional level, the regression helped David understand his desire to become a Thai massage therapist in this lifetime. More importantly, it made him realize that he doesn't need to learn a lot of techniques. The healing power is in his hands.

Akashic Records: The soul's book of life

Once you begin acquainting yourself with intuitives and healers, it is only a matter of time before you will meet an Akashic Record reader.

The Akashic Record, simply put, is the soul's book of life. Every soul has its own book of lifetimes, experiences, thoughts, and deeds. The books, which exist in the spiritual dimension, are housed in the Hall of Records. This Great Hall or Library of Records is depicted in the Robin Williams movie *What Dreams May Come* (1998) in one of the first scenes in the afterlife.

Amy, the same girlfriend who introduced me to Reiki, also introduced me to the Akashic Records. In an attempt to understand and deal with the loss and disconnectedness I felt after our relationship ended, I went for an Akashic reading with Chava Leah.

Although I do not recall any specific messages that came through, people who have done readings for me frequently comment on how open I am and how easily they are able to access the messages. Although it has been awhile, what I suspect happened is that Chava Leah had a sense that my openness would make me a decent reader. I found the Akashic Records so fascinating that I leapt at the chance to attend a training that Chava Leah offered to teach people to read and access the Records.

About 12 people gathered in Chava Leah's apartment for the class. Most of the participants were women, although two or three older gentlemen attended as well. Although the group consisted of people of different faiths, Chava Leah, who was Jewish, led us in prayer with the specific intention that our experiences and efforts would lead to whatever was in the highest good for the people involved. After teaching us a prayer to access the Records, we spent the rest of the time practicing in pairs and sharing our experiences.

My first partner, Jennifer, and I sat across from each other with less than a foot separating our knees. I recited the opening prayer and did my best to ignore the doubts in my mind. I seriously questioned my ability to access any accurate information in the reading, but the moment Jennifer asked me about her two children, I received an immediate impression about their differences in temperament, personality, and interest in spiritual connection. What I saw in my mind's eye was the physical form of each child as if in silhouette. The best way I can describe the impressions I received about Jennifer's children was a knowing – one moment my mind was blank, the next I had a strong sense of who her children were.

Despite what felt strangely like an information download, part of me still felt like I was making it up until the end of the reading when Jennifer told me how accurate my impressions had been. Her excitement at my understanding of her children gave me a strong boost of confidence.

One of the possibilities that fascinated me was the ability to read my own records. However, we were taught that accessing our own records was virtually impossible because much of the information would not be accessible. Except in cases where the information can help us through an immediate challenge, we are not meant to know about the experiences and lessons we may have planned for our current lifetime. This is all related to what is often referred to as the "veil of forgetfulness" that we assume before any incarnation.

The basic idea is that if remembered our past lives or knew what challenges we were to face before returning to the spiritual realm, the lessons would be much less impactful. The experiences have to feel real in every respect. Because so much is hidden from each person about his or her own Records, someone else reading the Records will have an easier time accessing whatever information is available. This may not be entirely accurate, but it is my general understanding. Apparently, the same principles are at play with psychics who are rarely psychic about themselves or their own situations.

Accessing the Insights

From a practitioner standpoint, there are a wide variety of ways to help people access the insights and wisdom from previous incarnations not limited to the hypnotic regressions done by Dr. Brian Weiss and other therapists. Many intuitives, like Therese Rowley and Veronica Rae Cowen, often tap into that information when they do readings for people. Veronica not only uses this information to help people release energetic blocks with past life origins, but also has used it to make hiring decisions at her company:

> In working with children through summer camps, and teaching meditation and awareness tools, I hear many amazing stories of kids who speak with their guides, remember before they were born and recall past lives. Children are extremely tapped into the spirit world, especially before the age of five when they shut that door in order to "fit in and be normal."
>
> I do much past life healing work, personally, as well as with others. Once that door becomes opened in adulthood, there is

much possibility for remembering the past, and healing it as well. Just like we can have a scar on our body, our spirit can have a scar too – and experiences from past lives can affect us in this life.

Recently when I was working with someone, we were just beginning to look at her past lives and I saw her as a sword smith creating beautiful and detailed swords and knives. She was well known for her work at that time and had a real skill in craftsmanship of sword making. When I finished telling her what I was seeing she looked at me with shock in her eyes, "I only have porcelain knives in my home." She said, "My whole life I have been terrified of metal knives and I have never known why!" The next piece of information that came to me was that because her swords and knives had been used in battle, and used to kill so many people she felt an immense guilt (unconsciously of course) every time she saw or used a metal knife. Out of reaction, and in an attempt to heal, she only used porcelain knives in this life. However, she was not really healing the issue by avoiding metal. The ability to heal it was in the opportunity to confront what had happened in the past and forgive herself. Only through self-forgiveness could she move on from that "spirit scar."

Often in life there are little quirks we have – things we are drawn to, and things we avoid – and many of them are actually the result of past life experiences we have buried deep away. When we clear the charge of the memories or experiences from past lives, we are actually freeing ourselves in real time. Freeing ourselves from past hurt and from playing out old patterns and habits. Conversely, we also have gifts and abilities that we have brought into this life that we are not even fully aware of or tapped into.

I recall working with one woman who had a hard time speaking the truth in this life. When we went to view the past life where this pattern was created, we saw that she was actually a young girl who had strong psychic abilities. Her job in the village was to warn the tribe of pending threats. One day she had gone before the elders of the group to explain what she saw coming. They did not like what she shared, and so she was killed. This experience had created an imprint in her that limits her ability to be honest in this life, today – for fear of being killed! She had subsequently been through many experiences where she lied and could not figure out why. As she released the charge of the memory from long ago, she was freed from the experience in this life as well.

Last year I was working with another woman who had a gift brought forth from a past life of being able to work with children – and see the light in them. As I saw this in her, I invited her to come and check out my Summer Camp. I could see she had the potential to be a great Site Director, although this was not something she had much experience with, and the idea of it made her nervous. I have since been working with her, training her, and supporting her in bringing that *ability to the forefront of her awareness. Watching her growth and expansion has been amazing – and she now runs one of my Summer Camps!*

To an outsider, it might seem crazy to have hired someone with little or no experience in the field, however I could see she did indeed have much experience, just not from this incarnation.

In the literature on past lives, there are many who believe souls tend to incarnate together across multiple lifetimes. Whenever fate or destiny is discussed, it always fascinates me to hear the stories people share. One of my favorite stories comes from Dan, who, several years ago, was set up on a blind date with a woman. After going out three or four times, neither Dan nor Emily felt any particular chemistry so they stopped seeing each other. One year later, a different couple set Dan up on a blind date with a woman they were certain he needed to meet. They did not tell Dan her name, and simply arranged the meeting. When Dan arrived, he was genuinely amused to find himself face-to-face with Emily. In getting reacquainted, Dan and Emily experienced the spark of chemistry that had somehow been missing before. The last time I saw them, they were happily married with a child on the way.

Patterns and Past Lives

One of the patterns I have noticed over the years is that whenever I have a session with an intuitive, I often receive a sign confirming some aspect of the session. One of the most memorable examples happened after a session I had with Sally, an intuitive friend of Robin and Jennifer, the women I first met at the Akashic Records class and who later trained me in Reiki. I only met Sally in person once and do not remember much about her, aside from her loving energy. So, I decided to get a reading with her.

During the session, Sally talked about a past life I had in the 12th century as Native American medicine man. At the time of our session, I was busy reading books by Tom Brown, Jr. about his years with Stalking Wolf (aka Grandfather), the Lipan Apache shaman and scout I mentioned earlier.

My first question to Sally when she talked about that lifetime was, "What was my name?"

After a brief pause, Sally replied, "I'm getting that's not important." Undeterred, I asked, "What tribe was I from?"

Despite my relative ignorance about the many Native American tribes, I secretly prayed Sally would say, Lipan Apache, Sioux, or some other tribe that seemed cool. Instead, she replied, "You were a Chippewa." My initial reaction was disappointment because I really wanted there to be a connection with Stalking Wolf. Also, Chippewa somehow didn't sound terribly exciting. That all changed the following day when I searched Google for more information on the tribe. Scanning the results of my search, I gasped upon seeing the third entry: The Chippewa of Sault Ste. Marie, Michigan.

Seeing my birthplace in the Google results for Chippewa Indians was the first of three signs I received within 48 hours of Sally's reading. This might not seem terribly significant, but Sault Ste. Marie is an incredibly small town and I am the only person, of all of my relatives, who was born there rather than Chicago.

The following day, I was in the weight room at Lakeshore Athletic Club in Lincoln Park when a t-shirt caught my eye. Despite the fact that I was in the gym almost every day, I had never seen either the person or the t-shirt before. The shirt had a picture of Native Americans on horseback and the words, "Sault Ste. Marie, Michigan" on one sleeve. At that point, I had been on the planet for 34 years and had never once seen anyone wearing a shirt from my birthplace; to this day, I have not seen another. Later, when I told my dad about the reading and the Sault Ste. Marie connection, he reminded me that I was born in Chippewa County. It's on my birth certificate, but I would not have remembered. As a result, for the third time in two days, a chill rushed up my spine as I recalled my reading with Sally.

Putting It into Practice

In his book *Through Time Into Healing*, Dr. Brian Weiss talks extensively about the healing power of past life regression and the insights that can come through hypnosis. Even though it is clear Wiess believes in past lives and the power of regression therapy, he is quick to point out that it doesn't matter if people believe or not. What matters is that patients who haven't achieved healing any other way often experience dramatic, life-changing, permanent results.

The alternative that Weiss doesn't mention, but is no less real, is the past-life insight that can come from a gifted intuitive like Veronica Rae Cowen or Therese Rowley. Some people are even able to achieve past-life insights from dreams or self-guided meditation. It doesn't matter how you get there. What matters is that exploring a possible past-life connection may be both insightful and helpful – especially if you are dealing with an issue that is frustrating you or getting in the way of your enjoyment of life and you don't understand it or know what caused it.

CHAPTER 12:

Angels Watching and Protecting

We're lifted up by angels
Given wings to fly
Leave the night behind us
Trust the light to find us
Even as we rise
We're lifted up by angels
*-- from the song **"Angels":** Words & Music by Tom Kimmel & Jennifer Kimball*
Copyright © 1990 Night Rainbow Music/ASCAP/Morrissette Music ASCAP/Colgems-EMI Music, Inc. ASCAP/Sweet Angel Music (ASCAP) - Used with permission of the artist.

When people open up about their stories, I am often struck by how often their experiences share the common theme of being watched over in the most loving and wonderful ways. That is definitely true in my own case as well.

In Chapter 6, I described how the number 555 appeared with a growing frequency, bordering on urgency, as if to prepare me for the major life changes I experienced with the tumors and simultaneous career transitions. But by far, the more awe-inspiring was a completely different synchronicity that began around the same time the doctors believe the tumors started developing.

My friend Liliana called me one day to ask if I would consider renting my extra room to her friend, Christina, who was looking for a roommate. Christina, who moved to Chicago from Venezuela a few years before, had been sharing a studio apartment with Liliana while she was looking for a job.

Even though I was not looking for a roommate, I had the strong feeling I needed to be open to the possibility. Maybe because I grew up with three brothers and two sisters, I enjoy being around people every bit as much as I value my alone time. That, combined with the fact that I travel a lot, made it a great potential fit for both of us. A few weeks after seeing my place, Christina texted to say she was interested in renting the room.

Two weeks before the first noticeable symptoms occurred, Christina moved in. At this point, you may be thinking, "So what?" I might agree with you, except for the fact that Christina worked for Imerman's Angels, a non-profit that pairs cancer patients with people who survived the same diagnosis and treatment regimen. In order to work for Imerman Angels, you must have experienced cancer personally or been a caregiver for a cancer patient. What a wonderful way for the Universe to give me peace of mind. Besides connecting me with an official mentor, Christina provided a wealth of knowledge about other support services as well as introductions to her equally supportive colleagues. Better still, Christina proved to be a great listener. Even though I never needed any special attention, it was comforting to know she was there. My intention all along was to remain completely independent and not have to rely on anyone for help. However, I had no way of knowing how my body would react to the chemo or how sick I would get.

The entire experience, which rises way beyond a simple synchronicity, gave me the most incredible feeling because I truly felt loved and watched over by the Universe. It reminded me of the Albert Einstein quote: "Coincidence is God's way of remaining anonymous."

Sometimes, it isn't anonymous at all. People like Hailey Brasser are fortunate to know exactly who is watching over them. What I love most about Hailey's story is that her angelic companion explained the truth of their relationship long before Hailey confirmed it with her parents. Ever since she was little, Hailey has known about her twin, though her mother had never mentioned it to her. Hailey's mother had vanishing twin syndrome – this occurs when, in utero, one of the twins is reabsorbed and the remaining twin is carried to term. Here is Hailey's story in her own words:

> *My twin and I communicate through my dreams. I have never had a dream that she is not in. Some dreams I have are more fun where we fly through the clouds together, but some are way more serious. Occasionally, when I am not listening to the whispering angels, my twin will yell very loudly in my ear. My twin is really funny and I often wake up laughing. Even when I was a baby, my mom said that I would laugh in my sleep. In my dreams, [my twin] is never in the same body or form. I know exactly what she would look like if she was born: bright green eyes, a little taller than me, looks more like my mom,*

darker hair with more highlights than mine, and a lot more freckles on her nose and cheeks.

One day, I was wishing that my twin had been born because I knew how much fun we would have together. That night in my dream, she showed me exactly what it would be like if she had been born with me. We were both in the same wheelchair with somebody wheeling us down the hallway on the way to Mrs. King's classroom (my teacher at the time). Our arms and legs were super skinny, probably around two inches thick. We were sitting in front of the room...I saw all my classmates and wanted to talk to them when I suddenly realized that I could not talk. I was getting really mad and had to show everybody that this is not who I was: "I am Hailey Brasser your classmate and friend. I am not somebody that you just look at with sad eyes and feel bad for."

To show everybody this, I decided to stand up and show I could walk. I fell painfully on my face the second I tried to put pressure on my knees. I could not get up and felt tons of hands on me lifting me back up into my chair. I heard whispers through the classroom things like "Why did she try to stand?" and "She has never done that before." I woke up angry and terrified, only to realize how lucky I am. I was relieved and tried to sit up, but could not move at all. I began to feel terrified again until it felt like somebody had ripped the covers off me and I could move again. Nobody was there and the covers were still on my body. That day, all I could think about was how lucky I am to be so healthy and that God does everything for a reason. When asked, my twin said that she has a lot of names. The only one I could remember was Sarah. My twin's name is Sarah and she will always be my guardian angel.

Hailey's dream about what life would be like had Sarah been born is particularly noteworthy because she had the dream before confirming the vanishing twin phenomenon with her mother. Only then did she find out that doctors had expressed a serious concern when they thought her mother would be giving birth to twins. Given her mother's history, doctors were deeply concerned both babies would be born with deformities, exactly like what Hailey's twin described.

Considering the tendency for psychic abilities to be passed down in families, it will not come as surprise that Hailey's mother, Megan, has her own stories and her own take on being pregnant with Hailey and the vanishing twin:

I have always had "experiences" that I just can't explain. In fact, I learned as a child to brush them off with laughter as my dad obviously did at cocktail hour with neighbors. He would ask me to talk about one of my latest dreams or events. I would be excited to be heard and then they would all laugh at my four-year-old self and my entertaining story, which was sometimes a painful nightmare.

Now, in all fairness, I adore my dad and have every day of my life. And I have always known my father adores me. I even knew, because of his deep love, he was actually interested in my dreams and perceptions. But I also knew he dismissed them when they got "too crazy" because they are not at all in line with his Midwestern "farm kid" upbringing and what he could accept as part of the "real world." My mom, on the other hand, asked many questions...too many. I knew instinctively whatever this is, I got it from her.

Through the years, I slowly adapted to my dad's way of thinking and rarely took myself seriously. Yet my mom's questions after a troubling dream told me to hold on to it — to hold on somehow and not entirely dismiss my intuitions, my dreams, my knowings without any possible explanation for what I knew about people. My mom's questions kept my gift alive. I have come to believe a powerful intuition is every child's gift. Mine was preserved by a curious mother who always came to me with her big, inquisitive, believing eyes.

I was just 21 when I met similar eyes in my future husband, Richard. He would also ask me a lot of questions about the feelings I still didn't take very seriously. It almost felt foreign by now and weird to me how curious he was about the things I couldn't explain. His mother, who died when he was young, was very open to and fascinated with psychic abilities. He recognized that events I randomly and light-heartedly chattered about tended to happen and impossible things I knew about someone would later prove to be true. Again, I practically made fun of myself as who wants to listen to another weird dream of mine? They were long, detailed and usually pretty boring to everyone but me. Or so I thought. Richard always listened to the details. I actually loved him for it, but had no idea he was actually helping me to exercise a gift I could barely acknowledge.

Through our 20 married years together, it feels as though my intuition has grown into more forms. It has been said that intuition lives in the imagination. I suppose I play there a lot…even in daydreams. I could always tell the sex of our baby because of my dreams. Four pregnancies equalled four correct predictions. Even In my second pregnancy when I was pregnant with twins, I told the nurse at six weeks, "there are two." I already knew there were twins and warned her my bloodwork would be higher than usual because there were two baby girls who come to me in my dreams. She laughed — until my eight-week ultrasound. Honestly, I laughed, too, until there they were! I remember asking if Baby B was ok and they assured me "it" measures exactly the same as A and there was nothing to worry about. They seemed puzzled as to why I asked.

I am equally sure I felt the moment one of our twin's souls left my body. Strangely, I didn't recall the moment until several years later. But I now have the memory of that moment as clear as the morning I was laying in my bed around 13 weeks pregnant when I felt a shooting star glittering down my abdomen. It was like a shimmering, trickling flash that was all too powerful and too beautiful. I have never felt anything like it before or since. The only way I can describe it was exactly how a shooting star would feel inside one's womb. I knew instantly and said aloud, "If you have left us, this is when you did, I felt that, I felt you leave me, you are like a shooting star, so beautiful."

Not only did I suppress that memory for years, but also along with it vanished my memory of a heart pleading prayer one night. Upon one haphazard try for pregnancy, Richard and I were pregnant with TWINS! Meanwhile, I had three of my dearest friends who had no success getting pregnant. My best friend, Jocelyn, had been trying for years, suffering one miscarriage after another heartbreaking miscarriage. It was gut wrenching to witness her struggle because she deserved the baby she was dreaming of more than anyone I knew, including me. While still in my first trimester, I pleaded with God about how easily I get pregnant and how fast. I told God he could take my babies and give them to my three friends struggling to get pregnant. I promised him I would understand but to please take this guilt (of my healthy, fast, easy pregnancies) from me and just give them their sweet babies.

A couple weeks later, I was the most accepting one in that (16 week) ultrasound room, when they announced "vanishing twin syndrome" after I asked "where is the other one?" But I wouldn't remember why I was so peacefully prepared until years later.

The brain is an amazing and funny machine when it serves to protect. I thought "I already knew" that day because my stomach was still too flat for two babies and I had also caught someone giving my tummy that thought. But the real reason I actually knew was because her sweet soul had gifted me a very dazzling, sensational farewell. It was such a sweet gift that it allowed for the one healthy, beautiful baby girl still thriving and literally tumbling all around on the screen and completely showing off, to be fully celebrated. We welcomed God's plan with open arms. We would name her Hailey the following April. By July of the same year, all three of my friends had gotten pregnant and delivered beautiful baby girls! They are all sweet friends of Hailey's to this day.

As I completed one of the final read-throughs of the manuscript, I re-read Megan's story and was struck by the line "her sweet soul had gifted me a very dazzling, sensational farewell." Inspired, I texted Megan:

Me:

Random question: I am going through Josseline's edits of the book and re-reading your story. I so love the shooting star image. I'm curious if that's why you named her Hailey (as in the comet)?

Megan:

Omg

No

I never thought of that!!!

You have to add that epiphany of yours!!!

Spirit Twins

When Marjorie was a little girl growing up in France, she had a friend at school named Mathilde who occasionally showed up in her dreams as well. They were constant companions and playmates until Marjorie turned six and her family moved to a nearby town. Marjorie never saw Mathilde at school again, but dreamt about her occasionally over the next nine years.

Around the time Marjorie turned 15, she found a towel that was part of a school art project the class did when she was four years old. The towel included a self-portrait of every child in the class along with his or her name. When Marjorie found the towel, she looked all over for Mathilde's name but couldn't find it anywhere. When she asked her mom why Mathilde's name wasn't included, her mother insisted there was no Mathilde in the class. Convinced that her mom was wrong, Marjorie found the class picture, identified Mathilde immediately, and said, "Look, there she is. I knew there was a Mathilde"

To Marjorie's surprise, her mother said, "No, Marjorie, that's you."

This was the moment Marjorie realized what happened. When Marjorie was nine or ten, her mother told her that she had been pregnant with twins, but had an accident and fell on her side. Her mom knew immediately something was wrong and went to the hospital where she learned that one of the twins had died. The original plan was to name the twins Stefanie and Mathilde, but her parents decided instead to name the remaining twin Marjorie.

It was only when Marjorie turned 15 and found the class towel that she realized that Mathilde, the friend who always looked exactly like her, was her twin who had only ever been with her in spirit form.

Marjorie hasn't seen Mathilde since she was seventeen and misses her still.

I am so grateful to Hailey, Megan, and Marjorie for sharing their stories because it is such a gift to hear about the same miracle from different perspectives. For most of us, our experience of being watched over is not quite as dramatic and soul-affirming as Hailey, Megan, and Marjorie, but it does not make it any less hopeful or miraculous.

The most common instances seem to happen when people get a sense of a deceased loved one through distinctive scents. For example, you might smell their pipe or cigar smoke even though no one in the vicinity is smoking. I remember stepping into an elevator one day when, halfway to my destination, the unmistakable scent of my late grandmother's perfume appeared out of nowhere and gave me the strong sense that she was there, lovingly watching over me. In those moments, I find it helpful to do three things. First, ask if the person has a message for you. Second, watch and listen. Third, say "Thank you!" Even if you did not express gratitude in the moment, as I am quite sure I didn't, it is never too late.

Spirit Guides

When it comes to spiritual guidance, there seem to be at least three groups — people who are not open to the possibility, people who are open and accept the possibility based on faith and experience (I would fall into this category), and people who know exactly who their Spirit Guides are and maintain an active relationship with them. My friend, Veronica Rae Cowen, falls into the third category. As you will soon see, she and I have her Spirit Guides to thank for our friendship.

> *Over the last 11 years I have developed a strong and trusting relationship with my Spirit Guides. I find their counsel to be extraordinarily helpful - as they have access to a bigger picture I cannot even begin to see. The guidance they give me from seemingly mundane nudges that help me find the perfect parking spots - to big dialogues which have paved the way to open and oversee a successful business - have all helped me to live life with greater ease, flow and grace. I call my Spirit Council my "Dream Team," because the support and information they share (when I am open to receive it and call upon it) is truly a miracle. My whole life, from my relationship, to my work, even my overall health, I attribute to the commitment I have to my spiritual growth, my guides and Creator.*

> *Often my guides will support me in accomplishing my To Do lists. They give me guidance about the order in which to do each task. And I find that (again with their view of the bigger picture) things flow more smoothly. I also notice how resistant*

I am to doing as they suggest thinking that "my way" will work out better (it usually doesn't). Sometimes I will be guided to only complete half of the tasks I intend to take on for the day. They will tell me the order, as well as which tasks are top priority (which sometimes counter my mind's plan). As I make my way through the list, something comes up and I am suddenly called elsewhere, now unable to complete the day's "needs." However, magically everything that either solves itself or can wait until tomorrow was at the bottom of the "Guides' List!!" Again, they prove themselves.

One day I found myself channeling my list for the day when my guides said, "Email Rob Sullivan."

"Rob Sullivan?" I asked, "Who is that?"

"Google search him, and email him." they replied.

"Well, that is ridiculous!" I was quick to retort.

However, I had learned by this point that they usually knew what I was needing - and perhaps Rob Sullivan and I needed to cross paths. So, I searched his name and looked through his website – feeling overcome with a sense of familiarity, I emailed him:

Hello Rob,

I hope this email finds you well. Although we have never met, I have a strange sense that I know you. I was guided to email you and I feel as though we can help each other in some way. I am in a place of transition in life, and it seems I may have an ability to support you in connecting with universal guidance in a way you had not previously considered.

I know this seems strange, as believe me it does for me as well! But I did find it interesting that I was led to the computer to google your name, and here you are. The work that you do interests me- as I feel this is the type of work I am being led towards however on a different basis – more in the area of education, and supporting schools and teachers in shifting the way we teach children. As you may be aware, there are more and more conscious kids being born.

Like I said above I feel as though I am out on a limb- as I am not really sure why I am emailing you, other than that I was guided to by my intuition.

Thank You for your time :-)

~Veronica

Within a few hours Rob had replied:

Hi Veronica,

Wow! I loved your email. I am very spiritual and am forever amazed at the wonderful insights that come when we trust our intuition.

I would welcome the opportunity to talk with you and explore the possibilities. I looked at your site and am definitely interested in buying a copy of your book.

I'd love to hear more about what led you to google me. Did you get an intuitive hit on my name or had you heard of me somehow before? Give me a call when you get a chance and we'll talk.

* * *

From there Rob and I began a conversation, in the weeks that followed I introduced him to his guides and for more than 10 years Rob and I have maintained contact and exchanged healing and transformative experiences. Thanks, Guides, for this beautiful friendship and connection!

Veronica's guides not only help with her To Do lists and introductions, but they have also been instrumental in building her business:

I have always had a knowingness inside of me that I am being looked after or protected. I vividly recall one night in my early twenties, living in Thailand, when I got into a minor motorbike accident. I flew off the bike and spun around the handle bars, and the only scrape I had was on my toe. As I got up and walked away, I looked around and said aloud, "Thank You!" I knew I was being watched over! I also just so happened to be living on the grounds of a Buddhist temple, and this little accident had happened at the entrance to the temple property. I knew there was a guardian there looking out for me. And for that, I was grateful.

In 2013, I was invited to start a summer camp. It is an industry I have worked in for many, many years and in 2010 I left the last summer camp I ran thinking with an assured cockiness "I am not going to be a camp counselor forever! I am going to do bigger and better things!" Little did I know Creator and my guides had something else in store for my life! So in 2013, with reluctance, I opened a new camp - I had had a reading from a teacher I greatly respect and he told me "You will get out of this everything you could want!" So hesitantly, I agreed.

I moved forward and began the process of starting a new camp venture. Although I am usually good at tapping into guidance and coming up with creative names, I found myself struggling to name the camp. One afternoon I sat with my mother and calmly asked her; "Mom, can you please look into the future and tell me what this camp is called?" She agreed to do it, closed her eyes, got really still, and then 10 seconds later joyfully said, "It's called Camp Funderblast!"

"Yes it is!" I replied! And so it was.

I love telling the kids at camp this story - it breaks the box of limitation in their minds. Occasionally a child will say to me, "Your mom didn't really look into the future to see what the camp is called, did she?!"

To which I reply, "Of course she did - it's called Camp Funderblast isn't it!?"

A couple weeks later after I had created the logo — a ring of light with a lightning bolt inside and the words "I'm a Funderblaster!" (which has come to mean "I spread love and positive energy") — I sat on my bed deep in meditation. A vibrant spirit appeared before me and said,

"That is the lightning bolt of love on your logo and on your camp shirts"

"Really? I like that!" I replied.

"It's me - I am Louie - the lightning bolt of love! And you can make a lightning bolt stuffed animal for the kids, and call it Louie. I will be your guide, and the guardian angel of Camp Funderblast."

Over the next month Louie guided me on many things, including how to sew his stuffed animal body! After we had made the stuffed lightning bolt, wherever I took him, people started hugging him, and asking me if I had purposefully made the stuffed animal hugging size? To which I replied. "I am not doing any of this on purpose! It is just coming through me!"

On the first day of camp, the kids came running up to me yelling, "When you hug Louie he hugs you back!!!! You can actually feel his energy hug you back!" And so the legend of Louie became realized. I have even had parents arrive at camp to pick up their children after a stressful day at work and say to me, "Where is Louie, I need a hug."

Five years later there are three Camp Funderblast locations, two after School programs and three Louie stuffies. Everyone loves to hug Louie and I have yet to hear someone say they do not feel the hug returned. But it's not just a hug you receive from squeezing Louie, it's a healing. And just as we always tell the kids - you do not need to hug Louie to get the love and healing energy he holds. You can close your eyes and ask for it any time with your intention. – Try it now – Ask Louie for a healing, you might feel goose bumps, chills, warmth or simply a sense of peace wash over you. Louie the Lightning Bolt of Love is certainly real.

I don't know what will come next, but it seems Camp Funderblast has been in a process of growth since its conception. Louie the Lightning Bolt of Love continues to support Funderblast and all its families in spreading love and positive energy. For this I am abundantly grateful!

Signs as Unanswered Prayers

Reading Veronica's words above, the positive energy is so clear it is not hard to imagine that she has a wide-open channel of communication when it comes to prayer and asking for signs. For others, like Rachel, signs come in the form of spontaneous job offers, paid-for apartments, and unanswered prayers.

> *"I was married when I was 20 to a worship leader with a heart of gold. He helped everyone and was so incredibly kind. When I first met him, I was agnostic and I thought his love for me was a gift from God. I thought being with him made me a better person. I am naturally outgoing, but he told me that drawing attention to myself is wrong. If we went out, he would praise me if I was sweet and quiet.*
>
> *About 8 months into our marriage, he told me that he made a mistake and had "listened to the wrong voice" when he married me. He said I was a "dark cloud". I thought I hadn't been good enough. I was never so hurt. I prayed that he would have a change of heart. I walked on eggshells. He would sleep with me because I was his wife but then ignore me for a week so as to not give me hope. I didn't tell anyone because I didn't want anyone to think badly of him. People would ask me how it felt to be married to someone so "anointed by God." I loved him so much and thought God must be saving him from me.*
>
> *I prayed and prayed, but the more time I spent in prayer, the more freedom I found. About five months into the verbal abuse, my parents told me to move out. I did. I didn't know*

where I would go, but I wanted to move to Colorado to be with my mom and dad. I kept waiting for an answer. I never had a clear sign. So, I packed my car and went to film a commercial in Oklahoma City. I would leave that afternoon for Colorado. I prayed the whole way there for God to stop me if I wasn't supposed to leave. In my heart, I wanted to stay so my marriage wouldn't fall apart — even though it was so far gone.

When I got to the shoot, the producer asked if I would like to intern with their production company over the summer. I said possibly. Then, the makeup artist invited me to her church. I told God after the shoot, "Well, that's great and everything, but I can't just live in my car here all summer, so I'm still going to Colorado." I got to my friend's house to pick up my dog and head out when her little sister came out and said, "Hey, I'm leaving for the summer. You can have my room. The rent is already paid." And I stayed.

That Sunday, I went to church with the makeup artist who invited me, and I met Marty, my new husband. My first husband did finally divorce me, though I held out to the end, never even signing the papers. But today looking back, I see why the prayer was unanswered. I was in a narcissistic relationship. Because of it and because of the isolation, I realized that I am ENOUGH and that God/the universe/whatever you want to call it, creates paths for the people who are genuinely seeking. I was meant to be with Marty. He loves ME. I can be free in so many ways. I wasn't just trapped by the marriage I prayed so hard to keep, but I was trapped by myself and my own insecurities. I'm so thankful for that unanswered prayer."

Warnings from the Universe

Not long ago, a somewhat skeptical friend asked me sincerely, "Psychics always predict good things in readings. Do they ever tell you when something bad is going to happen?"

The short answer is yes. The good news is always more exciting and hopeful, but the fact is, they often share warnings, bad news, and other information that would be helpful to know. Whether the communication is from psychics, dreams, or other signs, the message is often a warning.

PyschicDave Tillman is particularly good at that. I can remember several accurate warnings he gave me in advance. First, as I mentioned in Chapter 4, he warned me that my accountant was "missing some things." He was right – the accountant missed thousands in airfare deductions on my tax returns. A few years later, he warned me about an emotional period that would prove particularly challenging. He said, "I'm worried about you. This situation has nothing to do with you, but I see it dragging you down and getting worse by summer." Right again.

Insights from Psychics/Intuitives

Nadia, another gifted intuitive I have worked with, has also been helpful in this regard. Of the countless predictions she has made that have come to pass, there was one in particular that I find especially fascinating. In the early summer of 2018 right before my dad died, I began experiencing a strange numbness and tingling sensation in the thumb and first finger of my left hand I had been told was the direct result of an issue with my neck that some had speculated was a bulging disc. When I first asked about it, Nadia replied that she wasn't allowed to give medical information. Thinking about it from her point-of-view, I decided to ask the question differently. First, I assured her that I had follow-up appointments scheduled with a neurologist as well as a chiropractor. To my surprise, Nadia said the issue was muscular and related to my shoulder blade.

In an effort to resolve the issue as quickly as possible, I shared this information with a massage therapist, the neurologist and the physical therapist the neurologist sent me to see. In hindsight, my mistake was sharing the source of the information. All three listened politely and proceeded to ignore it. This was especially interesting because the physical therapist had shared with me her fascination and openness to intuitives.

Why is this important? After nine months of physical therapy, Kayla, one of the other therapists on the team, started our appointment by saying the insurance company was asking for an assessment since we hadn't made the kind of progress any of us had hoped to see. When she started pushing down on the area between my left shoulder and neck, she asked, "What do you feel when I press here?"

I replied, "That's a knot, but it's always been there."

To my surprise, Kayla responded, "It's not a knot; it's a bone."

When I said I didn't think there was supposed to be a bone there, she said, "You're right. There isn't supposed to be."

It was at that moment, almost a full year after my session with Nadia, that her prediction came to pass. Once it was determined that my shoulder blade was out of place – possibly as a result of the many months I spent on crutches as a child – Kayla was able to come up with an effective treatment plan.

Over the past few years, so much of what I have learned from Nadia and her guide, Fred, has come to pass that I know not to question them. At the same time, I am well aware the rest of the world doesn't necessarily share my faith. So, if a psychic/intuitive gives you a warning that you have a strong sense would be helpful to share, it may be equally helpful to be vague about where you got the information. Otherwise, it is likely to get politely – or impolitely – ignored.

Warnings do not always come from psychics, however. Many people receive messages and impressions that help by putting them on a heightened sense of alert. Not surprisingly, warnings focus on a person's well-being, and often are about health and safety as the stories below demonstrate.

When Tiffany, a friend and classmate from high school, started her story she said, "I don't know if this counts as a sign or a warning that my life was headed in the wrong direction, but I'm grateful I listened to the warning." Tiffany was driving from New Jersey back to Chicago when she pulled into a rest stop in Ohio. Moments later, she was shocked when her left arm "went completely dead/paralyzed for about five minutes." Once she regained movement, she continued driving to Chicago, arrived at her parents' house, and immediately recounted the weird, temporary paralysis of her arm. Her parents made her promise she would get it checked out when she returned to New Jersey after the holidays. Since she had arrived relatively late, her mother went upstairs to help her father get ready for bed leaving Tiffany in the kitchen by herself. That's when she heard the words, "Don't go to sleep" repeated three times in a row, "as if someone were standing next to me saying them."

"I heeded the words (freaked out as I was), went to Evanston Hospital, and discovered a whole host of serious underlying health issues that likely would have resulted in another more serious stroke had I just gone to sleep that night instead." Tiffany went on to say, "While not everything about my life changed overnight, some things did, and have remained so to this day. And I'm grateful I 'listened' to the warning I was given that night."

The next few stories detail other wellness-related warnings that go beyond one individual's health and well-being. Megan's story is a good example of this.

When Megan had to go to Las Vegas for a work conference, she and her husband Mike decided to have some fun and make it a family trip. They brought along their five-month-old daughter, and noticed right away how different Vegas was with an infant. Now they needed to worry about second-hand smoke and noise, in addition to learning how to navigate a stroller through the hordes of people walking up and down the Strip.

Looking at things in "parent vision" led them to have a chilling conversation about what they would do if they saw an active shooter. Would they try and push the stroller to safety, with the baby still inside, or would they take the baby out of the stroller and run? An unpleasant conundrum to be sure, but after discussing it for a few minutes, they went on with their day. They discussed spending another night in the city so they could have some more time to see the sites – Mike and the baby had spent the day at Mandalay Bay the day before, but Megan had been too busy at the conference to do much exploring. They eventually decided they felt it was best to return home.

On their drive back to Los Angeles, they learned that a gunman had opened fire on a country music concert in Las Vegas, killing 58 people and injuring 489. While they did not have tickets to the concert, they would likely have been stuck amidst the chaos. They now see the seemingly random conversation as a warning from the Universe that it was important that they leave.

A number of other people shared similar stories. On September 10, 2001, the day before the terrorist attack on the Twin Towers, Robbie, a pilot for a regional airline, was driving into work from his home in Michigan. When he saw the gorgeous Chicago skyline, he wondered aloud about whether a building would be able to remain standing if it were struck by a plane.

The week before Robbie's unexplainable thought, Matt Gordon had a dream that took place in a skyscraper with his friend, Dani. The building was struck by a plane during daylight hours on a clear day. As Matt put it, "We all needed to evacuate down the stairwell and I had to plead with Dani to leave the building because she was frightened."

As it happens, the warnings are not always about man-made disasters. Bo, an American who spent several years in Japan, discovered that he had a strange and unexplainable ability to predict the timing and severity of earthquakes. Japan has so many earthquakes every year that Bo had ample time to practice. Here is how he describes it:

I first became aware of my earthquake-predicting ability shortly following a 6.2 earthquake that shook Tokyo around 9:30 P.M. on Friday, October 4th, one month to the day after I had moved to Japan.

I was aware that Japan had frequent earthquakes, so I tried not to freak out and stuck my head out of the dormitory I was visiting to see if I could see any high rises in the Shinjuku area sway. As it happened, that first earthquake I experienced was the largest to hit the area in 62 years, and was centered 35 miles from Tokyo. Luckily, it was centered 50 miles below the surface; thus, little damage occurred to buildings or infrastructures. It must have triggered an "animal instinct" in me, because what I can only describe as my inner core became disturbed and I could sense energy released from the ground shortly before aftershocks occurred. I did not feel the disturbance when there weren't any aftershocks.

As the months passed, I grew to recognize the disturbing feeling and would test my intuition by telling friends and co-

workers a few days in advance when I expected earthquakes. From the start, I was quite accurate with an 85% success rate.

I returned to my Ohio hometown [of] Miamisburg for my brother's wedding in April of 1987 [and] I stayed home for over a month before starting a new job. The last week at home, I started to experience the disturbance in my inner core and mentioned it to my mother as we chatted late one night. Later, as my father drove me to the airport for my return to Japan, my mother mentioned my feeling about a potential earthquake to my father, who acted like I was crazy. Sure enough, on June 11th, just before 7:00 P.M. Central Time, the U.S. Midwest experienced the largest earthquake in 20 years, a 5.0 centered in southern Illinois. As a result, one of the first phone calls I received at my new job was from my mother, who shouted "You were right, you were right...we just had a big earthquake here in Ohio."

My ability lasted the entire 14 years I lived in Japan. Before long, co-workers began asking me to post on my desk the level of "disturbance" I felt. Others would bet me on my predictions and I always won those bets...a dinner here, a bottle of liquor there, etc.

At one point, a friend of mine connected me with a seismologist from the University of Tokyo. The very day I went to meet him, I began to experience that familiar feeling. I shared my story and predicted one in the next four days with a rather significant intensity (in Japan, they use a different scale based on the "shaking intensity"). Once again, I was right on the money, but strangely enough, I never heard from the professor again.

Now that I am back in the Midwest where there is rarely any seismic activity, I don't get that familiar feeling because there is very little energy released here. But if it happens again, I'll know, because the disturbing feeling is not one I could ever forget.

Some people theorize that with earthquakes and severe storms, there is an initial release of energy and a change in negative and positive ions that animals detect and respond to. For some reason, I am highly sensitive to whatever is happening and seem to be able to tune into that energy I feel as a "disturbance in my inner core." I may not be able to explain it fully, but it's definitely a gift.

From what psychic friends have shared, the ability to pick up on negative future events is actually far more common than the ability to make positive predictions. People theorize that this may be a reflection of the fact that negative events have so much more energetic weight than positive events.

You can test this yourself. Spend a few moments and visualize all of your dreams coming true. Imagine what that would feel like. Once you have that feeling, pause and imagine the most catastrophic, horrible events you could experience personally. Which one is heavier? For whatever reason, the negative possibility always outweighs the positive one.

For Megan, Robbie, Matt, and Bo, the warnings were not about events that would impact them personally, but they almost certainly served the purpose of placing them on a heightened state of alert with a deeper appreciation and awareness of the messages and the source behind them.

Guardian Grandma

For Kathleen Knorr, her warning came not as a premonition, but as an awareness of her grandmother's presence:

At 2:00AM, when I was in the midst of my partying 20s, I was in my car driving when a breeze literally blew through the car that smelled exactly like my grandmother. I mentioned it to my friends, who didn't think much of it. (Grandma died when I was 10). About a mile later, two of my friends start razzing me for stopping at a green light. I wasn't even sure why I paused, but I did.

Seconds later, a car came out of nowhere and blew through the red light, going at least 70 miles per hour. Had I not stopped, it would have hit us for sure. It didn't take long for my friends to appreciate my grandma's timely visit. We were all thanking my guardian angel grandma that night for our lives.

Like Kathleen, Nina Ring from Trier, Germany knows exactly who her guardian angel is:

Almost two years ago, Jonas, my best friend, protector, source of peace, and [my] better half, died of cancer. Although he is not on the planet anymore, I feel this extremely strong connection and can feel his presence everywhere. No matter where I go, I see and feel him with me. Sometimes he is a butterfly, sometimes a tree, and every day he is my sunlight. The moment Jonas passed away, the sun rose and glowed so bright[ly], as if his always-smiling facial expression was somehow transferred to the sky. Even friends and family who weren't present when Jonas closed his eyes forever recognized the warmth and peace of the sun.

One of my favorite memories of his presence occurred during a trip to Thailand a year or so after he died. In the midst of a rather unpleasant bout with food poisoning, I slept on a mat and awoke with a grey cat right beside me. The cat had the same beautiful energy and the same ocean blue eyes as Jonas. The similarity was so striking it felt like the rebirth of Jonas. Better still, this adorable fellow stayed by my side for the next few days while I recovered. Thanks to a constant array of experiences like this, I have not felt alone or afraid since the moment Jonas died. I know that he is always with me - as a tree, a bird, a cat, or some other form. Thanks to Jonas, I have found peace and know my little angel is with me all the time.

In Kathleen Gold's case, the angel showed up not in the form of a dearly departed grandmother or as an animal protector, but as a homeless person who unintentionally scared her at first:

> I was working in Orlando for a jewelry store at Church St. Station, which is right downtown. I was not having very good luck with jobs and not enjoying Orlando so much. That day, the manager ran out to get lunch or coffee, leaving me alone in the store. I saw a man approaching, and the closer he got the more nervous I became, because a: I was alone in the jewelry store (something that is never supposed to happen) and b: I realized he was homeless.
>
> The man walked into the store, approached me, and told me not to be scared. Then he said, "I just wanted to tell you everything is going to be all right." He said it with absolute certainty and, knowing he had delivered the message, turned around and walked out. The message was powerful because at that time my life was very unsettled in Orlando and filled with The Clash-type "Should I Stay or Should I Go?" moments. So, when he said everything would be alright, it literally took the worry out of what would come next in my day, world, life, and universe. I needed to hear those words at that time.

A Day of Miraculous Synchronicities

What I love most about the way the Universe works is the way so many of us have the opportunity to serve as the angels doing the watching. At the suggestion of my friend, Lauren, I started reading *The Five*

Secrets You Must Discover Before You Die by John Izzo. The book, which is based on interviews with over 200 people who found happiness and meaning in their lives, has a number of interesting suggestions. One of the first to catch my attention was the simple prayer a woman named Lea says every morning:

> *"Make me open to love from the time I leave my house until the time I come home. Help me so that when I meet those in my path for whom a kind word, a smile, a thank you might be life-changing, please do not let me be so busy I miss it."*

Lea's intention really struck me because it isn't simply about being too busy to notice. If I just missed those opportunities, that would be one thing. The bigger issues for me are those moments in which I let impatience and everyday frustrations take the place of compassion.

Why do I mention this? Because when I did my gratitude meditation the following morning, for the first time ever I added the intention to be open to opportunities to demonstrate love to those who most need it. I am in awe how quickly it worked.

At 9:41am, less than two hours later, I received the following message on Couchsurfing from Nicole (not her real name):

> *"Hi Rob, I've just arrived in Chicago from Cleveland via Megabus. It was a spur of the moment trip to try and clear my head and see some friends, but as I've arrived so hastily I was wondering if I may stay at your home until I make more proper arrangements, which should be by tomorrow. Thank you!"*

Whenever I read a Couchsurfing request, I immediately check with my gut to get a read on the person who wrote the message. It's fascinating how well this technique works and how much is communicated by the energy behind the words. In this case, getting a read wasn't hard because the phrases "try and clear my head" and "I've arrived so hastily" painted a clear picture that this was, at the very least, a woman who needed a friend. Sensing the urgency, I immediately offered her a place to stay, but didn't acknowledge the underlying need the way I should have. Nevertheless, she replied at 3:53pm saying: *"Great. Thank you. When would be a good time to show up?"*

After a few quick text messages and a phone call, Nicole jumped in an Uber and arrived about 4:30pm. Having missed my earlier opportunity to acknowledge her situation, I gave her a warm welcome and made it a point to say something like, "Sounds like you've got a lot going on." She responded with a warm smile and expressed her gratitude for my willingness to host last-minute.

I don't remember our exact words, but that isn't the point. What was more important was communicating the intention that I cared and was ready to listen if that was what she needed most. Nicole immediately opened up and shared a few of the personal challenges that led to a recent suicide attempt and subsequent hospitalization. Later she described the intense 15 minutes she spent that afternoon on a downtown bridge staring at the cold Chicago River below. In a moment that sounded eerily like the scene from the movie *It's A Wonderful Life*, Nicole thought about jumping and succumbing under the weight of her backpack. While it was heartbreaking to listen to Nicole's story, I found tremendous hope as she talked about the strong feeling that suicide wasn't the answer and that she was being called to choose another path.

The hard part for any of us who have experienced feelings of hopelessness is trusting that life will get better. At the same time, what I have come to understand since my best friend, Charlie, killed himself, is the firm belief that whatever we experience emotionally — whether it is soul-nurturing joy or the deepest despair — comes with us as we move from state to state, country to country, or even life to death. In the case of despair, the only escape is resolution. No matter where you are, there is no different than here.

Having said that, I freely acknowledge several important points. First, I don't pretend to understand all of the intricacies of mental illness and recognize that there are no easy answers, and in many cases, no cures. Second, for those who, for whatever reason, aren't able to deal with or resolve their issues, I make no judgment and offer only compassion. While I have certainly experienced the bitter taste of sadness and hopelessness, I cannot begin to comprehend what it would be like to deal with mental illness. What I am certain of, for those of us who are not debilitated by chemical imbalances, is the incredible power of thought and the awe-inspiring capacity we have to change our situation by thinking and acting differently.

Not long after Nicole arrived, we both realized we were hungry so we ordered a pizza. On the way to pick it up, Nicole brought up the possibility that she had limiting beliefs she needed to confront. I was relieved to hear this because, unlike people for whom mental illness makes rational thought challenging or impossible, it was clear Nicole was open to other ways of interpreting and resolving her situation. In this case, the belief I most wanted to challenge was that killing herself would somehow be an improvement.

In the movie *What Dreams May Come* (1998), Robin Williams goes on a journey into the afterlife to rescue the soul of his wife, Annie, who committed suicide. When he finally finds Annie, he discovers that her overwhelming despair and guilt make communicating with her virtually impossible. When I told Nicole about the movie, she eagerly agreed to watch it with me after dinner. Not surprisingly, it was an intense experience that led to a conversation that extended well past 3am. It also led to even more synchronicities.

At one point, Nicole talked about how painful transitions have been — specifically transitions marking the end of important relationships. As she shared, I was reminded of the beautiful image of a seed becoming a plant. From the point-of-view of a seed, having your outer shell destroyed and cast away is almost unspeakably violent. Yet the end result — a plant that is exponentially larger and infinitely more beautiful — makes the complete destruction of the shell worthwhile. Even aspirational. When I looked at Nicole, that's what I saw — a seed in the midst of one of nature's most violent transitions. The following morning, I awoke to a beautiful daily email from my friend, Veronica. In yet another wonderful synchronicity, here is what she wrote:

Today's Practice: A Crack

Somewhere in your space is a crack. A crack where the light begins to seep in. A crack in your reality, in your resistance, a crack in your tendency to hang on to the past. Let the light into this crack. And as the light comes in - allow the shell to shatter. Sometimes we have to break to be healed. We have to feel drained to ask for help. We have to shatter to allow and accept the assistance of God. Rather than breaking by some external force - choose to do it yourself. Calling upon, asking for, and allowing in the healing that has always been present for you. Close your eyes and imagine one spot in your bubble becoming illuminated where there is an energetic crack. Then let God's light flow into the crack. And let the shell break. Let the valence go. The delusion of who you think you need to be - dissolve and disappear. A crack is not a bad thing, it is an opportunity for light to enter.

I shouldn't be amazed by this because the Universe clearly works in miraculous ways. Nevertheless, I take it as a sign that I was exactly where I needed to be. And so was Nicole.

Putting It into Practice

If you accept that spiritual guidance like the examples described above happen, stay present for that possibility in your own life. You don't have to have a relative or friend who has passed on to have someone watching out for you. It could be an angel or someone with whom you experienced a past life but who chose not to incarnate in this one.

There are two levels of openness if you want to get the best results. First, be open to the possibility. Second, actually make yourself open. I remember hearing one intuitive share that deceased relatives, in particular, may see and sense that we are experiencing difficulty, but they can't read our thoughts. For this reason, it's a good idea to speak to them directly or to give them permission to know your thoughts.

Another common approach is to ask for signs from the spirits or angels who are watching over you. I can't say this with absolute certainty, but I would be cautious about asking excessively for signs. After all, if the roles were reversed and you were the one being tested, it wouldn't take long for you to get annoyed. You'd almost certainly appreciate someone who approached the relationship with faith and gratitude.

CHAPTER 13:

Laughing in the Face of Danger

One of the best lessons you can learn in life
is to master how to remain calm.
– Catherine Pulsifier

One of my fondest memories of the entire tumor experience occurred in response to the second of eleven journal entries I posted online. Suzie Eckard, a friend from high school, wrote:

> *"Love that you are able to impart your wisdom with morsels of humor! I have been reading this while Jim is sitting here saying, 'Uh, aren't you reading about cancer? What is so funny?' Then I read him what you have written and he understands."*

I made a number of important choices in terms of how I thought about, spoke about, and handled the tumors, but one of the most vital turned out to be the decision not to lose my sense of humor. As a kid, I remember feeling sorry for myself and refusing to smile during situations that had other people close to hysterics. I'm not sure exactly when or why the turning point occurred, but eventually I decided to take life less seriously. I am glad I did because it probably saved my life.

Perhaps it was part of the Universe's plan all along, but there were more than a few legitimately funny moments that began the afternoon Dr. Stephen Becker called with the CT scan results to tell me there was an eight by five by seven-centimeter tumor in my chest just above my heart. It was February 18th, my 48th birthday, and I scheduled the scan at 6:30 A.M. so I could take the rest of the day off and enjoy myself.

For whatever reason, the possibility that the lump in my neck would turn out to be a tumor had never entered my mind — the swirl of feelings that followed included surprise, confusion, concern, and fear, but not anger or denial. I accepted what Dr. Becker said because I knew in my heart it was true. Even though the doctors did not know exactly what type of tumors we were dealing with, I took some comfort in Dr. Becker's certainty that they could be treated. I was also relieved that he had already called my dad to let him know what was happening. I didn't want to have to make that phone call.

From my initial place of acceptance emerged a powerful desire to remain positive and optimistic. A big part of this came from the responsibility I felt to manage expectations. More specifically, from an energetic perspective, I knew it would be important to keep friends and family focused on health and healing rather than the possibility of me checking out early.

Thankfully, more than a few funny moments started within minutes of that life-altering diagnosis. The first came in the form of a Facebook birthday greeting from Sue Spalt Davis, one of my best friends and someone I have known for over 25 years. She wrote simply, "Happy Birthday, Buddy! Hope there is a surprise somewhere in your day."

Having already received the preliminary diagnosis, I laughed out loud. A few weeks later, when I knew more about the prognosis and treatment plan, Sue laughed when I teased her and said, "Next year, I need you to be more specific." It felt great to share a laugh, if only to assure her that nothing changed.

Lymphomania and a Visit to the Sperm Bank

Strangely, the initial visit to Dr. Leo Gordon, the oncologist, also led to a few funny moments. First, I loved the fact that Dr. Gordon, an understated guy and one of the foremost experts on lymphoma, is referred to by his colleagues as a "lymphomaniac". It is such an odd way to describe someone who spends his days interacting with people who are experiencing tumors. Despite, or perhaps because of the fear and negativity that abound in that environment, Dr. Gordon maintains a calm, peaceful demeanor that could give anyone hope.

I vividly remember my first visit, when Dr. Gordon matter-of-factly asked if I planned to have children. Being still single I replied, "I'm not sure. That's a team sport."

"In that case," he said, "we'll get someone up here from urology to talk to you about freezing your sperm."

Moments later, Valerie, an attractive woman who appeared to be in her mid-20s, walked into the exam room, quickly introduced herself and excitedly started talking about reproduction, sperm counts, and frozen storage. I loved her energy and enthusiasm from the start and found myself smiling when she paused to check in with me, "So, what are you thinking right now?"

When I said, "Well, I think you've got a really interesting job," she laughed and said, "I know, right? I get to talk about sperm and ejaculations all day."

With a slightly more serious tone, she asked sincerely, "So, how are you feeling right now about all of this?"

I replied, "I think it's funny."

Clearly confused, Valerie asked, "What do you mean?"

"Well," I said, "I spent my entire life teaching them to swim backwards and now you're telling me I have to pay for their storage."

Valerie burst out laughing and said with a smile, "Great. So you are not somebody I'm going to have to worry about. Some people have a really hard time with this."

When I shared that story in an early Facebook post, friends teased me about my subsequent visit to the sperm bank. My brother, Bill, described it as "uniquely awkward" which is absolutely perfect. It also made me laugh when my friends Penney and Ilanit wondered why I didn't just show up with "a few hot European couchsurfers" to make the process more enjoyable.

When I decided to share the diagnosis publicly, it felt pretty emasculating to do so. It was like raising my hand and saying, "I'm sick, I need help, and I can't do this by myself." Instead, I was shocked when people used words like "grace" and "strength" to describe my approach. Nevertheless, it did not feel that way at first.

At the time, my biggest fear was that people would suddenly treat me differently, look at me with sad, pathetic eyes, and feel sorry for me. My friend, Paul Wiltberger, put all of those fears to rest in an instant in response to the post in which I first shared the diagnosis:

> *"I'm just going straight to the important question, do you wanna give me any concert tickets you can't attend? I'll still bring the date you have for the evening also!"*

Sharing the News

Well aware that the mere mention of words like tumor, lymphoma, and chemo can send shockwaves of terror through people (myself included), I gave considerable thought to the people I needed to tell personally, either face-to-face or via telephone.

Right near the top of the list was my little friend, Steele, who was 10 at the time. Steele is the son of my friend, Penney. He and I met when he was three months old and have had a special connection ever since.

It has got to be some sort of horrific record that none of my five siblings started having grandchildren until my parents had been married for 48 ½ years. So, for a while, Steele – who calls me Uncle Robby – was the closest thing my parents had to a grandchild. When I called Penney to share the diagnosis, we talked about the pros and cons of telling Steele. Even though he and I do not see each other as often as we did when he was a baby, I knew in my heart it was not something I could hide. Knowing how incredibly compassionate and sensitive he has always been, I planned my words carefully.

That Sunday, Steele and I had plans to go to the Grand Opening of Mondo Meatball, a restaurant opened by my friend, Dean Casagrande, and where my brother John was the executive chef. As we sat across the table from each other, Steele told me he was getting bullied at school. It was heartbreaking to hear, but I was glad to know the right people were aware of the issue. I told him my own story of having been bullied in grade school and we spent quite a bit of time talking about different ways to think about the situation.

Once the bullying conversation came to its natural conclusion, I took a deep breath and started to tell Steele about the tumors. I do not remember exactly what I said, but I kept everything factual, low-key, and prefaced my story saying I would be fine so he would know there was no need to worry. Leading up to the conversation, I had visions of tears, hugs, and me doing my best to comfort Steele, but I must say he took it exceptionally well. So well that a little part of me laughed when I thought, "Aren't you going to cry even a little?" Instead, he flashed his bright smile, walked back to the makeshift buffet, and helped himself to another serving of the cookies that came with his gelato. Mission accomplished.

Laughing from the First Admission

In a most welcome surprise, my friend Ross Parr came to the hospital and hung out for a few hours right before my first admission. His timing was perfect because it set the tone for the entire stay. Within minutes of our arrival in 1548, Ross and I were laughing and having fun with Annette, my primary nurse. Annette had the thankless task of performing some necessary, but rather inelegant tests, which led to a few hilarious moments in the room that were a bit too graphic to recount when I posted my next Facebook update. Ross, however, had the following brilliant response to my efforts to be discrete:

> *"Rob mentioned she had to perform an 'inelegant task.' I've been sworn to secrecy but, in my world, I would have called it a 'rockin Saturday night with a wild nurse,' but that's just me."*

Rockin, inelegant, or however you choose to describe it, I decided in that moment to show up for my second admission with candles and mood music to set the stage for the next hospital-directed invasion of my privacy.

Unfortunately, Annette was not on duty the day I arrived for my second treatment, but she laughed when she saw the candles the following day. Instead, Corrine (pronounced kahr-in) had the joy of welcoming me to unit for the second treatment. One of her first tasks was to walk through an intake questionnaire that asked a wide range of questions clearly designed to assess a rapidly deteriorating mental state and a massive degree of hopelessness. Hopelessness was so far from what I was feeling that I had a hard time taking the survey seriously.

Toward the end of the survey, Corrine asked, "Do you utilize a visiting nurse, special services, assistance, or care at home?" I looked at her with a completely straight face and said, "No. But I'm thinking about getting an au pair. Or two."

In that moment, Corrine perked up and asked, "Oh, do you have kids?"

I replied, "No. That would just be for me."

Corrine never took her eyes off the computer, but I would love to know what was going through her mind in the few awkward seconds that followed.

My Hairless Life

Considering that hair loss was a side effect of three of the six chemotherapy drugs I was on, I knew there would be no escaping it. I also knew I did not want to watch the hair on my head thin and fall out. I'm strong. But I'm not that strong.

Knowing I would never quite be ready, I chose the Sunday after my first treatment as the night I would shave my head. The day before, I had searched the cabinet below my bathroom sink on a whim and was surprised to find a hair trimmer I did not recall purchasing. Although I could not find a charger, the trimmer worked for almost an hour while I stood freezing on my back porch watching clumps of my hair blow across the deck. When my fingers could not take it anymore, I went upstairs, jumped in the shower, and almost finished the job with a razor. I say "almost" because I truly believed I shaved it all even though I was not using mirror. That was not exactly the case though.

When I stepped out of the shower and saw myself in the mirror, I burst out laughing. There were patches of relatively long hair on the top and back of my head I had somehow missed. I thought about taking pictures but knew this was not something I could unsee or easily forget. I do, however, regret that I completely forgot to stop and give myself a Mohawk on my 90-minute journey to baldness.

Knowing that she always makes me laugh, I decided to send one of my first hairless selfies to Amy Karasick. That proved to be a good choice because it was only a matter of moments before I started getting texts with hairy emoticons. If you have not seen a hairy, yellow smiley face, trust me, it is a strong argument for baldness.

For the first few weeks, it was a somewhat out-of-body experience to walk past a mirror and not recognize myself. It was also fascinating to see that not all of the hair on my body was impacted by the treatment. Within a few weeks of chemo, I no longer had to shave my face. In addition, most of the hair on my head stopped growing – except my eyebrows and eyelashes.

Strangely, the hair on my arms and legs also remained intact, even though it had fallen off everywhere else. One morning, I was drying myself off after a shower and thought, "Hey, I don't remember shaving my armpits." This was a particularly odd thought given that I have never once shaved my armpits. That is when I realized it fell out on its own. In case you have lost track, that left me with the head and torso of a prepubescent 12-year-old and the arms and legs of a missing evolutionary link. I looked hilarious.

Fun on the Unit

During the second hospitalization, the white board with treatment notes that hung in my hospital room inspired my brother Bill to start a trend by writing in his own irreverent comments. The board has categories for basic information the day, date, room number, the name of the nurse, doctor, and Patient Care Technician (PCT) on duty. It also captures patient specific information like height, weight, diet, today's goals, mobility plan, and pain plan. Here are a few of my favorite "Today's Goals" from Bill:

- **Day:** Today (Let's try to be in the moment. Namaste.)

- **Date:** Whenever you are free.

- **Planned Activities:** Walking. Irritating Annette.

- **Pain Plan:** Safe Word = "That tickles."

- **Today's Goals:** Fret over my inadequacy less.

The safe word was my favorite, by far. It is so not very Christian Gray. The following treatment, I decided to get a little more aggressive with Today's Goals:

1. World Peace

2. Inspire Annette to exceptional levels of patient care.

3. Patience (see #2)

I also used it to lobby my favorite nurses for a group sponge bath, whether I needed one or not. With each subsequent hospitalization, I found an increasing number of friendly and familiar faces greeting me with an enthusiastic, "Nice to see you again." In some ways, it felt strange, but it was certainly better than checking out to, "Come back soon."

After getting used to seeing the same nurses, I was surprised to discover I would be doing my last treatments on the 14th floor instead of the 15th. The constant, however, remained countless friends who brightened my days with funny and heartfelt messages on my Facebook wall. One of my favorite messages came from my college classmate, John Forsythe, in response to the update I posted on at the start of my fifth treatment:

Status Update:

>"Uh oh. After four treatments on the 15th floor of Prentice, they put me on 14. A whole new team of nurses to torment...um, I mean charm."

John's Response:

>"Rob, all good to hear and I am sure they will all be charmed. Also, while you're going through this, please don't start another Facebook post with 'Uh oh'. Thanks." [smile]

Unexpected Uncertainty

Even the unexpected uncertainty following the ending of treatment led to a few funny moments. The three weeks or so between my last PET scan and the robotic surgery to remove and biopsy the small mass (that was still lighting up the scan the way a tumor might) were legitimately scary. After all, if the mass proved to be an active tumor, the next step would not be more chemo, but a bone marrow transplant.

It was mind-blowing to consider that technology has advanced to the point that robotic chest surgery is considered minimally invasive. I always thought the only operation more maximally invasive than chest surgery was brain surgery. No doubt I would have found the procedure even more interesting and inspiring had it been done to someone else.

The morning of the procedure, I headed to the gym early and bumped into my friend, Nikki Grieco. As we talked about the procedure, she encouraged me to call the next day if I needed any help. I casually replied, "Oh, I'll be fine. I'm actually planning to go hear Heather Horton play at Underground Wonder Bar on Saturday night."

Nikki, looking somewhat concerned, said, "I think you should stay in."

Not able to suppress my smirk, I replied, "Thanks, Mom." Doing my best to reassure her, I continued: "Actually, my understanding is that the procedure would be outpatient, except that it's chest surgery."

Nikki looked at me incredulously and exclaimed: "Say it again! CHEST. SURGERY." I wish I had her reaction on video. I'm still laughing.

Though these are far from all the funny moments that happened during the six months of treatment, this is enough of an illustration to see what a blessing it was to find reasons to smile and laugh throughout. There is no question in my mind that this positive attitude had a huge, vitally important impact on the course of my treatment and my body's ability to recover.

My challenge to myself and to everyone else is to look for reasons to smile in the face of adversity. If you can laugh when others would cry or recoil in fear, you will get through difficult experiences more quickly and easily. If you make the choice to wallow in self-pity, whatever you are dealing with will seem to last forever.

Putting It into Practice

The temptation during periods of stress and sadness is to adopt an air of solemnity and sorrow that may be understandable, but misses the opportunity to lighten the moment and take ourselves less seriously. The experiences I described above are directly attributable to my decision to view the tumors as a gift. Without that positive foundation, it's very likely that I would have missed out on the months of laughter and fun that happened as a result.

Some events are so tragic and horrific that they don't lend themselves to humor. I get that. Fortunately, those aren't every day occurrences for most of us. The more common, day-to-day challenges are the ones where humor can be found.

For example, Kristen Murray Endre, whose story appears in the Epilogue, shares a wonderful example about how she passed this attitude to her son, Brendan, in dealing with his older brother, Conor, who has special needs:

> *"In the early years, Brendan's playdates were consciously/unconsciously limited to friends with siblings with special needs, or the like. At some point we both got brave and invited over someone outside that circle. Sensing Brendan's concerns about the 'what ifs', we talked. It was like a team meeting before a big game: 'B, this is like any other playdate, we've got this. I will explain why our house looks different (we still had child gates and infant toys), and your most important job is to have fun.'*

Conor was practicing some newly found skills at the time, and B was worried that Conor might do something embarrassing. I promised nothing would happen, but if it did, just don't make fun of Conor or make a fuss. Just ignore it and I'll be there to fix it.

Sure enough, I left Conor out of eyesight when I heard the younger boys come running down the stairs. I got to the living room just in time to see that Conor had removed his clothing, and to hear this - Friend: "Um, Brendan, your brother...." Brendan: "Don't worry, he's just wearing his invisible pants."

Hearing examples of people who find humor in the face of difficulty is particularly inspiring because it serves as a reminder that we truly do have a choice in how we respond. If you have a great example of your own, please share it on www.atrekwithin.com

CHAPTER 14:

Accepting (and Surviving) the Pain

"

Because sometimes you need the darkness
In order to ever see the light
*-- from the song **"I Know a Place"** by Michael McDermott*
Reprinted with permission: Michael McDermott/Pauper Sky Songs (ASCAP)

D iving into one's emotions can be a challenge, without a doubt, and this was definitely the case when it came to dealing with the suicide of my best friend, Charlie.

I met Charlie in my advisory period (think homeroom), and he and I quickly became best friends. Even though we both had many other friends, he and I were almost always together. One year, Charlie and his family even invited me to spend Spring Break with them on Sanibel Island in Florida.

For the three years Charlie and I knew each other, friends and girlfriends came and went, but our friendship remained constant. Senior year, thanks to my friend Christopher Brown, I got my own radio show on our high school station, WNTH-FM. Charlie and I did the show together every week and had a blast.

What I loved about Charlie was his casual approach to life and his professed desire to do as little as possible to get by academically. I can still hear the excitement in his voice the morning our grades were passed out along with our class rank. With a huge grin, Charlie said, "I did it." Looking to the bottom of the page, I was surprised to see in the slightly faded print "532 out of 1,065." Confused, I asked, "What do you mean?"

Charlie gleefully exclaimed, "Don't you get it? This is an improvement. My parents begged me to at least finish in the top half of the class. I did it!" He was truly one of the funniest people I have ever met. He made it by one person. Who does that?

Two weeks after graduation, the last of the parties had taken place, so Charlie and I compared schedules and decided we would get together on Thursday night, June 20. When the day arrived, I called Charlie in the afternoon to confirm our plans. When his mom told me Charlie was playing golf with his dad, my first thought was, "Oh, great. Now he won't be up for going out tonight." Fully expecting Charlie to cancel, I was surprised to get a message from him indicating otherwise and expressing great enthusiasm for getting together.

When we got in the car, Charlie initially seemed a bit rushed, but then was in a perfectly good mood. Since we did not have a plan and there weren't any parties to go to, we sat there for a few minutes and decided we would pick up a six-pack of beer at the liquor store and head to the beach. For the next few hours, the two of us sat by the pier and talked about the many friends we had made, the people we hoped to stay in touch with, and what an amazing journey the previous three years had been. I even remember Charlie talking about the graphite tennis racquet his dad had purchased for him as a graduation gift, which he planned to pick up the following week.

After three years of creating memories, it was nice to spend a night where all we did was reminisce about the many adventures we had had in the three short years we had known each other. Although it was sad to know that he was going off to the University of Iowa and I would be near Boston (nearly 1,150 miles away), I did not think much about it. I figured we would have the whole summer to hang out and have fun.

A few hours after I dropped Charlie off at home, he went to the garage, turned on the car, and killed himself. Suicide is difficult to accept under any circumstances, but even harder when you know the person had second thoughts: Charlie's family found his jean jacket on a chair in the backyard the following day, reeking of car fumes.

Although I had absolutely no clue as to Charlie's intentions, in hindsight it is clear he had it all planned: his urgency to get out of the house, despite the fact that we did not have anywhere to go, suddenly made sense. I am honored he chose to spend his last night with me, but that did not lessen the deep grief I experienced. For over a year, I struggled with the fact that he had been such a great friend to me, yet never shared what was bothering him most. I felt like a failure as a friend and it broke my heart.

Since Charlie did not leave a note – he was never really one to explain himself – it is doubtful that anyone knows exactly what prompted him to take his own life. The following night, when I went to Charlie's house to be with his parents and siblings, his mother thanked me for being such a good friend and for spending so much time with him. She went on to say how good it was to see him going out and having fun. I had no idea until that moment that he was not particularly social before he met me. I was shocked; Charlie was always the life of the party.

The day I found out about Charlie's death, I was volunteering at the children's hospital and getting ready to take the train back up to the suburbs. My mom called the hospital and left an urgent message for me to call home. I met her at the office of Dr. Michael Tansey, a psychologist I went to during my senior year of high school, where she frantically delivered the news. Dr. Tansey and I spent the hour talking about Charlie's death while my mom waited outside. I was devastated but did not cry. Strangely, it took a week until I shed the first tears.

After the appointment, as my mom and I drove back on Lake Shore Drive in the warm June sunshine, I remember having the urge to turn on the radio. Hearing the opening notes to "Don't Fear the Reaper" by the Blue Oyster Cult gave me an unforgettable chill. Considering Charlie's love for music, I knew immediately that it was his way of communicating.

For a long time after Charlie's death, I had been awakened several times a year by dreams in which he appeared. The strange, almost eerie quality of each dream reinforces the awareness that I am interacting with him after his death. It is almost as if his energy is weak so he fades in and out of awareness as he did on Feb. 20, 2009, when I awoke and recorded the following dream:

Charlie and I were on a long pontoon boat that probably could have seated 30 or more people. One minute he was there, but the next minute he seemed pre-occupied or was not there at all. I asked him where he had been, referring to after he died, but he seemed reluctant to answer with other people around.

The dream above is one of many in which Charlie was there but not fully present. This eerie quality was so striking and memorable that it reminds me of the Robin Williams movie *What Dreams May Come.* Even before this movie was released, my communication with Charlie in the dreams had a similar, although less intense, quality.

Many of the spiritually-oriented books I have read talk about suicide as an act that violates the sanctity of our lives and leaves the guilt-ridden soul in a somewhat lengthy state of disorientation until it can heal. Judging by my own experiences after Charlie's death, it would appear there is truth to this.

Even though I have never brought up the topic of suicide or asked about Charlie specifically in any of my sessions with psychics, it is not uncommon to have people pick up on his energy during readings. Whenever the subject comes up, the person is not probing for information, but rather stating fact: "You lost a very close friend at a relatively young age. I'm getting it was a suicide."

A few years ago, a reader named Judy Crookes took it a step further in a reading when she said, "Whenever you think about Charlie, pray for him. He is struggling now and needs your prayers."

It made me sad to hear those words, but I knew in my heart Judy was right. It also explained why Charlie seemed so preoccupied and his energy in my dream seemed so distant and sporadic. Now that he has been gone for over 30 years, the dreams come less frequently and I no longer think of him every day. Whenever I do think about him, I take Judy's advice and let Charlie know I love him and forgive him for hurting himself and so many others in the process. Most of all, I ask him to forgive himself. That is always the hardest part.

Update (July 17, 2023): I awoke from the first dream I've had about Charlie in ages and the only one I can recall where he was his usual fun self. That definitely made me smile.

The Littlest Angels and Teachers

In my early years as a volunteer at the children's hospital, many of the patients who came to the playrooms were being treated for asthma, tonsillectomies, and other issues that would not even warrant a hospitalization in today's healthcare environment. We had playrooms on every floor where I found myself doing a lot of coloring and face painting. Over time, however, the hospital began to admit only the most serious cases, so my work shifted from the playroom to the bedside.

With the exposure to patients with life-threatening conditions, it was only a matter of time before I was touched by the death of children at the hospital. Experiencing hope, anticipation, anguish, and heartbreak on a weekly basis naturally made me think more about the nature of life, death, the soul, and what happens when we die. This coincided with the rising popularity of books on near-death experiences and angel encounters: *Embraced by the Light*, *Life After Life*, *Where Angels Walk*, and *Angels Among Us*, to name a few. I loved reading these stories because they were so hopeful, and, for the most part, consistent. I found it fascinating that so many people, from so many different cultures and backgrounds, reported similar, life-changing experiences.

But it was not just the near-death experiences or miracles that caught my attention; it was the courageous young souls for whom miracles did not happen. Of all the patients who have inspired me with their courage, there are three whose experiences impacted me most profoundly. For confidentiality reasons, all names and identifying information have been changed.)

Kevin

One Thursday night, my supervisor Jami asked me to give some special attention to Kevin, a boy who was about 12. When I arrived on the floor, I checked in with Kevin's nurse to see if there was anything I needed to know about his condition or frame of mind in order to interact effectively. She surprised me by telling me Kevin did not have much longer to live, and went on to say he had not slept in two days because he was literally terrified to die. Also, Kevin's mother had tragically died a few years before. This level of detail was unusual, given patient confidentiality laws, but since I would be spending a few hours with him, the nurse thought it important for me to know what Kevin was experiencing.

When I met him, I was surprised to see an active, intelligent boy, who, although weakened by his condition, was not only able to walk, but was also allowed to leave the floor. Although 12-year-olds are not technically allowed in the Teen Lounge at the hospital, we made an exception in order to distract him and to ease his mind.

Kevin walked into the Teen Lounge slowly, with one hand on his portable I.V. pole, struggling somewhat to keep his balance. His eyes lit up within seconds when he saw our showcase piece: a gigantic leather chair shaped like a baseball glove. For the next two hours, Kevin sat in the chair, talked about baseball, and seemed to relax.

I do not remember many of the specifics of my conversation with Kevin, but when I asked him if he would like to stay after the Teen Lounge officially closed, he eagerly agreed. After watching the last two teens head back to their respective rooms, I was surprised to look back and see Kevin shut his eyes for a brief moment. Knowing how terrified he was of going to sleep, I quietly made a few phone calls to see if we could move the baseball chair to his room for the night.

When I explained the situation, the supervisor for the Teen Lounge quickly gave me her permission. I crouched down next to the big chair and said: *"Hey Kevin, I have an idea. You look so comfortable in that chair; how would you like it if I got special permission to move it to your room for the night? It might help you get some sleep."*

Kevin smiled softly and agreed the plan might work. After taking Kevin back to his room, I returned to the Teen Lounge to get the chair.

That night, Kevin tried to relax in the chair but once again was overwhelmed by the fear that he would die in his sleep. He was agitated and restless all night, but relatively calm the following morning as he stood outside his room talking to the nurse. A little while later, after his nurse had changed his sheets, Kevin looked at her and said softly, "I'm going to see my mom." With that, he walked back in the room, laid down on the bed, and died.

While I still mourn for him, nearly 20 years later, I find myself filled with a sense of relief and hope that Kevin, who had been terrified of death, somehow found peace, comfort, and an absolute certainty that he would see his deceased mother. The deathbed enlightenment, inner peace, or whatever you want to call it, is fascinating because it is often observed by caregivers and family when people reach their final moments.

Meeting Kevin in his final hours made an impression on me; he was the first person I met who has experienced such a profound shift from terror to peace. On the one hand, it served as a strong confirmation that death does not have to be a scary process, even if you do not experience the luxury of a full and healthy life, but on a more personal note, it reinforced what I had come to belief about life after life because it so closely mirrored other experiences I had only read about at that point.

Annabel

Annabel was just a few months old when I first saw her in the Pediatric Intensive Care Unit. At the time, Catherine, another volunteer, and I used to do our bedside visits together. Every week for more than a year, Catherine and I spent time playing with and getting to know Annabel. Neither Catherine nor I knew much about Annabel's diagnosis or prognosis; all we knew was that this beautiful little baby had an exceptionally positive personality and magnetic energy.

Only through working with other patients did I recently learn that one of Annabel's issues was likely Spinal Muscle Atrophy, a brutal disease the robs the person of the ability to move. Despite what must have been a very uncomfortable, or even painful, condition Annabel never seemed unhappy.

Since her parents did not visit frequently, Catherine and I made it a point to give Annabel as much love and attention as we could squeeze into our weekly visits, though her condition was so fragile she could not even be held. As a result, we spent a lot of time playing tug-of-war with a multi-colored plastic Slinky.

When Annabel turned 18 months old, the doctors determined that nothing more could be done and made the decision, along with her parents, to discharge her so she could spend her last weeks at home. After 14 months of weekly visits, I knew Annabel and I had a special bond, but it was not until after she left the hospital that I had any idea how special.

One gorgeous Saturday afternoon, a few weeks after Annabel went home, I passed the hospital and walked toward the beach, marveling at the warm, sunny weather. Suddenly, I was enveloped in what I can only describe as a profound and comforting awareness that Annabel had died and was now at peace. The initial feeling lasted less than a minute, but the peace lingered for quite some time. The moment was so unexpected and touched me so deeply there was no question in my mind I had experienced a connection that was both otherworldly and very real.

That afternoon, before starting her next journey, Annabel stopped to give me a hug and leave me with a clear, unmistakable message:

> *"Rob, I wanted you to know I am finally at peace. Goodbye, and thank you for being my friend."*

When I arrived at the hospital the following Thursday, Jami Harris, the Child Life supervisor, confirmed what I already knew: Annabel had died on Saturday afternoon around the same time I experienced her beautiful goodbye. To this day, I still get tears in my eyes whenever I think of her final message.

Tommy

Tommy and I met following an incredibly frustrating workday. When I arrived at the hospital, Jami Harris said, "Rob, I need you to go see Tommy up in 786. He's in isolation, and could really use some attention. I really think you two will hit it off."

Ordinarily, I would have asked more questions, but I was too preoccupied with the aforementioned work issues. Given the almost urgent tone of Jami's request, I made Tommy my priority, knowing that if he and I did get along, I would spend the entire two-hour shift with him.

When I arrived at his room, the wooden door was slightly ajar. Through the narrow window in the door, I could see that Tommy was sitting on the edge of his bed dressed in a black t-shirt and scrubs. He appeared to be about 17 years old.

From my previous experience with teens at the hospital, I knew there was an excellent chance that Tommy would tell me he wanted to be alone. Nevertheless, I knocked on the door. When Tommy looked up, I smiled, walked in the room, and said, "Hi, Tommy. My name is Rob. I'm one of the volunteers, and I came by to say hi."

By the time I got to the bed, I was close enough to see that the t-shirt Tommy had on was from the Chicago punk band Naked Raygun. Knowing that my familiarity with the band would mean instant credibility, I smiled and said, "Naked Raygun. Cool. I saw them open for the Ramones at the Aragon." Tommy's eyes immediately lit up with envy and we launched into a passionate discussion about music, bouncing effortlessly from one topic to the next. The conversation shifted when Tommy casually mentioned his status on the waiting list for a life-saving organ transplant. What surprised me most was his delivery of this shattering news – if he was scared, it did not show.

But it was not Tommy's willingness to share his condition that struck me; it was his positive attitude and his outlook on life. There was no question in Tommy's mind that he would get a transplant before it was too late. To him, the transplant was not particularly urgent, important, or even inconvenient; it was simply something that had to be done.

I did my best not to show it, but when Tommy shared his condition, I was deeply ashamed of myself. Except for my interaction with Tommy, which had completely taken my mind off of my work issues, I willingly surrendered the keys to my sanity to the people and relatively trivial circumstances at work. In that moment, I realized my problems were not problems at all – they were deadlines. By the same time the next week, they would be replaced with other deadlines. For more than two hours, Tommy and I talked about music and looked at his artwork.

Jami said later, "No one has been able to get through to him. He's been here three weeks and hasn't talked with anybody before you. He sent everyone away."

It's important to point out that there is nothing special about me. The credit goes to Jami for planting the idea that we would get along. Had she instead told me he was an angry teenager who sent everyone away, it's almost a certainty I would have had the same experience – simply because I would have expected the same. That's the Law of Attraction: we get whatever we give attention, energy, and focus.

Knowing I had helped Tommy in some small way meant a lot to me. However, I had a hard time forgiving myself for wasting so much time feeling sorry for myself. With so much on my mind, I left the hospital and went for a long walk along the lakefront to clear my mind and pray about what really mattered – Tommy's transplant.

Over the next few months, I spent a lot of time with Tommy before and after his successful transplant. A few years later, I bumped into him at the World Music Theater during a concert by the Cure. Sadly, that was the last time I ever saw him; he died a few years later of health complications. I never had the chance to thank him. More than any other person I have ever met, he gave me the gift of perspective.

It has often been said that people who volunteer get more out of the experience than the people who are being helped; that is certainly true in my case. What started out as a way to improve my college applications turned into a mind-expanding adventure that changed the way I view faith, life, death, reincarnation, and the ongoing opportunities I have to better distinguish between passing annoyances and serious issues. Countless patients have been exceptionally good teachers in that regard, but Kevin, Annabel, and Tommy stand out among them. Although all three have passed on, they live on in the wisdom they shared. And for that I am eternally grateful.

Putting It into Practice

None of us will escape loss in our lifetime. It's an inevitable part of the human experience. Therefore, there are two important questions we need to keep in mind:

- How will we handle grief when it happens to us?
- How will we show up for those we love when they are experiencing grief?

Sadly, there is no adequate answer to the first question. The closest I've ever been able to come is through remembering a short poem my high school classmate, Anne Hoban Moore, wrote after Charlie died:

His presence made me smile

His absence makes me cry

But the memories make me smile once more

How we show up for others – or more importantly THAT we show up for others is really the key question.

Every so often, I have a conversation with someone that I find myself replaying in my mind. I'm not talking about obsessing in a "winning imaginary arguments in the shower" sort of way. Instead, I am referring to the almost involuntary reflection that happens when I need to process and understand.

I recently went to visit an old friend. Before long, she and I started talking about those times we are comfortable being alone, the experiences that are more fun when shared, and the times we sometimes find ourselves alone when we'd rather we weren't. It was at that moment that my friend, who had lost her husband five years before, shared an experience that surprised me.

Over several decades of marriage, she and her husband built a life together that included a grown son, a beautiful granddaughter, co-ownership and active involvement in a successful business, and a nice group of friends. Unfortunately, after the husband died, a strange thing happened. Most of the friends they shared stopped calling. Overnight, the social life she once knew came to an unexpected halt. Confused, she turned to a lifelong friend who had also lost a husband and shared her experience. Knowing she could count on her friend to be completely honest, she fully expected to hear, "Don't worry. You're imagining it" or "This won't last."

Instead, her friend said, "Oh, yes. That's exactly what happens. People stop calling. Everything changes."

Listening to my friend's story and looking beyond her strong, poised, and genuinely positive exterior, I could clearly feel the hurt, sadness, and disappointment. It was heartbreaking. First, I can't begin to imagine how hard it must have been to lose her husband of so many years. But to effectively lose friends at the same time had to have been even more devastating.

In a very real way, my friend's experience is reminiscent of my experience after Charlie's suicide. Many of the people we had hung out with weren't comfortable calling me. I didn't keep a scorecard of who checked in on me and who didn't, but I will say that the people who made the biggest impression were the ones who reached out even when they didn't know what to say. Interestingly, this group included strangers who quickly became cherished friends.

The compassionate side of me is well aware that it is absolutely human to worry about what to say to people who are suffering. But it isn't about the words. I don't remember what people said and I doubt I even heard it in the moment. Intention is what matters, not the words.

I also have a feeling that some people avoid friends who are experiencing grief because they fear they won't know what to do if the person goes on and on about their lost love one. In many cases though, the opposite is true. The grief-stricken may not want to talk much at all. They certainly aren't going to talk about their loss very time we see them. Thinking about my friend's situation made me wonder if a similar phenomenon occurs with couples who divorce after long marriages. I strongly suspect it does — especially when the couple once shared a core group of friends.

I share this not to be judgmental, but to raise awareness about this strange and sad phenomenon. My sincere hope is that anyone who reads this is inspired to think hard about people they know who might be going through the same heartbreak as my friend. If someone comes to mind, consider doing your part to minimize the loneliness of loss — not as a one-time outreach but as a sustained effort to help someone who may be quietly struggling to re-create their social life.

Shortly after I shared the thoughts above on Facebook, a few friends pointed out that some of the people closest to us are not always the ones who are there for us during illnesses or other difficult situations. They asked if I had the same experience when I went through chemo.

First, I have to preface my comments acknowledging how blown away I was, in the best of all possible ways, by friends, strangers, and acquaintances alike. In fairness, I suspect some of this is attributable to the fact that the type of lymphoma I experienced is no longer a death sentence. This makes a difference because not everyone is comfortable with uncertainty — especially when that uncertainty can lead to what my dad sometimes playfully referred to as "an acute shortness of breath". That's why I did my best to make it clear I wasn't checking out early.

Had the prognosis been worse, it's not hard to imagine that the responses might have been different as well. Some people would have stepped up to an even greater degree. Others might not have shown up at all. In any case, I made the decision to give my attention, energy, focus, and gratitude to the people who consciously decided to walk with me. At the same time, I am human. It didn't escape my attention that a few people never reached out and still haven't. Whatever their reasons, I do my best not to judge or take it personally. If the person lost a parent or loved one to cancer, the diagnosis alone might have been enough to cause a sudden and overwhelming surge of sadness. In other cases, people may simply lack the communication skills or emotional development to deal with their feelings effectively. Still others may not trust themselves to find the right words, without ever realizing it isn't about the words at all. Kindness, after all, needs no vocabulary.

Thanks to Facebook, I was surprised to discover another category I hadn't considered — the Silent Supporters. Throughout the treatment and even more recently, I have bumped into Silent Supporters who knew exactly what was going on and, in many cases, had read every word of every update. Until the chance encounters, I had no idea these people even knew about the tumors. Nevertheless, these Silent Supporters cared, they were concerned, they prayed, they visualized, and they ultimately cheered. But they never reached out. I have no idea why, and it isn't important. When I see these people — and there were many — I can feel their genuine compassion and concern. That energy is real and I'm quite sure it helped. So, how can I be anything other than grateful and happy for what they contributed anonymously? Ask any nonprofit organization: checks from anonymous donors do just as much good as the ones from people who are more visible in their support.

Silent Supporters are important. Visible supporters are even better. So, if your goal is to be a more visible supporter, remember, it doesn't matter what you say. Don't put that kind of pressure on yourself. In the midst of grief, especially when Charlie died, I don't remember what people said. But I do remember that they were there and that they cared.

CHAPTER 15:

Piecing It Together:
The Mental, Physical, and Spiritual

Nothing truly stops you. Nothing truly holds you back. For your own will is always within your control. Sickness may challenge your body. But are you merely your body? Lameness may impede your legs. But you are not merely your legs. Your will is bigger than your legs. Your will needn't be affected by an incident unless you let it.

-- Epictetus

My journey with lymphoma was not an adventure I planned, nor was it like anything I had ever experienced. Yet, in a most unexpected way, it marked the convergence of many seemingly unrelated experiences of my life. For most of the journey, I viewed the tumors as a gift that brought lessons, exponential personal growth, and an outpouring of love and support I could never have predicted. From this perspective, I feel like the luckiest, happiest guy on earth. That feeling provides a nice answer to the question, "What did you get out of this experience?"

However, it does not address the deeper question that has been on my mind from the beginning: "Why and how did the tumors develop in the first place?"

Knowing that risk factors exist for certain types of tumors, I casually asked Dr. Gordon and his nurse Betsy what causes lymphoma. I remember the conversation vividly because both of our reactions took me by surprise.

Betsy instantly and insistently replied, "You didn't cause these!" The investigative reporter in me had asked the question out of genuine curiosity with no particular agenda in mind, yet Betsy answered as if I had asked "What did I do to cause these tumors?"

As Betsy went on to say that little is known about what triggers lymphoma, I experienced an unexpectedly powerful, gut level disagreement with her contention that I was somehow blameless. I did not know why, but I knew at a deep, soul level that was not completely true.

Our Minds and Our Health

The connection between what we think and what we experience from a health standpoint is well-known, although not necessarily universally appreciated or accepted.

I certainly cannot attribute every illness or injury to my state of mind, nor is it necessary to do so. However, having recognized certain patterns over the years, I have found it helpful to consider the possibility whenever I am faced with a health issue because our bodies can be very literal. For example, lower back pain is almost always a sign that I am concerned about money and may be slipping into a scarcity mentality. In other words, it is not unusual to experience stiffness and pain in the part of my body that plays a key role in overall physical stability when my mind raises questions about my financial stability.

Similarly, congestion is a warning sign that often appears when I am avoiding important conversations. The words I need to speak are literally trapped and show up in the form of congestion. While I do not particularly enjoy this symptom, I do appreciate having an internal warning system that encourages me to think about concerns I should express rather than repress.

In the case of the tumors, the situation is a bit more complicated. As mentioned previously, due to my neck-related fears, I was not surprised the tumors were discovered there first. Given my fear of choking, the pressure on the front of my throat made me wonder how the tumors would impact my breathing. The way the tumors surrounded and put pressure near my voice box, I also spent the first few days wondering if there was a connection to communication, perhaps a more advanced form of congestion.

The first CT scan told a markedly different story: the tumor that bulged out above my collar bone was the tip of a much bigger mass centered in my chest. The largest tumor, which was not visible until we looked deeper, was sitting right on my heart. The symbolism of that did not escape me; in a real sense, the scan gave me a rare glimpse of a much deeper emotional issue of which communication was only a part.

As I pieced together the signs, it was not difficult to understand what my intuition leads me to believe happened in this case. Given the heart connection, it probably will not come as a surprise that there was a woman involved.

The discovery of the tumors corresponded almost exactly with the one-year anniversary of the last time I had seen a woman with whom I had been in a brief but particularly promising relationship.

As the one-year anniversary of our last contact approached, feelings of disappointment, mixed with a dose of frustration, bubbled to the surface. I did my best to hold onto the happy memories and gratitude, but it did not always work.

In light of what felt like a year-long emotional circling of the drain, it is not at all surprising that I had unknowingly and energetically created an environment in which the lymphoma took hold and began to thrive. Aggressively. It is also no surprise the largest tumor started closest to my heart.

Am I saying this was the only factor? Absolutely not. If that were the case, we would all have gigantic tumors. Instead, I think of it as a contributing factor that operated as a warning sign in the same way congestion and lower back pain shows up in my body. What is true for me is that intensity of the physical manifestation often mirrors the intensity of the underlying feelings. That is certainly true in this case.

It was not the treatment experience, or even the tumors themselves, however, that made this part of my journey the missing chapter. After all, millions of people have experienced tumors and treatment. What made this experience a unifying thread is the way it incorporated Western and Eastern medicine, prayer, meditation, visualization, and spirituality, as well as the contributions and insights of intuitives. For the first time, it finally made sense how my previous experiences and shifts in perspective had prepared me to handle adversity in a way that surprised everyone, myself included.

My consultations with Eastern healers started immediately with Shen Robinson who told me I had lymphoma days before the test results came back. Around the same time, I spoke with Jei Atacama about the tumors. Jei was confident in his ability to cure them, but he was completely supportive of my decision to pursue a traditional, Western approach. After all, since Western medicine offered a cure, there was no reason to turn away from it. Instead, he agreed to work with me to manage the symptoms.

And manage them he did. I made it through six R-EPOCH chemo treatments – the first four of which increased steadily in intensity – without ever needing a transfusion. Although I experienced some uncomfortable stomach cramps, I never experienced nausea. Of all the side effects I managed to avoid, that meant the most because my neck-related fears directly contributed to an additional fear of vomiting that I have had since I was 10, possibly longer.

Along the way, I also turned to Christie Jordan and her staff at Source Healing for frequent acupuncture sessions to help minimize the intestinal discomfort. Other interventions included a fantastic Reiki session from Silvia and Letizia Romero and an hour on a sound bed donated to Gail Volpe by Brazilian healer, John of God for use, free of charge, by cancer patients.

But it was not just Reiki, acupuncture, and energy work that got me through. I am absolutely convinced that two other factors played a significant role. First, there were the prayers and visualizations of friends and strangers alike who followed every step of the journey through my Facebook posts. I am still amazed by the number of people who visualized the tumors shrinking.

Two of the most powerful visualizations came from my friends, Cynthia Block Feuer and Tracy. Cynthia wrote to let me know her surprise when the tumors actually melted in her visualization. Not long afterwards, "melt" is the exact word one of the oncology professionals used to describe how the tumors respond to treatment. Later, toward the end of the treatment, Tracy, a yoga teacher and friend from high school, sent the following beautiful message:

> I want to share with you a vision I had. I was lying in Savasana at the end of a recent yoga class. I've been working hard to be able to clear my mind during this pose and usually do so by finding my way to my "happy place" – a beach on the ocean.
>
> On this day, with my eyes closed, I found my mind at peace when a bright light came into view. It was a bright white light, filled with love and healing and in the center of the light was you. Not you as a person – I didn't actually see a human standing in the light – but you as a spirit. It was clear it was you. It was almost as if this light was bursting out of you. After about 15 seconds, the vision slowly disappeared and I was filled with an even greater peace and a sense of your body in perfect health."

In addition to the power of visualizations, the second factor that got me through this experience is the positive attitude and appreciation for the power of language I gained from studying the teachings of Abraham, as described by Esther and Jerry Hicks.

Esther, who channels Abraham, talks frequently about the tendency for so many of us to swim upstream and make life more difficult than it needs to be. To me, the concept of battling cancer seemed like the ultimate expression of swimming upstream. So, I chose not to do that. Rather than battling the tumors or attempting to "kick cancer's ass," I chose to walk with and learn from the tumors; I chose to see them as a gift.

At the same time, I was careful to separate myself energetically from them. As I mentioned earlier, I did not refer to them in a possessive sense. They were not "my" tumors and I did not "have" them. Instead, I paid particular attention to the words I used. I distanced myself by saying that I was "experiencing" tumors or "going through treatment for tumors." This way, I made it clear to my body through my words that the tumors were not mine; they were not going to stick around forever. More importantly, walking with the tumors rather than fighting them helped me honor them and learn from them without being attached to them.

When I reflect back on the journey, I see clearly how Western and alternative medicine, combined with a positive focus proved absolutely instrumental in getting through the treatment. In addition to my deepest appreciation to Dr. Leo Gordon, the oncologist, and his nurse, Betsy, I am grateful to my dear friend, Jackie Hart, who gave me the words to accompany my approach when she talked about "walking with the tumors." I am equally grateful to Jei Atacama, the late Japanese healer. The best evidence of Jei's effectiveness came toward the end of the treatment when I found myself dealing with tongue pain. To picture this, imagine the pain you feel when you bite your tongue. Now imagine that localized pain spreading across your entire tongue, top, bottom, and sides. That's tongue pain.

One morning when the pain was particularly bad, I texted Jei's office to ask for a treatment. Debbie and Aviva, his assistants, told me he was treating another patient but they would get back to me as quickly as possible. At 8:55am, I was getting on my bike after leaving Dr. Gordon's office. In that moment, the tongue pain reduced by 40-50% in an instant. It was as if a light switch shut off the pain. A minute or two later, his office called and said, "Jei just treated you." But I already knew.

My dad, as mentioned previously, had always been open-minded about alternatives like Chinese medicine, acupuncture, and the power of medicinal plants. As he put it, "Western medicine, as we know it, has only been around a few hundred years. Chinese doctors, shamans, and others have been healing people for thousands of years. We'd be naïve to think we couldn't learn from them."

And learn from them he has. When dad was in Evanston Hospital recovering from pneumonia, he had so much trouble breathing he sat in a chair and did not move his arms for over a week. This led to a nerve issue in both arms so severe he could not hold a pen. A neurologist who evaluated him said his arms might be 50% better after a year or they might not improve at all. In search of more hopeful treatment options, dad turned to acupuncture and experienced an 80% improvement after just two treatments.

As it happens, both Western medicine and alternative medicine have the power to heal. It is not necessary to swear an ill-conceived allegiance to one or the other. What does make a difference, however, is attitude: our thoughts are a creative force that have the power to heal our bodies. But thoughts can also make us sick.

Alan Wolf, a body work practitioner, is also a wonderful example of the power our bodies have to heal. In the late 1980s, Alan was one of the top two body-building contenders for Mr. Illinois when, during a workout, he ruptured and herniated nine discs in his back. After spending the next nine months hearing doctor after doctor tell him he would never be the same, Alan rejected the dire predictions and radical recommendations for surgery and took charge of his own healing. Through body work, yoga, and a dedication to stretching and training, Alan healed. Even though he had no desire to compete again, Alan worked his way back into competition shape. But more importantly, he discovered a passion for body work and now dedicates his time and energy to helping people train and heal.

To sum it up, this book is not about pretending to be some super-human person who learned a few lessons and is now somehow better than everyone else. It is about showing who I am and what I am becoming with the hope that others can learn from the many mistakes I continue to make. I am what I am, a flawed person gathering the lessons of yet another lifetime.

Where Do You Go from Here?

It is now an almost weekly occurrence that someone tells me they live vicariously through my social media posts and admire the positive attitude with which I approach life. All I can say is that it was not always this way; getting to this point took a lot of work. But the good news is that there is nothing particularly special about me. Everything I did, you can do as well. My only hope is that the stories of the book inspire you to learn the lessons without the pain of the experiences.

Lymphoma is no picnic, trust me. But my surviving that journey comes down to one concept: conscious choice.

I made a choice to address and resolve my scarcity mentality.

I made a choice to inspire abundance by maintaining a gratitude journal and capturing five things every day for which I was grateful.

I made a choice to remain open to concepts like reincarnation that, in some cases, contradicted beliefs passed on through religion.

I made a choice to keep journals of dreams and synchronicities.

I made a choice to find a cure for narcolepsy when Western medicine offered nothing more than a pharmaceutical Band-Aid for the symptoms.

I made a choice not to abandon Western medicine on the basis on one failure.

I made a choice to see the tumors as a gift and to walk with, rather than fight them.

I made a choice to share this journey publicly, knowing not everyone will agree or accept my conclusions.

These choices all add up to the most important decision of all: to be open to, to embrace, and to learn from the many experiences of life, while at the same time, to do my best not to attach a negative value judgment to the experiences themselves. Most people view cancer as a terrible thing, and that is a negative value judgment I consciously chose to avoid. Instead, I see the tumors as a gift that rewarded me with love, lessons, and, ultimately, life. When we look for the signs, the lessons, the wisdom, and the gifts in our everyday experiences, we cannot help but achieve a more positive and abundant mindset. Adopt it. It works.

You don't even have to talk about prosperity;
you just have to stop talking about lack.

-- Abraham-Hicks

EPILOGUE

Signposts on Our Inner Expeditions

> Basically, Intelligent Design is the idea that life on earth is too complex to have evolved without a guiding hand. We're not saying it's God, just someone with the basic skill set to create an entire working universe
>
> -- Jon Stewart, comedian

As I was putting together the material for this book, I put the word out to my network that I was looking for a few additional stories to include. As further evidence of the Universe's plan, I received the following letter from Alasdair, a friend and British ex-pat who now lives in Prague. Alasdair's experiences reflect exactly that manifestation of "God drawing straight with crooked lines" that led me to write this book. So, it's only fitting that I end with his letter:

> Rob, I feel a strong urge to write to you after reading your last post...I should say I am not looking to provide any particular stories for it, but I am (once again) blown away by the Universe's ability to provide. Signs, synchronicity, the gift of soul-mirrors (for want of a better term), twin flames, enlightenment, etc.
>
> When we met, I had no idea what you do – I understood some kind of coaching – I just figured you for a decent, kind,

generous, warm guy who dug music like I do. But of course, the Universe knew what She was doing in throwing us together.

My soul journey has undergone a lightspeed transformation in the last year and a half. I have "stumbled" upon epiphany after epiphany in my journey from darkness to light. In doing so, I have settled on the realisation that truth and understanding were in me all along. Revelations I had, and decisions I made, when I was 15-16 years old are only just becoming clear – rooted as they were in soul consciousness. Songs I wrote years ago are only now revealing their message to me.

One of them is my song 'Signposts', and I would like to share the lyrics with you. Maybe they will resonate with you:

> There's no landmarks out here,
> But I'm led by a feeling
> The road that I'm on
> Is slowly revealing its signs.
>
> There's no comfort out here,
> But I'm fed by the hunger
> & when the day closes
> I wish it were longer.
>
> So don't follow the path; let the path follow you.

There's no secrets out here,
Where all hearts are opened
& a man is still judged
By the words he has spoken & kept.

There's no warnings out here,
For we hold by the canon
Of natural law
That our forefathers swore on.

So don't follow the path; let the path follow you.

There's no sickness out here,
For we're spurred by the fever,
Not driven by blindness
That makes us believers

There's no answers out here,
Though we're all born with questions,
The truth will arise
If you just pay attention.

So don't follow the path; let the path follow you.

Lyric from "Signposts" by Alasdair Bouch. Copyright ©
2013 by Alasdair Bouch. Reprinted with permission.

My reasons for landing in Praha 11 years ago are only just now making sense to me. As I have progressed from lesson to lesson (some had to be 'learned' more than once, as you say), a path has appeared – the signs for which only appeared as I passed them, to show that I was on the right Way. My raison d'être is clearer than ever, and in harnessing the gifts the Universe has bestowed upon me, I hope to channel this light. As I am making sense of the complex web of connections, signs, gifts, meetings, teachings and lessons, a simple path of Truth, Righteousness, Goodness & Light is discernible – unafraid and rooted in the Now.

The path is manifesting in so many extraordinary ways – particularly in the Laws of Attraction, one thing I am being mindful of at the moment.

To paraphrase from another, far "greater" poet, Robert Frost: Two roads met in a wood, and we shared the one less traveled by. And that has made all the difference.

I am most grateful for your company on this road, my friend. All power to you, may the light of the Universe guide you.

Alasdair's message is beautiful because it touches on so many of the themes of this book – the angels we meet along the way, messages in songs, and the importance of trusting the path even when it is not clear to us in the moment.

Kristen Murray Endre, a friend and classmate from high school, is one person who clearly appreciates the importance of signposts on our journey that don't always make sense in the moment. Not long after we met sophomore year, Kristen tore the ACL in her knee. Today, that injury would be repaired with a scope and she would probably have walked out of the hospital within a few hours and with minimal assistance. When we were in high school, that wasn't the case. Repairing the ACL was a much more involved procedure that required a multi-day stay with her leg in traction, connected to a machine that kept it in continuous motion.

When Kristen returned to school, she found herself in an adaptive physical education class since she wasn't able to participate in regular gym. As a result, Kristen spent gym period in the boiler room of New Trier High School with a large group of special education students who dealt with a variety of physical, emotional, and intellectual issues. At first, Kristen found the situation incredibly frustrating, *"I spent the first week being pissed off thinking to myself 'What benefit is this to me? Why am I with these kids? I'm an athlete. I don't belong here.'"*

Over the next few months though, Kristen forged friendships with classmates she would otherwise never have met. Soon, she saw her new classmates as capable athletes, students, and friends. Those friendships led to Kristen's involvement as a volunteer with Special Olympics and later as a teacher's assistant in French class, two activities she continued throughout high school.

As it happened, interacting with people who experienced mental and physical challenges wasn't completely unfamiliar territory because Kristen had frequent weekend visits to see another classmate's brother in a Chicago-area facility that cares for people with a wide range of physical and mental challenges. As Kristen put it, "There was no fear of people with differences for me, but they were not part of the community in any way at all. You never saw them."

If you had known Kristen at the time, you might have assumed that her work with the Special Olympians was little more than a surgery-inspired happy coincidence made possible by her already huge heart, warm smile, and genuine concern for others.

But the Universe had other plans.

After marrying, Kristen gave birth to her first son, Conor. If you accept the possibility that, on a soul level, at least some of us chose our parents, Conor knew exactly what he was doing when he picked Kristen as his mom. Why? Because Conor was born with Angelman Syndrome, a complex chromosomal mutation that leads to profound medical challenges. The condition is somewhat similar to autism in terms of its impact on behavior and cognition. In Conor's case, it also came with a seizure disorder.

Kristen's experience with Special Olympians and her comfort around people like Conor would have made her an ideal mother under any circumstances. However, it is her advocacy that truly sets her apart. Having witnessed first-hand the institutionalization and marginalization of special needs children years before, Kristen wanted to make sure Conor was a visible and valued part of her community. She became an advocate for many and has spent over a decade working hard to create educational opportunities for other parents and supporting inclusive social and recreational programs. What remained missing was the chance for Conor to learn with all of his peers in a regular classroom. The work she does as a parent and advocate is not without its share of struggles, failures, and successes, but, as Kristen puts it, *"If you have special needs, you don't belong in an institution somewhere. You belong with your peers. The more people interact with each other, the more they appreciate, understand, accept, and welcome all of us."*

After more than 10 years of hard work, Kristen scored a major victory in her ongoing efforts on behalf of all children like Conor. He is now the first special needs child to take a general education language arts class in the local middle school. This has already led to some inspiring interactions. Conor, who is unable to read but who loves to be read to, was paired with a student who struggles with diction and pronunciation and needs practice reading out loud. A perfect match.

From her current vantage point, Kristen can see the many signposts on her journey that were not apparent at the time, but that make perfect sense in hindsight. Kristen describes it beautifully, *"The experience completely changed my outlook without me realizing it until 20 years later. The universe puts something in your path behind you, and sometimes it bubbles up to the surface at just the right moment."*

I love the concept of the Universe putting "something in your path behind you" because there is no way Kristen could possibly have been present to what was truly occurring. It would have been completely unrealistic for Kristen to sit in high school gym class and think to herself, "I'm probably going to have a special needs child someday so this experience will really be helpful."

That's not the way it works.

Knowing that she is exactly where she needs to be, doing exactly what needs to be done, is one of the main reasons Kristen is as happy and peaceful as she has ever been. Better still, future generations of families impacted by Angelman, autism, and other developmental differences will be able to look on her family's journey and find hope knowing that anyone can create their own possibilities.

If you have read this far, I am confident that you are a worthy companion for other travellers on the path. For that I am grateful. May you always follow your inner compass and may you always recognize and learn from the many signposts along the way.

APPENDIX

Different Ways of
Receiving Signs and Messages

When she took my hand
And traced every line
She said the answer you seek
Has been with you all this time
The secret of life is up to you
Cause every day is another dream come true
*-- from the song "**Another Dream Come True**"*
by Michael Lille and Dave Mallett
Downstream Lean Music / BMI Forerunner Music / ASCAP

To better appreciate the intuitive and spiritual messages we all have access to, it's helpful to look at the many ways these messages can be received. The following is not intended as an exhaustive list, but as a way to explain a few of the methods psychics often use. In the examples below, the 17th Century French word "clair" meaning "clear" is combined in each case with a more specific word that describes the type of sense or cognitive process used in the communication or perception.

Clairvoyance (sight)

The ability to perceive information or events that cannot be perceived through the five basic senses. People who are clairvoyant often "see" past and future events in their mind. I have never experienced what might be described as clairvoyance, but I know someone in my immediate family has on at least one occasion.

Claircognizance (knowing)

Claircognizance is an interesting phenomenon in which people suddenly become aware of certain facts, perceptions, or knowledge without being able to identify how they received the information. My first experience with this happened during the Akashic record reading with Jennifer. One minute I didn't even know she had children. The next moment, I found myself describing each in detail without knowing how I knew.

Clairsentience (feeling/touch)

People who possess clairsentience pick up information through the energy or vibration of others. More specifically, they might hold an item belonging to the person that has picked up the person's energy. PsychicDave Tillman used this method before his ability developed to the point where he no longer needs direct or indirect physical contact to connect with the people he reads. For example, he uses direct contact when he puts his hand on the shoulder of a person in order to do a reading. Similarly, indirect contact involves holding a personal item such as a watch or ring that came in close contact with the person for extended periods. My favorite example of this occurred when

PsychicDave did an in-person reading for Mike, one of my sister's ex-boyfriends. Within seconds of Mike handing him the watch he was wearing to hold, PsychicDave said, "This isn't going to work. You've owned the watch for a long time, but you've only been wearing it for a few weeks." Mike was stunned because he was exactly right on both counts.

Clairaudience (hearing)

Some psychics "hear" the information they receive through sounds that may not be perceived by recording equipment or anyone else in the room. People such as James Van Praagh and others who communicate with spirits and souls of the deceased often have this ability.

What I find especially fascinating about this modality is the fact that some of the people who have this ability report that the voices often sound more like chirping as if they were listening to a recording that was being played on fast forward. This is believed to be a result of the spirit world's faster vibration. The analogy that best describes this is the image of a high-speed fan. Our eyes and mind are not capable of seeing the individual blades when they are moving quickly, and we often have a fairly clear image of whatever is beyond the blades, but we know the blades are still there even though they appear to be invisible. Similarly, the vibration of spirits is so high that most people are not in tune enough to sense them. It is this higher and faster vibration that is thought to cause the fast, high-pitched sound clairaudient people perceive.

One of my only personal experiences with clairaudience happened on June 29, 2007. I was in a particularly upbeat mood that night because I was going to the House of Blues in Chicago to see one of my favorite live bands, The Psychedelic Furs, for the 18ᵗʰ time. I was on a second date with Emily (not her real name), a woman I knew was a party girl. We started with dinner and a few glasses of wine before the show and switched to martinis late in the evening.

The fact that I was buzzed but not drunk probably played a role in my heightened sensitivity because my conscious mind and rational thoughts weren't getting in the way of what I was sensing. Twice during the concert, I experienced claircognizance in which I knew with absolute certainty what song would be played next. In each case, I turned to Emily as one song ended and correctly predicted the next song. Judging by the look on her face, Emily didn't know whether to be impressed or spooked. I really should know better than to do psychic stuff on first or second dates, but it happens so rarely and I enjoy the experience so much I wanted to share it.

One could easily argue that what happened during the concert wasn't claircognizance at all, but rather intuition based on information gathered from the 17 previous Furs shows I had attended. I certainly won't argue the point. However, it was what happened later that got my attention — and Emily's as well.

After the show, we stopped by Enclave, a local club, to meet Emily's friend, Jill. After talking to Jill briefly, Emily and I walked down the street to Martini Ranch. On the way, we got into a conversation about middle names. Perhaps because of what happened at the concert,

Emily decided this would be a good opportunity to test me. Rather than tell me her middle name, she asked me to guess. I must have sensed that looking her in the eyes would give me a better chance to guess correctly, because without thinking, I grabbed her left arm, stopped her mid-stride, and spun her around so she was facing me with my hands on her shoulders. The moment I looked into Emily's eyes, I heard a voice loud and clear in my head say "Marie". The voice was odd in the sense that I couldn't be sure if it belonged to a man or woman. However, it sounded like a normal human voice in the sense that it wasn't high pitched like clairaudients often report.

Having had such an unexpected experience, there was no question in my mind about the accuracy of the information. With absolutely certainty, I said, "Marie", let go of Emily's shoulders, and started walking. I didn't need to wait for a reaction because I knew I was right. At that point, Emily's expression was somewhere between genuinely surprised and horrified.

Emily gasped, ran a few steps to catch up to me, and asked earnestly, "How did you know that?"

"This is probably going to sound strange", I replied, "because this has never happened to me before, but when I looked in your eyes, I actually heard a voice say, 'Marie'."

It probably also won't come as a complete surprise that Emily and I never had a third date. So much for honesty.

Most of the sessions I've had over the years with psychics have been with people who received information using one of more of the techniques mentioned above. In many cases, I have no idea how the person receives their information because it doesn't necessarily matter. No one technique is better than another. What matters is what works best for the person doing the perceiving.

www.ingramcontent.com/pod-product-compliance
Lightning Source LLC
Chambersburg PA
CBHW021702120626
46545CB00004B/1362